# Business Processes

*A bridge to SAP and. Guide to SAP TS410 Certification*

Robert Szymanski
Viswa Viswanathan

Infivista Inc

Business Processes : A bridge to SAP and a guide to SAP TS410 certification



ISBN: 978-1-941773-04-8

First Edition : February 2019

10 9 8 7 6 5 4 3 2 1

# CONTENTS

## Table of Contents

# The Big Picture

***THIS BOOK COVERS*** the core business processes and their realization within SAP. The book also emphasizes the integration of these business processes. We use the term business process very broadly to mean common organizational processes in businesses, governments and non-profit organizations. Although the sheer volume of material covered appears daunting, pure common sense can help us to navigate it quite easily. Much of the complexity actually arises from terminology.

You will encounter numerous terms, but as long as you can clearly associate the terms with common-sense business activities, you will progress smoothly through the material. In this chapter we provide a bird's-eye view of some of the important business processes and the associated SAP terms.

## Study Strategy

The SAP course material (henceforth SAPCM) seems daunting just in terms of volume. Although very informative, you will probably not find the material to be self-contained. We have therefore created this book to help you navigate each unit of SAPCM. In this book, you will find different kinds of supporting material for each unit of the SAPCM. In this section we suggest a sequence of activities that will help you to best absorb each unit. Figure 1 shows the suggested study strategy.

The following sections provide a whirlwind tour of some common business processes in manufacturing organizations. Along the way, we introduce some terms that we will encounter in later chapters as we delve deeper into these business processes. Be sure to memorize these terms and to connect them with real world business situations. Try to gain a common sense understanding of what each term represents.

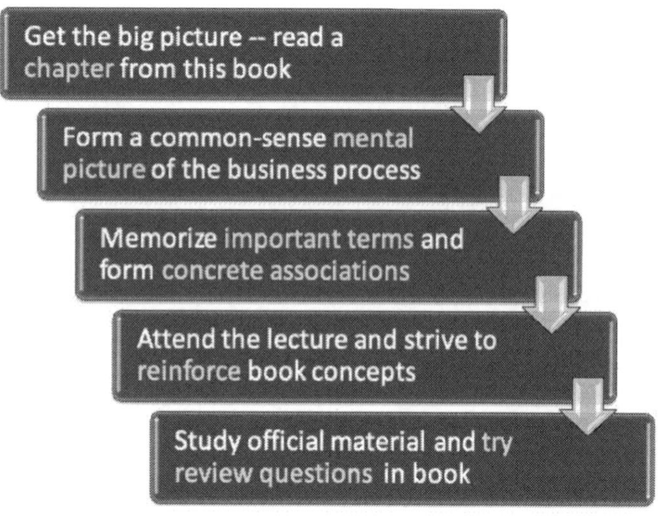


*Figure 1: Suggested study strategy*

## Setting the stage

Manufacturing organizations purchase raw materials and convert them into finished products for sale. Such organizations need to plan carefully for materials to ensure that material availability meshes properly with production plans. Otherwise they may realize they are short of some of the required materials just as they are about to begin a production shift. That could be disastrous.

They cannot just play safe and have huge quantities of materials either – because that would mean holding a lot of inventory and incurring working capital costs. The material can also get spoiled or even go to waste if they decide to discontinue making some products. You can see how proper material planning plays a big role in profitability. With very stiff competition among companies, even a 2-3% increase in costs can hurt.

We consider a trivial example to unveil some of the main issues involved in Material Planning.

TablesRUs (TRUS) produces and sells study tables. TRUS buys the legs and the top as raw materials, assembles them into tables and then paints them to ready them for sale. TRUS makes only one kind of table.

To make one table, they need:

- Four legs
- One top
- 2 liters of primer
- 2 liters of paint

We see a very simple list above because of our simplifying assumptions. The list would be more complex in more realistic situations. Business organizations use the term Bill of Materials – or just BOM for short – to refer to such lists. Table 1 shows the BOM for a TRUS study table.

Manufacturing organizations deal with raw materials and finished goods. They use raw materials to make finished goods. SAP uses the generic term material to refer to raw materials and finished goods (as well as trading goods, which we will shortly encounter).

As *Table 1* shows, a BOM for a material mentions the raw materials and the quantity of each one needed to manufacture or assemble the material. Materials that we make by putting together – or assembling – other materials are referred to as assemblies.

| Sno | Material | Quantity | Units |
|---|---|---|---|
| 1 | Legs | 4 | nos |
| 2 | Top | 1 | nos |
| 3 | Primer | 2 | liters |
| 4 | Paint | 2 | liters |

*Table 1: BOM for a TRUS table*

BOMs play an important role in determining how much of each material a company should buy (or make) while considering the production plans, current inventory, anticipated deliveries, how much time suppliers need to deliver the materials, and many other such factors. When companies deal with thousands of materials, the task becomes large and complex. Enterprise systems like SAP help companies to efficiently manage this complexity.

Let us consider another example (see *Table 2* and *Table 3*): to make one unit of a material A, we need 3 units of material B and one unit of material C.

However, in this example, material B itself is an assembly and has its own BOM; to make one unit of material B we might require 2 units of material D and 5 units of material E.

| Sno | Material | Quantity | Units |
|---|---|---|---|
| 1 | B | 3 | nos |
| 2 | C | 1 | nos |

*Table 2: Another BOM*

| Sno | Material | Quantity | Units |
|---|---|---|---|
| 1 | D | 2 | nos |
| 2 | E | 5 | nos |

*Table 3: BOM for item B from Table 2*

Let us assume that materials C, D and E are atomic and not assemblies – that is, they do not need their own BOMs. We do not need to assemble any other parts to make materials C, D or E.

The above example shows a multi-level BOM, that is, one in which materials that form a part of a BOM for one material could themselves be assemblies – and therefore have their own BOMs. SAP uses the term BOM exactly in the sense that we have used it above. However, BOM is a generic term used in industry and is not SAP specific.

The first set of review questions in this chapter appears below. You can find suggested answers to all the questions in this chapter on page 201.

***Review 1:*** *Look around you and select an object. Make up a BOM for it.*

***Review 2:*** *If TRUS has to make 50 tables and already has 100 legs, 12 tops, 60 liters of primer and 80 liters of paint in inventory, how much of each material would it need to buy or procure?*

***Review 3:*** *Refer to tables 2 and 3. If we have to make 10 pieces of material A and have no stock of materials B, C, D and E, how much of each of these materials would we need to procure?*

BOMs help in material planning. Let us also understand an important SAP-specific term that often goes along with BOMs – Routing. Whereas a BOM specifies the materials and their quantities needed to make a product, a Routing specifies the operations to be carried out to make a finished product or assembly. *Table 4* shows the routing for the study table.

| Opn no | Description | Materials needed | Work center | Standard time |
|---|---|---|---|---|
| **10** | Fix legs to table | Top and four legs | Assembly area | 20 min |
| **20** | Sand and apply primer | Primer | Finishing area | 15 min |
| **30** | Paint | Paint | Finishing area | 15 min |
| **40** | Dry | -- | Finishing area | 2 hrs |

*Table 4: Routing for TRUS study table*

TRUS buys table legs and the tops from vendor Country Lumber, and primer and paint from vendor Village Depot. While purchasing these materials from vendors, let us suppose that the vendors cannot supply the materials immediately and that there is a delay between ordering these and their arrival at the factory. We refer to this delay as Purchasing lead time.

Companies also do not usually buy items in arbitrary quantities. Instead they buy most materials in multiples of certain quantities – called the lot size – which could differ from material to material. For example, it might be the case that TRUS has a lot size of 100 for legs. In this case, if the company needed 360 legs, it would buy four lots of 100 each. This represents an example of fixed lot size. *Table 5* shows the lead times and lot sizes for the materials that TRUS uses.

| Material | Vendor | Purch lead time | Lot size |
|---|---|---|---|
| **Legs** | Country lumber | 1 month | 100 nos |
| **Tops** | Country lumber | 2 months | 25 nos |
| **Primer** | Village depot | 2 weeks | 100 ltrs |
| **Paint** | Village depot | 3 weeks | 25 ltrs |

*Table 5: Purchasing lead times and lot sizes for TRUS materials*

TRUS buys raw materials from these vendors regularly. To do so, TRUS places Purchase Orders with these vendors. Let us suppose that TRUS prints and sends out Purchase Orders by regular mail. Since TRUS does business regularly with several vendors, it might be beneficial for them to be able to pull up vendor information on demand. Also, assuming that TRUS uses a computerized system to generate the Purchase Orders, the program can pull relevant information about a vendor automatically. Some items of information that companies might store about their vendors include (among many others) Vendor name and Vendor address. Of course, companies need to maintain such information for all the vendors they do business with. Obviously, the same situation applies to customers as well – companies maintain information about all their registered customers – same with materials and lots of other things.

Information Systems professionals refer to such information as Master Records. The master record for a specific vendor would thus be a Vendor Master Record for that particular vendor. We refer to the collection of all vendor information as the Vendor Master. If a company does business with 1,000 vendors, then its Vendor Master would contain 1,000 Vendor Master Records, one for each vendor. Table 6 shows an example of a vendor master.

| Vendor no | Name | Address | email | ... | ... |
|---|---|---|---|---|---|
| **1** | Country lumber | 100 Main st, ... | ... | ... | ... |
| **2** | Village depot | 150 South ave, ... | ... | ... | ... |
| **3** | Ace hardware | 95 Brooklyn st, ... | ... | ... | ... |
| ... | .. | ... | ... | ... | ... |

*Table 6: Vendor master, containing one vendor master record for each vendor*

Similarly, companies maintain Customer Masters with Customer Master Records and Material Masters with Material Master Records and so on.

To generate a Purchase Order, TRUS would obviously need information about the materials that it wants to order. You can easily see that some of this information would come from the Material Master Records of the corresponding materials.

Thus far, we have talked about two different types of materials that TRUS deals with – the table that TRUS sells is a Finished Good while the materials that TRUS uses to make the table are Raw Materials. Sometimes companies do not manufacture any of the products that they sell – they simply buy from vendors and sell them to end customers without any additional processing. Amazon.com's book and digital media business is an example. WalMart would be another. Sometimes companies do both – that is, they make and sell some materials and also simply resell others. SAP refers to materials that a company simply buys and sells without further processing – that is, material that a company trades in – as Trading Goods.

Suppose TRUS, in addition to manufacturing and selling tables, also sold chairs, but did not manufacture them. Instead TRUS just buys chairs from another manufacturer and simply resells them (at a profit). In this case, we should not treat chairs as finished goods; these chairs represent Trading Goods.

The Material Master contains information for all three types of materials raw materials, finished goods and trading goods, one Material Master Record per individual material. If a company deals with 500 raw materials, 25 finished goods and 4 trading goods, its Material Master would contain 529 Material Master Records.

BOM and routing for our finished product are also considered master data.

***Review 4:*** *Answer the following:*

1. What information does a BOM contain?
2. What information does a routing contain?
3. What is purchasing lead time?
4. What is lot size?
5. How many different lot sizes have been mentioned in this document? What are they?
6. What is the name of the document that indicates to a vendor what materials and in what quantities we want to buy them?
7. Where is information about a particular material stored?
8. What is the name given to the entity that keeps information about all materials?
9. What contains information about a particular vendor?
10. What is the name given to the entity that keeps information about all vendors?
11. To store information about the vendors mentioned in Table 5, how many vendor master records would we need? Explain.
12. To store information about the materials mentioned in Table 1 as well as information about a TRUS table itself, how many material master records would we need? Explain
13. What type of material is a TRUS table?
14. What type of material is paint in the context of TRUS?

15. List the different types of materials discussed in this chapter.
16. What is a Trading Good?

Armed with this basic information about TRUS we can readily imagine the following business processes that would be absolutely essential for it to operate:

- purchasing raw materials (procurement cycle)
- producing finished goods (manufacturing execution)
- selling finished products (sales order processing)

Would these processes alone suffice? Think of what else the company would need to do in order to function. However, looking closer, we can see that, in addition to the above processes, TRUS also needs to perform various other activities. For example:

- **Sales and operations planning (SOP)**: How much of finished goods should the company produce in various time periods – next week, the following week, and so on. TRUS will need to base this on several things:
    - forecasted demand for its products
    - finished goods already in stock
    - production capacity constraints
- **Materials requirement planning:** Once TRUS has a SOP, it needs to then translate that into raw material requirements and prepare a plan for how much of each material to buy at specific times. In more complex situations companies may buy raw materials and create intermediate products or sub-assemblies that they then incorporate into their final products. In such cases, they would also need to plan when to make these sub-assemblies as well and determine the timing and quantities of raw material purchases accordingly. When companies deal with many raw materials and finished products, all this can become too complex to track manually. Furthermore, these processes happen continuously with prior plans being changed often to accommodate changes in the environment.

Suppose for example, that TRUS needs to produce 140 study tables on March 31 and has nothing in stock – no raw materials and no finished goods. How much raw materials would they need to purchase and by when should the purchase orders be sent out to the vendors? Assume for simplicity that all of the tables will be made in one day and that we are concerned with planning for just that one day of production.

***Review 5:*** *Answer the following:*

1. How many tables are to be made on March 31?
2. How many legs are needed?
3. How many tops are needed?
4. How many liters of primer are needed?
5. How many liters of paint are needed?

6. At the latest, when should the purchase order for legs go out?
7. How many legs should be ordered?
8. At the latest, when should the purchase order for tops go out?
9. How many tops should be ordered?
10. At the latest, when should the purchase order for primer go out?
11. How many liters of primer should be ordered?
12. At the latest, when should the purchase order for paint go out?
13. How many liters of paint should be ordered?

Given a BOM for a material M – which could be a finished good or a subassembly – the process of finding out how much of various other materials we need for producing a certain quantity of M is called BOM Explosion. This might look trivial, but when we have complex BOMs with several levels of nesting and numerous materials, BOM Explosion can be tedious. Automating it can increase efficiency. When we consider that companies often make many finished goods, with several of them having at least some common raw materials and sub-assemblies, you can see how useful automated BOM explosion can be for Materials Requirement Planning or MRP.

***Review 6:*** *Answer the following:*

1. What is BOM explosion?
2. What is MRP? Don't just expand the acronym. Instead, give a concrete example of your own.
3. In the TRUS case, what information should be considered in determining when a purchase order should be sent out?
4. What information determines the quantity of an item to be ordered?
5. In the TRUS case, all materials needed for producing a table are bought from vendors and therefore MRP only has to produce purchasing documents. Suppose some of the parts to assemble a table are themselves assembled in our own factory, using materials bought from outside, then what additional considerations enter the MRP process?

## So, what is this book about?

Thus far, we have looked at some obvious business processes in a simple manufacturing company. In a real-life situation, companies obviously have to do more:

- At the very least, companies are required by law to do Financial Accounting.
- To operate efficiently, we can imagine that companies will also perform Management Accounting to make good decisions based on accounting information.

- Most companies, especially manufacturing and trading companies, deal with materials and have to handle Inventory and warehouse management and Procurement
- Any company with a reasonable number of employees has to also perform Human Resources Management.
- A company with manufacturing facilities certainly has to perform Plant Maintenance or Enterprise Asset Management. This will encompass both routine Preventive Maintenance to reduce the risk of mechanical breakdowns (like oil changes for cars), as well as Breakdown Maintenance when things do go wrong.
- In addition, companies often execute projects – like constructing new manufacturing facilities, conducting sales conferences, building new information systems and so on. Companies therefore need to do Project Management as well.

The business world generally classifies processes directly related to the production and sale of the end products of a business as Main Value Chain activities and classifies other processes as Supporting Value Chain activities. Figure 2 lists the main and supporting value chain processes we have discussed thus far.

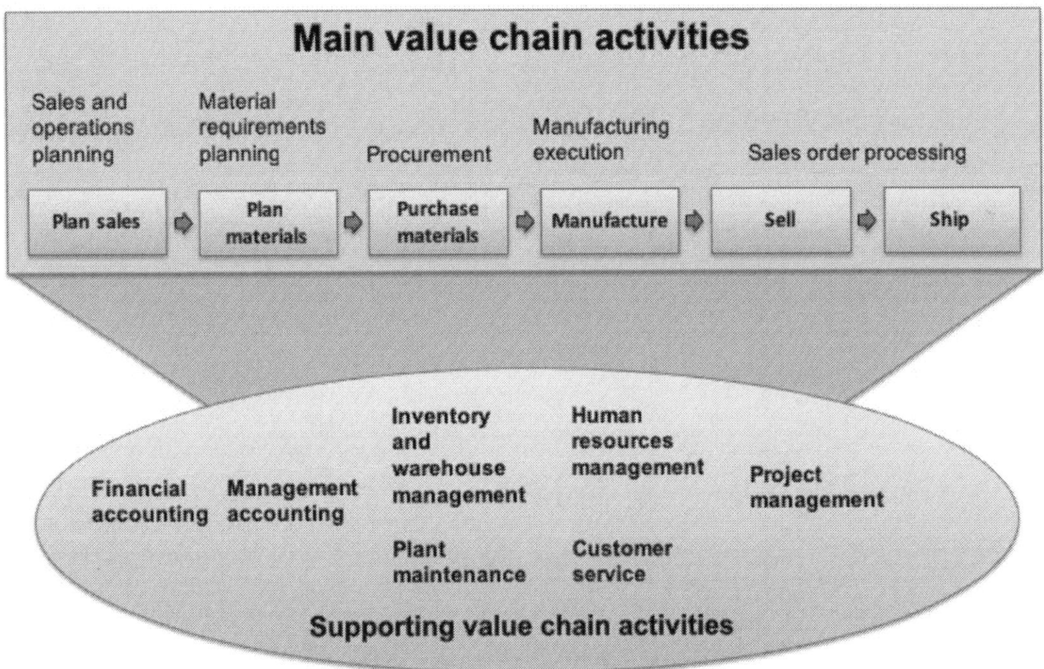


*Figure 2: Main and supporting value chain business processes*

This book addresses how SAP models each of the above business processes and highlights their inter-linkages.

To benefit from the course or to pass the SAP TS410 certification examination, you need to clearly understand the above business processes and their inter-linkages. Rather than just seeing each process and term we cover as something abstract that you need to memorize, you should be able to relate everything we talk about to concrete real-world occurrences.

We cover a lot of ground and get down to fairly minute details about many things. It might seem complex but grasping everything well only requires you to attach a common-sense meaning to the numerous terms that you will encounter. This chapter has already introduced many terms and will introduce some more before we are done.

**As a solid first step you should master the exact meaning of the terms and be able to recall their meanings as soon as you see them. With that kind of mastery, you will be able to handle the course and the SAP certification examination quite easily. Most crucially, you will understand much more of what goes on in the organization that you already work for, or will soon work for.**

## Key process flows

After that overview of the book's topics, let us turn our attention to some key process flows in SAP. You will grasp the upcoming chapters much better once you have this broad picture.

In this section, we want to show you a common theme that underlies many business processes in SAP. Before we look at that common theme, let us look at a concrete process. We start with Sales Order Processing – also called as the Order to Cash Process.

The Order to Cash process covers all the steps involved in customers ordering products from a company, the company fulfilling the order and the customer paying for the products.

The formal process starts when a customer places a concrete Sales Order with the company. However, in a business-to-business (B2B) situation some steps will usually precede the formal step of placing a Sales Order. The unit that covers the Sales Order or Order to Cash process in detail will discuss many possible preliminary steps. We discuss one of them in this chapter.

A customer could initiate the process with a Sales Inquiry. Through a Sales Inquiry, a prospective customer merely seeks some information about the products, pricing and availability, with no contractual obligation involved. After getting the information, the customer could decide not to buy and that will end the process.

Alternately, the customer might proceed to place a Sales Order – which is a legally binding document. The company will start the process of shipping the product and the customer will be bound to pay for the shipped products. Note the key difference between a Sales Inquiry and a Sales Order.

As we mentioned earlier, instead of with a Sales Inquiry, the overall Order to Cash process might begin in other ways as well. For example, a prospective buyer might send an RFQ – Request for Quotation. We will cover those in a later chapter.

Once the company receives a Sales Order from the customer, it will need to start the process of fulfilling the order. That is, the sales department has to give the green signal to initiate the process of picking the materials from the warehouse and shipping them out to the customer.

Although the Sales department might receive the Sales Order, other departments will take care of many of the subsequent steps.

The finished goods stock from which the company will fulfill the order might be located in a warehouse in some other part of the country or even elsewhere around the globe. Therefore, someone in the warehouse will need to see that they have a new delivery to fulfill and initiate the steps to pick the materials from the warehouse shelves. The sales department, after verifying that everything about the Sales Order is correct, initiates the shipping process by creating a document called the Outbound Delivery. This document authorizes the subsequent steps to take place.

In large companies, picking an item out of a warehouse shelf might not be as trivial an operation as it sounds. The warehouse could be huge – the size of several football fields – and so someone with a forklift, or a robot, will need to go to the correct location and pick out the material. In large warehouses, picking materials each time an order comes in could be woefully inefficient and hence warehouse operators will need to optimize the whole process. For example, they might accumulate orders for a while and then determine an optimal routing through the warehouse to pick out the materials while expending as little energy as possible in the process (and incurring as little wear and tear on the equipment as possible). Given all of these intricacies in warehouse operations, companies typically use complex software to manage warehouse operations. SAP also supports warehouse operations. Thus, the picking step involves an integration between the Sales Order Processing system and the Warehouse Management system.

Once the warehouse completes the operation of taking a material off the shelves – picking, the material can then be formally removed from the company's stock. Suppose the company had 1000 laptops of a certain model in stock for sale and some customer ordered 90 of these. Once the 90 units are allocated to the customer sales order, the company now has only 910 units in stock. Which department tracks this?

Warehouse management is only concerned with the warehouse logistics of efficiently putting materials away and retrieving them. Inventory Management is the entity that tracks the quantities of various materials in stock at various storage locations.

Thus, we see that in fulfilling a Sales Order, we also have an interaction between Warehouse Management and Inventory Management.

The step of reducing the inventory once the warehouse operation is completed is called Posting of

Goods Issue. At this step, the company allocates the picked materials to the concerned sales order and records the fact that it now has fewer units of the concerned material in stock. The company does not own these materials anymore. Who owns them?

At this point, the customer who ordered the items owns the material and therefore owes the company some money.

To initiate the process of receiving payment, the company sends an Invoice to the customer for payment. This step shows an interface between the sales process and Financial Accounting.

Eventually, the customer sends a payment and the company's Accounting department will post the payment to the customer's account. This completes the process.

Figure 3 shows the major steps in the Order to Cash process.

*Figure 3: Order to cash business process*

Enterprise Systems strive to provide smooth integration across departmental boundaries. Individual steps of business processes must, of necessity, be initiated within some module of the enterprise system. However, completing a step in all but the most trivial business processes involve interfacing with one or more other modules of the enterprise system.

Figure 4 shows the Order to Cash process with additional details about the module in which each step might be initiated and the other key modules with which each step might interface.

| Step | Initiated in SAP module | Possible interfaces |
|---|---|---|
| Sales Inquiry | Sales and distribution | Inventory, procurement, production |
| Sales Order | | |
| Outbound Delivery | | |
| Pick and Pack | | Warehouse |
| Post goods issue | | Inventory |
| Ship | | Transportation |
| Invoice | | Financial accounting |
| Post payment | Financial Accounting | |

*Figure 4: Order to cash business process with integration details*

## Generic process structure in SAP

Several SAP business processes share a common structure and you might find it useful to understand this basic structure.

Many important processes begin with a preliminary step to initiate the process – like Sales Inquiry in the Order to Cash process.

This preliminary step is usually tentative, with no firm requirement for further action. For example, a customer could initiate a Sales Inquiry, but then not follow it up with a Sales Order. However, once the Sales Order is created, then the process goes forward.

Figure 5 shows the generic structure of many important processes in SAP and shows how the Order to Cash process maps to that generic structure.

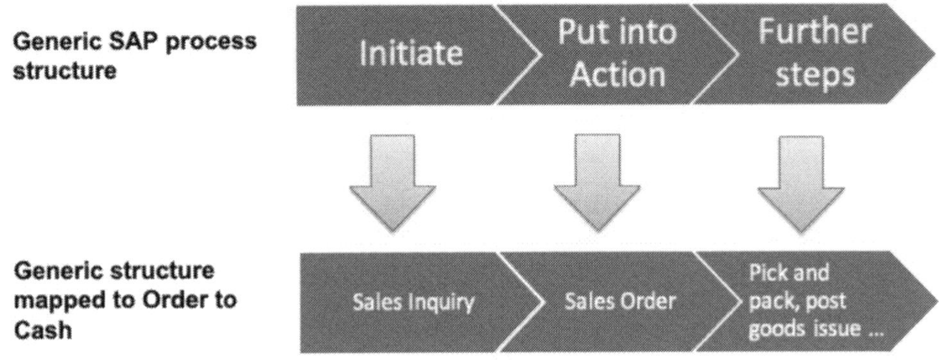


*Figure 5: SAP generic process structure and its mapping to the order to cash process*

Figure 6 shows a similar mapping for other business processes, with Order to Cash included for reference. Later chapters go into further details on these processes, but we briefly de- scribe each one below.

| | Initiate | Put into action | Further steps |
|---|---|---|---|
| Order to cash | Sales Inquiry | Sales Order | Outbound delivery, Pick and pack, Post goods issue, Ship, Invoice, Post customer payment |
| Purchasing | Purchase requisition | Purchase order | Goods receipt, Invoice verification, Payment |
| Manufacturing | Planned order | Production order | Goods issue, Confirmation, Goods receipt, Order settlement |
| Warehouse | Transfer request | Transfer order | Confirmation |
| Plant maintenance | Maintenance notification | Maintenance order | Goods issue, Confirmation, Settlement |

*Figure 6: SAP generic process structure and its mapping to several key business processes*

We see that each business process that Figure 6 covers has a preliminary step to initiate the process – Sales Inquiry, Purchase Requisition, Planned Order, Transfer Request and Maintenance Notification. All of these represent preliminary steps with no guarantee that the process will actually be executed to completion. The formal step occurs when these informal steps result in a corresponding Order – Sales Order, Purchase Order, Production Order, Transfer Order or Maintenance Order.

The subsequent steps differ from process to process.

Not all the steps in the above process template occur all the time. It is entirely possible that the process stops with the informal step itself – an Order might never be created. For example, a Sales Inquiry might never get converted into a Sales Order; a Purchase Requisition might not be converted into a Purchase Order.

The informal step is not mandatory. For example, it is possible for the Order to Cash process to start with the creation of a Sales Order directly and for the Purchasing process to begin with the creation of a Purchase Order.

We now provide a thumbnail description of each of the above processes. Be sure to see the commonsense nature of these processes and to memorize the steps and the documents in each one. That will significantly ease the process for you of integrating more intricate details in later chapters.

*Figure 7* shows the steps in the Procure to Pay business process and re-emphasizes their mapping to our generic process template.

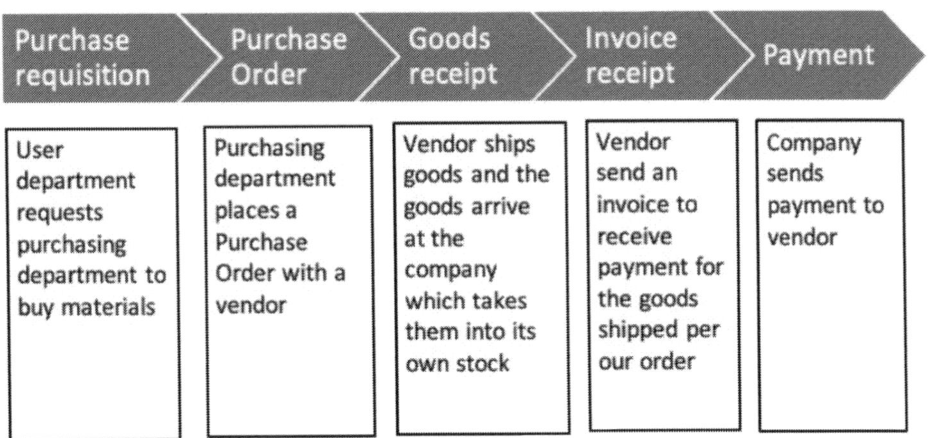


*Figure 7: Outline of the procure to pay process*

The Purchasing or Procure to Pay business process starts with some department requesting the purchasing department to buy some materials. The department needing the materials does this by creating a Purchase Requisition. Assuming that this requisition progresses further, the purchasing department might create a Purchase Order and send it to a vendor. You will see the details of vendor selection as well as other options for initiating the purchasing process in the corresponding course unit.

After receiving the Purchase Order, the vendor eventually ships the ordered materials and these materials show up at our company's warehouse. Thus far, the materials do not belong

to our company and we execute the step of Goods Receipt to formally receive the goods into our possession. Naturally this increases our stock of the materials received. We might some- times have additional steps – like quality inspection – before we take in the goods. We will cover these aspects later in the book.

The vendor will then send an invoice for the materials shipped. The Invoice Receipt step covers the process of verifying the invoice – after all we have to make sure that the invoice is for materials that we have actually ordered and received.

Finally, our company sends out a Payment to the vendor, thereby completing the process.

*Figure 8* briefly describes the steps in the Manufacturing business process.

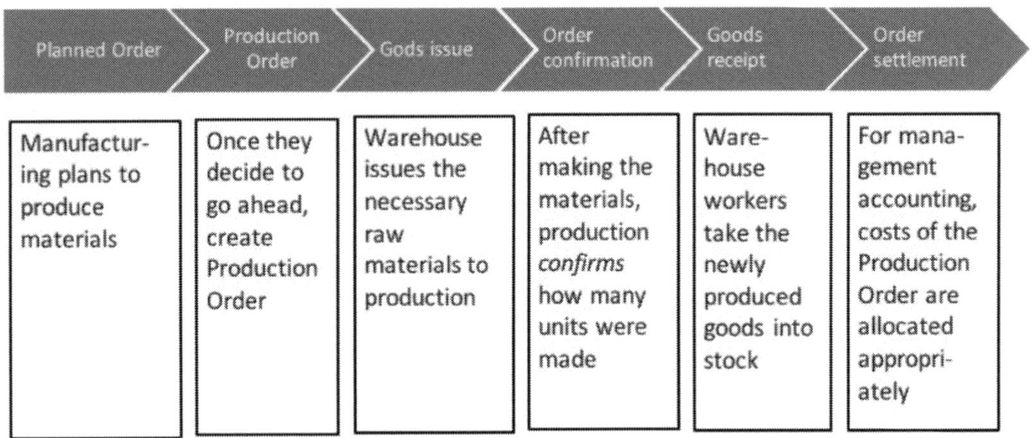
Planned Order
Production Order
Gods issue
Order confirmation
Goods receipt
Order settlement
Manufacturing plans to produce materials
Once they decide to go ahead, create Production Order
Warehouse issues the necessary raw materials to production
After making the materials, production *confirms* how many units were made
Warehouse workers take the newly produced goods into stock
For management accounting, costs of the Production Order are allocated appropriately

*Figure 8:Outline of the manufacturing business process*

The Manufacturing business process begins with the creation of a Planned Order – just a plan and not yet anything that causes any action. Planned Orders can be created manually but are usually automatically generated by the material requirements planning, or MRP, process.

Once the company decides to go ahead and actually execute the Planned Order, it creates a Production Order that authorizes actual manufacturing work.

Once the Production Order is released – and not before that – the manufacturing department can go ahead and issue the materials needed for the Production Order via the step, Goods Issue.

In SAP, the term release has a special connotation from a cost accounting viewpoint. From the viewpoint of production, a company would clearly be interested in tracking production costs. Let us suppose that a company has created a Production Order to produce 1000 units of some material. The company will surely want to track the production cost for this batch of 1000 units. The company should therefore accurately track all costs that go into this Production Order. In SAP, so-called Cost Objects can accumulate costs. To do this, whenever we record an expense, we can indicate the Cost Object to which the expense applies.

To facilitate this tracking, once the Production Order is released, SAP treats it as a Cost Object. This applies not just to Production Orders, but to all Order objects once they are released – it is at this point in time that they become cost objects. They are called Order-Related Cost Objects (discussed in greater detail in the Management Accounting chapter).

As production progresses, the manufacturing department confirms the number of units of the materials produced. Why would they need to do this – did they not start out to make a specific quantity of the material anyway? Well, actual production could come out quite different from what was intended. This could be because of quality or productivity issues. For management accounting, the company will need to know the exact quantity produced. This would be needed for computing the unit cost of manufacturing, and for other purposes.

In SAP, you will come across the term confirmation in a few different contexts. In manufacturing it denotes the completion of manufacture of some materials. In general, it confirms that some activity that was started has been completed and often causes other dependent activities to start.

Once manufacturing has produced the goods, the resulting materials have to go into our company's stock. Let us suppose our company had 200 tables in stock and manufacturing just completed making 50 more, we need to take those new tables into stock by executing the Goods Receipt step.

Although this seems to complete the manufacturing process, the process is not complete until the corresponding management accounting steps are complete. In the process of manufacturing some materials, the company has incurred some costs and these costs have to be allocated to the appropriate entities in the company. That whole process is called Order Settlement. You will also encounter the term Settlement quite a bit in SAP and it represents the step of allocating costs or revenues.

*Figure 9* briefly describes the steps in the Warehouse logistics process. This simple figure needs no further elaboration.

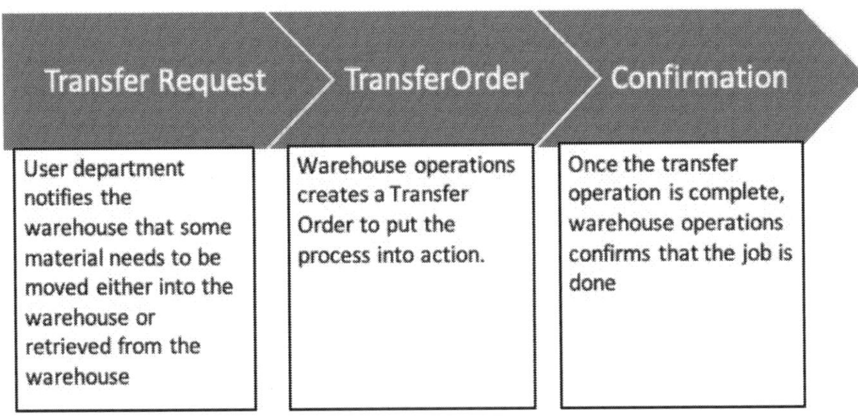


*Figure 9: Outline of the warehousing business process*

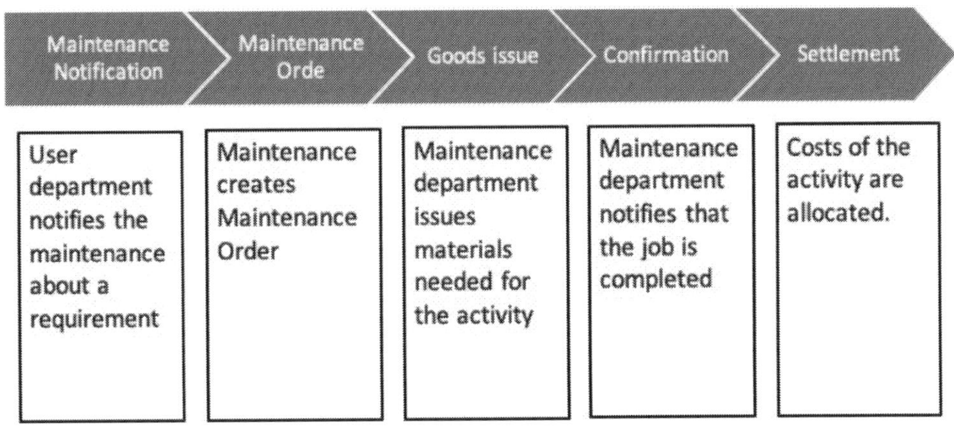

*Figure 10: Plant Maintenance or Enterprise Asset Management business process*

Figure 10 describes the steps in the Plant Maintenance process (Enterprise asset management).

## Configuring and customizing an ERP system

SAP provides a packaged solution that a user organization can adapt to its needs. Organizations differ significantly in their internal structures and operational policies and therefore we cannot expect a packaged solution like SAP to work out of the box for its user organizations. Of course, packaged ERP solution vendors like SAP know that organizations differ in many ways and provide features that allow user organizations to configure the ERP system to meet their requirements. In other words, ERP products ship with built-in functionality for several different ways in which companies do business and a particular company can choose the specific variants it needs.

For example, a user organization might not want all the standard steps that SAP provides in its Sales Order Processing module and might choose to turn off some of the steps. People implementing SAP for a user organization expend considerable effort. The process involves extensive discussions with managers in the user organizations to clearly understand their requirements, and to configure SAP accordingly. Configuration does not involve changing any code in the system or adding new code.

Given how businesses differ significantly, organizations often have specific features or practices that none of the built-in configuration settings can capture. In these cases, user organizations have to customize the ERP system by adding new code for their specific functionality. Customization calls for significantly more time, resources and effort than configuration.

Given the challenges of customization, organizations try to avoid it as much as possible. In some situations, organizations may choose to change their business processes to suit how the SAP software operates. Although this might sound like cutting your feet to fit the shoes, the approach might not be all that bad. After all, companies that sell packaged ERP offerings do so after extensive experience with numerous client organizations and often incorporate industry best-practices in their software. In most situations, adapting to their product is likely to be a wise choice.

Of course, organizations also try to gain competitive advantages in key areas by doing things differently and perhaps more efficiently than their competitors. In such situations, blindly adapting what an ERP system has to offer might not be in the best interests of a company. To summarize, companies might choose to customize the system in areas of their core competency where they would like to gain a strategic advantage by doing things differently. In other areas, they might just choose to go along with the features that the product has to offer.

***Review 7:*** *Explain in your own words the terms Configuration and Customization.*

***Review 8:*** *Find two reasons why Customization might require more time and resources than Configuration.*

## Organization levels in SAP

You already know that SAP is a packaged solution that is in- tended to meet the needs of many different organizations. Each organization adopts a structure to suit its own requirements. For example, one organization might divide its sales function in one way and another one might do it differently.

However, a packaged solution like SAP cannot possibly reflect the thousands of variations on how organizations could be structured. The SAP ERP system has its own structure. Mapping the structure of a user organization to those in the SAP system forms a key part of configuration.

SAP calls these basic structures as Organization Levels – do not confuse this with the common use of the term to represent levels in an organization's managerial reporting structure. Consider SAP Organizational Levels as a means for organizing data in the ERP system that support the various business processes.

To properly understand SAP, you need to master the concept of Organization Levels and the various Organization Levels it uses.

In SAP, a Client represents a conglomerate company – or a company that has several subsidiary companies within it. Take for example, the pharmaceutical giant Johnson and Johnson (J&J). Although J&J is a company in the legal sense of the term, internally it has several companies as legal entities and it is thus a conglomerate consisting of many companies.

Consider Google or Microsoft. These companies have their foreign subsidiaries – for example, Google UK, Google China, Google India and so on, with each of these being legal entities in their own right, registered in the respective countries.

Most large companies are actually conglomerates made up of other companies (legal entities). SAP uses the term Client to represent such a conglomerate entity. In SAP, Client is the highest organizational level.

The SAP term *Client* has no relationship to our normal use of the term.

SAP calls the individual companies that exist within a Client as Company codes. Each company code is a separate legal entity.

A company code is the smallest SAP entity to support a full set of books – or legal financial records. We will discuss this further in a later chapter. Figure 11 illustrates these ideas.

Company codes represent Legal entities from the viewpoint of statutory reporting requirements and other legal considerations. Thus, each company code has a Chart of Accounts and a General Ledger and can generate financial statements like the Balance Sheet and Income Statement.

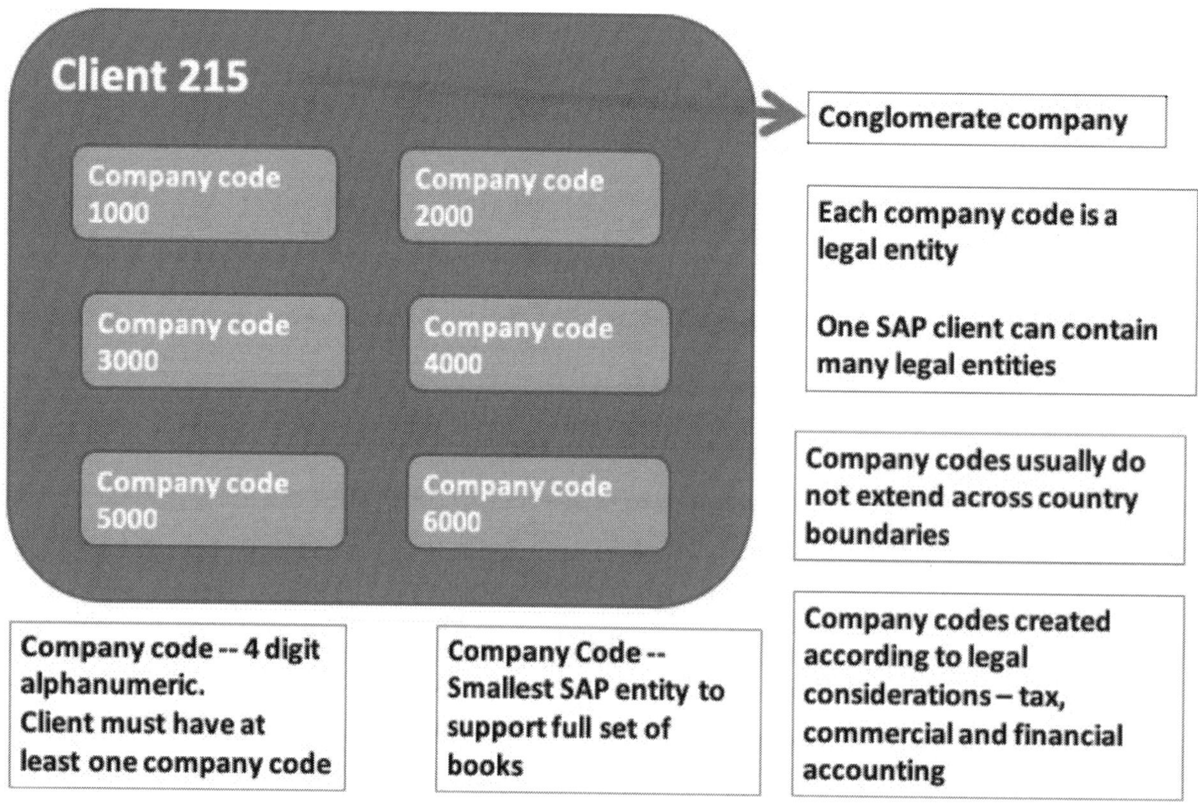


*Figure 11: Client and company codes in SAP*

Consider a conglomerate called ERPI with eight company codes as *Figure 12* shows.

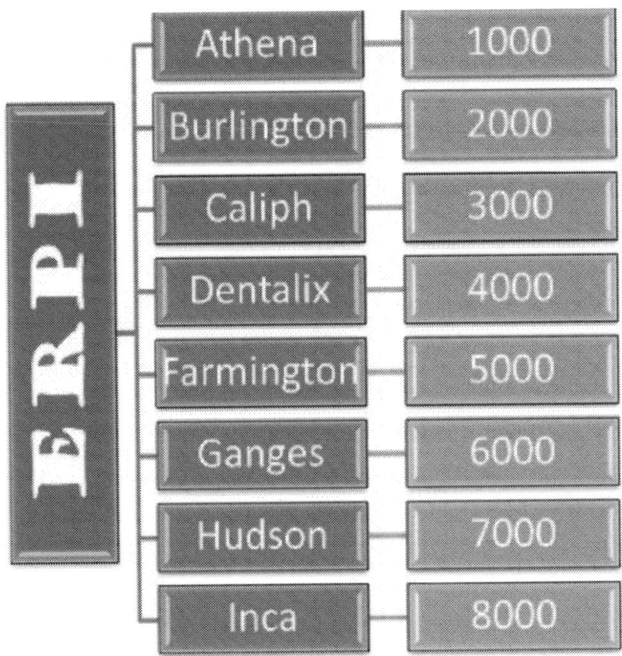


*Figure 12: ERPI – a conglomerate with eight company codes*

Each company code of conglomerate ERPI operates in one or more of the following market segments – Automotive, Pharmaceutical, Consumer Electronics and Medical Electronics.

Furthermore, large companies who do business in multiple countries often need to track the financial information for each of these segments. Since the company would create a company code for each of the countries in which it operates, there may be additional legal requirements to generate financial reports for each of these Business Segments. Using our ERPI example, *Figure 13* shows how these Business Segments can span across one or several company codes. As an example, it can be seen that the Medical Electronics business segment spans across every company code, while the Automotive Business Segment spans across all but company codes 1000 and 8000. Should company code 2000 (Burlington) require segment reporting, ERPI would be required to generate separate financial statements for each of the four business segments.

**Business segments**

**Company codes**

| | Automotive | Pharmaceutical | Consumer Electronics | Medical Electronics |
|---|---|---|---|---|
| 1000 | ☐ | ☑ | ☑ | ☑ |
| 2000 | ☑ | ☑ | ☑ | ☑ |
| 3000 | ☑ | ☑ | ☐ | ☑ |
| 4000 | ☑ | ☐ | ☑ | ☑ |
| 5000 | ☑ | ☐ | ☑ | ☑ |
| 6000 | ☑ | ☐ | ☐ | ☑ |
| 7000 | ☑ | ☑ | ☑ | ☑ |
| 8000 | ☐ | ☐ | ☑ | ☑ |

*Figure 13: ERPI – four Business Segments across eight company codes*

Each company code has individual financial reporting capabilities. However, companies may often need to generate financial statements for each business segment that spans across several company codes. To facilitate such a need, SAP makes use of business segments to support this process. If ERPI were to generate a set of financial statements for its overall Automotive business segment, it would include the relevant financial information from company codes 2000, 3000, 4000, 5000, 6000, and 7000.

In a conglomerate scenario, different company codes often share certain activities for efficiency. For example, ERPI could perform centralized purchasing for some company codes that use the same material. In such situations, the costs of shared activities need to be divided properly across the company codes that use these activities. Once again, we see the need to cut across company codes.

SAP uses the organization level called Controlling Area to facilitate management accounting across company codes. Only those companies belonging to the same Controlling Area can participate in cost sharing. We will see this in greater detail in the chapter on Management Accounting.

*Figure 14* shows an example of controlling areas and their mapping to company codes.

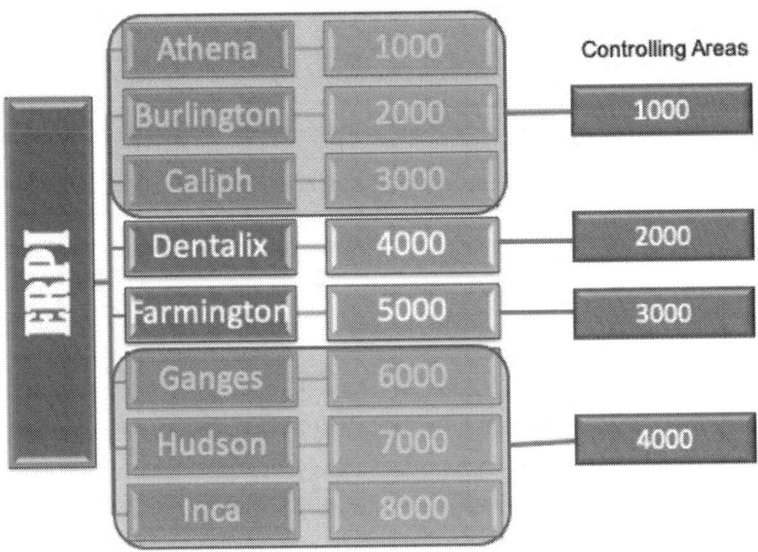


*Figure 14: ERPI – controlling areas and their mapping to company codes*

SAP uses four-digit numbers to represent company codes as well as controlling areas. Thus, a company code and a controlling area could have the same number. Do not let this confuse you. For example, company code 1000 is completely different from controlling area 1000.

Company codes 1000, 2000 and 3000 all belong to the con- trolling area 1000 and thus they can share some costs.

Likewise, company codes 6000, 7000 and 8000 all fall under controlling area 4000 and can share costs. Each of the company codes 4000 and 5000 has its own controlling area and therefore cannot share costs with any other company codes.

***Review** 9: Answer the following:*

1. Name two company codes in ERPI that cannot share costs with company code 7000.
2. Name two company codes in ERPI that can share costs with company code 3000.
3. Can company codes 1000 and 4000 have a common purchasing department? Why or why not?
4. Can company codes 6000 and 7000 share a power generating plant? Why or why not?

# Introduction to SAP S/4HANA

*SAP HAS BEEN AROUND* since 1972 and has undergone significant changes concurrently with the numerous momentous evolutions in hardware and software technologies. In this chapter, we cover the important stages in this evolution.

## The Evolution of SAP ERP

In 1979 SAP came out with their first ERP software product. At that time, it was known as SAP R/2. The goal and design of this software was to integrate business processes in a single software package and to do so in real-time. The architecture for R/2 was mainframe computing. In the early 1990's, R/2 was succeeded by R/3, in part because the technological architecture transitioned from mainframe to client/server. The year 2004 brought a growing business environment and the introduction of SAP NetWeaver. It also meant another change in architecture. The growing business environment and change in architecture is a common thread in the evolution of SAP ERP. MySAP ERP was not sufficient to meet the increasing demands of business. Businesses realized the need for software that extended beyond the enterprise. Additional applications such as CRM (Customer Relationship Management), SCM (Supply Chain Management), SRM (Supplier Relationship Management), and PLM (Product Lifecycle

Management) were included alongside SAP ERP. This suite of applications was called the SAP Business Suite. In 2004, SAP NetWeaver was introduced as an integration and application platform to support the SAP Business Suite as well as previous SAP products, and non-SAP products. The new technological architecture for MySAP ERP and its successor (ECC) was Service-Oriented Architecture (SOA). Figure 15 shows the evolution of SAP ERP.

*Figure 15: Evolution of SAP*

In the late 2000's, convergence of various technologies (mobility, in-memory processing, IoT, cloud computing, etc.) and critical mass (use of new technologies to create big data, social media, mobile users, etc.) led to innovative changes at SAP. SAP introduced HANA as a database. This was really SAP's first advancement in hardware. But HANA was more than just a database. HANA was labeled as an "appliance", which meant it offered characteristics beyond the standard database. For one, HANA was an in-memory database. This meant that all of the data stored in the database was stored memory and not on a physical disk like a traditional database. As such, SAP also had to incorporate capabilities for recovering data from the volatile memory storage. So, HANA also offers a persistence layer to log all of the data needed to support data recovery. (For a quick recap of HANA's persistence layer, you can link here: https://www.tutorialspoint.com/sap_hana/sap_hana_persistent_layer.htm).

In-memory capability also had the advantage of being able to process data faster. The SAP HANA appliance also allowed for columnar storage of data, not just row storage. This also leads to fast processing of the data in the database. This increase in speed is not linear. It's exponential, which means HANA has the power to process large amounts of data faster than ever before. HANA (as a database) serves as a means for meeting the Big Data needs of today's business environment. However, the problem was that HANA initially only supported processing data that was stored in SAP's Business Warehouse (data warehouse). But in 2012, SAP announced that SAP HANA would have the ability to run SAP ERP. And shortly thereafter, the entire SAP Business Suite could not be run on SAP HANA as a database.

Because SAP HANA was considered an "appliance", it was not a replacement for ERP or the Business Suite. It simply supported those applications on its database platform. But once again, changes in technologies led SAP to more innovation. SAP ERP and the SAP Business Suite were redesigned to leverage all of the capabilities of SAP HANA. And thus, SAP S/4HANA was born. S/4HANA is now the new "business suite". All of the applications available in the SAP Business Suite are included in

S/4HANA and rebranded to some degree as "Line of Business" (LOB) applications. What was traditionally referred to as ERP, is now called "Enterprise Management" in S/4HANA.

Some of the LOB solutions include:

- SAP S/4HANA Finance
- S/4HANA HR
- SAP S/4HANA Supply Chain & Asset Management
- SAP S/4HANA Sales, Services, and Marketing
- SAP S/4HANA Sourcing and Procurement

To support these new LOB's, SAP leverages solutions from some of its subsidiary companies. *Figure 16* shows some of these.

*Figure 16: SAP subsidiaries supporting various LOBs*

## S/4HANA Simplified Data Model

To make SAP S/4HANA successful, SAP not only re-branded their applications, they changed the entire data model. To accomplish this, SAP looked at their existing data model, which they found to be quite complex. One example of this can be found in how SAP traditionally managed the data for vendors and customers. Traditionally, this data was stored in two separate master data records. There was a record for the vendor and a separate record for the customer. Using the simplified approach, SAP realized that certain types of data stored for vendors and customers were the same. Figure 17 shows two separate records (one each for vendor and customer), however you can see that general and accounting data are needed for both. The only type of data that was truly unique, was the data relevant for purchasing or sales (vendor or customer).

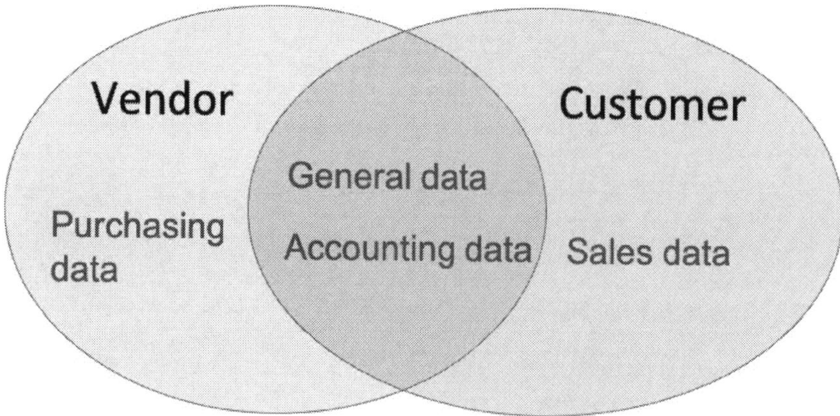


*Figure 17: Commonalities between customer and vendor masters*

This new simplified approach led to a new master record for the Business Partner. Whereby a business partner may be a vendor, customer, or both. As you can in Figure 18, a single business partner record can now be created to manage all types of data, dependent on the role of the business partner.

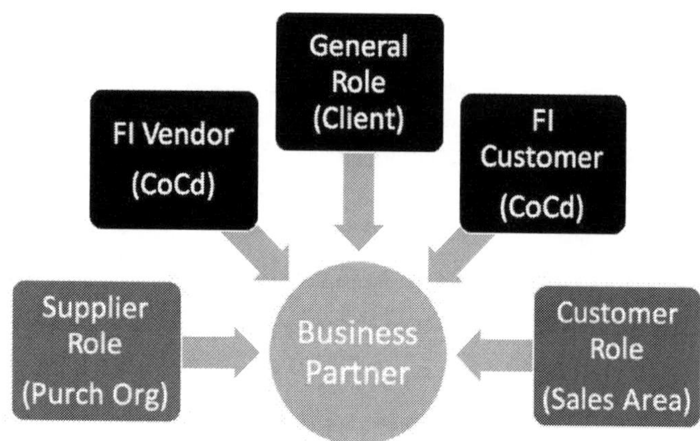


*Figure 18: Simplified business partner data model*

This simplified data model is not exclusive to vendors and customers. It is a common thread used to create a simpler and more unified data model throughout the entirety of S/4HANA.

## Simplification List

The Simplification List contains items to help SAP customers who are migrating from their current ERP environment to S/4HANA. This is a necessary step to ensure the data is modeled correctly and supported in S/4HANA. The simplification list provides the details for various types of data in S/4HANA and details the approach to creating the simplified data structure. Each new version of S/4HANA will include updates to this list to remain current and continue support for customers who are migrating to S/4HANA.

## New User Experience

Today's business person is mobile and needs a simpler interface to interact with SAP. With a simplified data model, along comes a simplified user experience, SAP Fiori User Experience (UX). Among the key driving forces behind the development of Fiori was the increase use of mobile devices by end users, management, analysts, and developers. These users don't necessarily interact with the system in the same manner. As a matter of fact, it's most likely they do not.

To support the needs of different users while creating a more simplified experience, SAP altered its way of thinking redesigned the user experience to one which shifted from a focus on the application/system, to a focus on the role of the user. One of the major advantages of this approach is that the Fiori UX has greatly reduced the navigational pain points as well as the number of clicks necessary to create data, run transactions, and run reports.

Today's user is also composed of a different demographic. We are referring to a demographic who grew up in the age of mobile devices and connectivity. Today's user is accustomed to working with a more contemporary interface. An interface that uses apps which can be downloaded and installed on mobile devices. The expectation is that the apps serve unique purposes and are streamlined in a manner which makes navigation simpler and the purpose more focused. The design of SAP Fiori takes these measures into account. Users work with apps to perform the necessary transactions required for a unique business purpose. The apps are housed on one screen, which SAP calls the SAP Fiori Launchpad. Figure 19 and Figure 20 show examples of the Fiori user interface. (As long as SAP continues to make it available, you can try SAP Fiori for free at: https://www.sapfioritrial.com/).

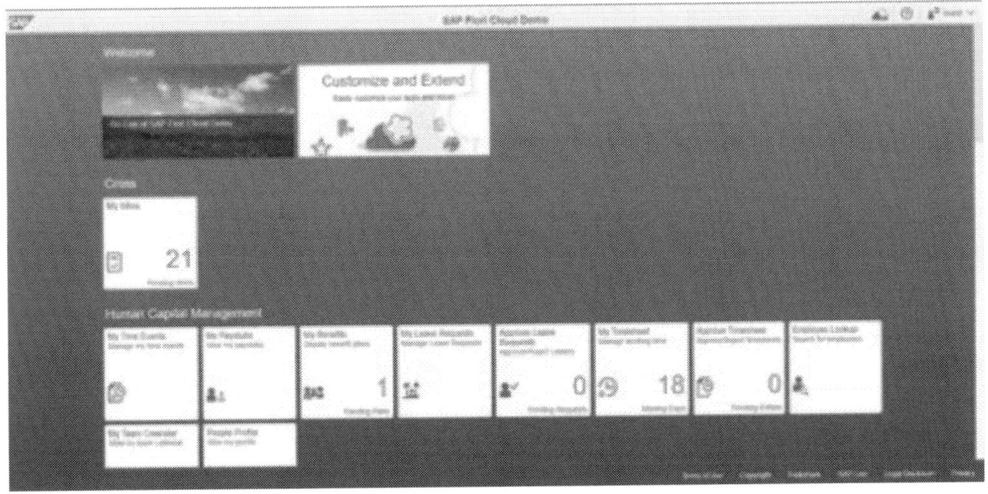


*Figure 19: An example of the Fiori user interface*

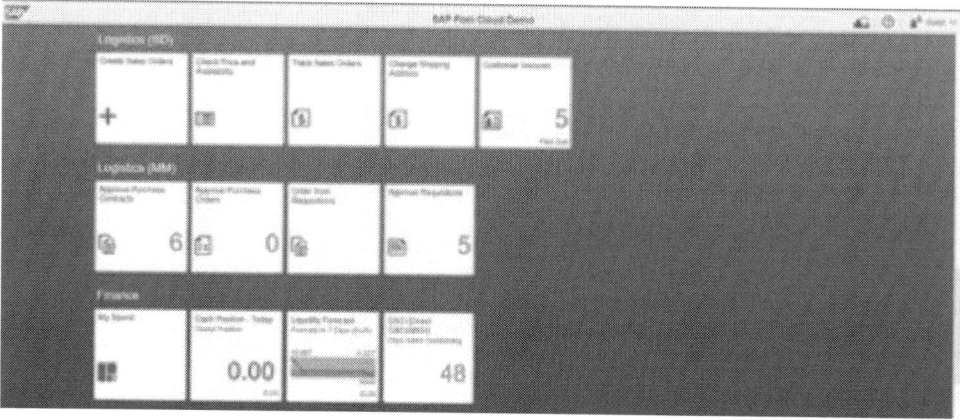


*Figure 20: Another example of the Fiori user interface*

## The Cloud Platform

Deploying SAP S/4HANA is pretty simple. SAP has done a good job at making S/4HANA flexible to be deployed in a variety of ways. First, it can be deployed on-premise which means the company manages all aspects of the technology and infrastructure necessary to run S/4HANA. This option may be good for some SAP customers, but not necessarily for all. SAP also offers S/4HANA in the Cloud. For SAP customers opting to run S/4HANA in the cloud, there is additional flexibility. An SAP customer can choose a "private" cloud or a "public" cloud. There are additional options depending on which cloud scenario the customer selects. SAP also offers hybrid solutions, allowing customers to manage some aspect of S/4HANA on-premise and other aspects in the cloud. But the most important takeaway from the various deployment options follow:

- On-premise
    - Highly customizable
    - Customers manage the infrastructure
    - Customers who are migrating from ERP, must address the Simplification list items
- Cloud (private)
    - Flexible deployment
    - less IT investment and complexity
    - Scalable
- Cloud (public)
    - IaaS (Infrastructure as a Service)
    - S/4HANA hosted by third partied (i.e. Amazon Web Services, Google Cloud et. al)
    - Pay as you go
- Hybrid
- Combining on-premise solutions with cloud solutions

# Financial Accounting (FI)

***FINANCIAL ACCOUNTING*** plays a key role in enterprise systems. Much of financial accounting goes on in the background as enterprise systems like SAP carry out transactions. Nevertheless, we cannot function effectively in an enterprise system without a basic grasp of financial accounting. SAP can perform seamlessly, by making the accounting postings quietly in the background. For this to occur, we have to set it up correctly to know which accounts to update at each stage of various business transactions. Setting this up properly requires us to understand basic accounting principles. This chapter provides the necessary background in accounting for you to be able to grasp the accounting implications of various steps in the business processes that we cover. By no means should you consider this brief introduction to even remotely reflect a complete coverage of financial accounting. The chapter covers the bare minimum that you will need to grasp what we cover in SAP.

## Introduction

The Financial Accounting process tracks the financial implications of business operations. Examples of business transactions with financial implications include:

- A vendor sends an invoice for products that we ordered
- We send out an invoice to a customer for products that they ordered, and we shipped
- A customer makes a payment against an invoice that we sent out
- We make a payment to a vendor based on an invoice that the vendor sent

- We pay our employees
- A tax payment is coming up
- We collect sales tax from our customers
- We use some material in production
- We receive goods at our warehouse
- A machine depreciates
- Value of land owned by the business appreciates
- ...

Businesses carry out numerous such transactions as they execute their operations and need an orderly means of keeping track of their financial implications. A simple-minded approach would involve just recording every transaction. The way we record our check transactions in a check ledger serves as a simple example of single-entry book-keeping. While being simple, the approach does not allow easy access to certain kinds of information that businesses need.

For example, with single-entry book-keeping:

- We cannot easily get an idea of the health of a business
- We will be hard-pressed to know much money is locked up in accounts receivable or inventories
- We will not be able to quickly find out how much money we owe others – our accounts payable.

We would need other systems outside of a single-entry bookkeeping system to track such things. Furthermore, the single-entry system does not allow us to easily spot errors.

Because of the shortcomings of single-entry book-keeping, organizations have been using double-entry book-keeping since the medieval times. Under this system, each financial transaction is entered in two places rather than in just one place. This approach reflects the simple fact that a financial transaction always has two sides to it. For example, when we pay cash and buy an item, our cash is reduced, but in exchange we get the item, and hence, the value inherent in it. Single-entry book-keeping does not reflect this basic balance. Double-entry book-keeping, on the other hand, is designed around this fundamental balance and it also erases many of the problems with single-entry book-keeping.

## The Accounting Equation and the Balance Sheet

At any point in time, a business has things of value or assets – directly as cash, or things it can sell and get cash in exchange. What might be some examples?

- Cash (direct currency, or money in the bank)

- Land
- Plant and machinery
- Raw materials and finished goods in stock
- Accounts receivable – money that people owe the business. While this might not appear to have a cash value, it actually does. After all, eventually some or all of the money owed will be paid back.
- Accounts receivable can indeed be sold. If you were to sell a business, the buyer of the business would inherit the accounts receivable and hence the rights to receive the payments as and when they are made.
- Investments that are held by the company

How did the business acquire all these assets? They certainly did not materialize from thin air and the business must have paid money to acquire these assets. Where did the business get the money to buy (or otherwise get) all of these things? The business used the owners' money, and perhaps other borrowings, to fund all these assets. For example, suppose the combined assets of a business are worth $1 million. This might be made up of, for example, cash and bank balances of $ 500,000, material stocks of $ 300,000, accounts receivable of $100,000 and investments worth $100,000. We need to account for how the business obtained assets worth $1 million. That is, how did they fund these assets? Here is one possible scenario:

- The owners started the business with an initial capital of $100,000
- The company has outstanding bank loans worth $700,000
- The company has $50,000 worth of raw materials that suppliers have supplied, but the company has yet to pay for (accounts payable)
- Over the years the company has ploughed back profits worth $150,000 into the business (accrued retained earnings)

This accounts for the $1 million in assets. The items: bank loans and accounts payable are called liabilities, and the items: initial capital and accrued retained earnings are together called owners' equity. The above exemplifies the basic accounting equation:

Assets = Liabilities + Owners' equity

or, in the current context:

*$1m assets = $750,000 liabilities + $250,000 owners' equity*

This just reflects the simple fact that whatever the company currently has by way of assets must have been obtained only by using the company's liabilities and owners' equity.

A company's Balance Sheet depicts the basic accounting equation as it applies to the company.

However, instead of just showing the assets, liabilities and owners' equity as single numbers, the balance sheet breaks these down further as we show below.

**Various kinds of assets:**

- current assets
- fixed assets
- land and buildings
- raw material inventories
- finished goods inventories
- marketable investments
- accounts receivable
- ...

**Various kinds of liabilities:**

- short term loans
- long term loans
- accounts payable
- ...

**Various kinds of owners' equity:**

- preferred stock
- ordinary stock
- retained earnings
- ...

We can also think of the balance sheet as a snapshot of a company at a specific point in time – like a photograph showing the assets, liabilities and owners' equity at that instant. If the company completely stops all its operations and comes to a complete halt (performs no activities that have any financial implications), the snapshot of its assets, liabilities and owners' equity represents its balance sheet. The balance sheet depicts a static view of the company. Of course, things are always happening, and the company seldom comes to a complete halt in all respects. Just like we never come to a complete stop, but people can still take an x-ray image to check on our health. A balance sheet is like an x-ray image to assess some aspects of the health of a company.

Accountants show the assets on the left-hand side and the liabilities and owners' equity on the right-hand side as Table 7 shows:

| Assets | | Liabilities and owners'equity | |
|---|---|---|---|
| **Cash and bank** | $500,000 | Bank loans | $700,000 |
| **Inventories** | $300,000 | Accounts payable | $50,000 |
| **Accounts receivable** | $100,000 | Initial capital | $100,000 |
| **Investments** | $100,000 | Accrued retained earnings | $150,000 |
| | $1,000000 | | $1,000000 |

*Table 7: Sample Balance Sheet*

The first set of review questions for this chapter appears below. You can find suggested answers to all the review questions in this chapter on page 204.

***Review 1:*** *For each of the following items, indicate whether it is an Asset, Liability, Owners' Equity or none of those:*

- New shares worth $450,000 that the company issued
- Shares worth $100,000 that this company purchases in other companies as a way of investing some of its earnings
- $26,500 that the company is yet to pay its suppliers for goods already supplied
- The value of goods supplied in the above item ($26,500, lying in inventory and not yet used)
- Money in a checking account maintained by the company
- Money that the company has paid as salary to its employees in the current month
- The value of a power generation plant that the company maintains to supply power to one of its factories
- Bank loans amounting to a total of $700,000 that the company has taken out to finance its business operations

***Review 2:*** *In your own words, explain the logic behind the accounting equation.*

***Review 3:*** *Draw up a balance sheet from the following information about John, a kid who operates a lemonade stand:*

- John borrowed $15 from his parents and put $7 from his profits back into his business
- John has equipment (glass jugs, drinking glasses, mixing spoons, etc.,) worth $10.
- John has borrowed 10 lemons from mom and will pay them back after the next weekend. These lemons cost $5.
- John has stocks of sugar worth $5
- Some of John's friends bought lemonade worth a total of $7 during the past weekend and have promised to pay him soon.

- John has $5 in his cash box.

***Review 4:*** *For each of the following business transactions, explain whether the total of assets (and therefore liabilities and owners' equity) will have a different value at the end of the transaction than it had at the beginning. If there will be a change, explain which components on the two sides of the accounting equation change. If the total does not change, explain whether there will be any redistribution among the components within a particular side of the equation. We have given two examples:*

***Example 1:*** *Company uses cash to buy raw materials worth $500.*

***Answer 1:*** *No change to total assets. Redistribution occurs only within the assets side. Cash decreases by $500 and inventory increases (the company now has additional raw material worth $500).*

***Example 2:*** *Company takes out a new long-term loan for $100,000*

***Answer 2:*** *Total assets increase because the company now has $100,000 more in cash (on the left-hand side of the equation). To compensate, there is now also an additional long-term liability (the new bank loan that the company now has to pay back) of $100,000 on the right-hand side. The two balancing entries therefore ensure that the accounting equation balances.*

a. The company receives raw material worth $50,000 and has been invoiced by the vendor in full. The company has not yet paid for this purchase.
b. The company uses $200,000 of its cash to buy back (repurchase) some of its own stock.
c. The company pays back $100,000 of its outstanding loan.
d. The company pays $50,000 to the vendor mentioned above.
e. The company places a new purchase order with a vendor to supply goods worth $35,000
f. The company sells some of its land for $1,000,000

## The Income Statement or Profit and Loss Statement

If we view the balance sheet as a snapshot of a company at some instant, the income statement summarizes the things a company did over a period of time as it moved from one state to another (or from one Balance Sheet to another). In this sense it presents a dynamic view of what a business did during a time interval – as opposed to the state of a business at some instant which the Balance Sheet shows.

For example, a company had a balance sheet on the start of January 1, 2017 and another at the end of December 31, 2017. These two are almost certain to be quite different. The income statement covering the period January 1, 2017 through December 31, 2017 will show the financial aspects of what the company did by way of operations during this period. Table 8 shows an example.

Table 8 shows an income statement with commonly occurring items.

| **Sales revenue** | **$200,000** |
|---|---|
| Less: Cost of goods sold (cost of raw materials, labor, and other things directly attributable to the products sold) | $100,000 |
| Less: Overhead expenses (selling, general and administrative expenses) | $50,000 |
| Less: Depreciation (to account for wear and tear of plant and machinery; discussed later.) | $10,000 |
| Less: Interest expenses (on bank loans) | $10,000 |
| Interest and other income | - |
| **Profit before taxation** | **$30,000** |
| Less: Taxes (@40%) | $12,000 |
| Profit after taxation | $18,000 |
| Less: Dividends paid to shareholders | $5,000 |
| **Retained earnings** | **$13,000** |

*Table 8: Income or profit and loss statement*

## Chart of Accounts

Thus far, we have seen the structure of the balance sheet and of the income statement. Within each, we have seen different broad headings under which financial accounts are aggregated. If we take a closer look, we can see that there are five different account categories:

- Asset accounts: To track things of value owned by the business
- Liability accounts: Track money that the business owes to outsiders
- Owners' equity: Track amounts the business owes its owners
- Revenue accounts: Track various incomes from business operations
- Expense accounts: Track payments necessary to run the business

Under each category, we might keep several different sub headings for convenience. For example, under asset accounts we could keep different accounts to track the following things separately:

- Raw material inventories
- Finished goods inventories
- Bank account

- Plant and machinery
- Land
- Investments and marketable securities
- ...

Similarly, under expense accounts, we could have many different accounts to separately track the following:

- Payments for raw materials
- Labor charges
- Rents
- Utility charges
- ...

Each company might choose to maintain a different set of accounts in each category depending on its individual needs and how fine-grained it wants the tracking to be. For example, a company could keep just one single expense account perhaps called rents paid to track all rents that it pays. A different company might keep four different expense accounts to track the rents it pays – office rents, equipment rents, executive residence rents and other rents. What a company actually uses depends on its own needs.

Can you think of three different revenue accounts that a company might keep?

A company that sells several products could keep separate revenue accounts for each product group. A company could also keep separate revenue accounts to track revenues from sale of products and sales of services.

The Chart of Accounts is a complete list of different accounts that a business chooses to maintain to keep track of its financial transactions.

As we already know, with double-entry book-keeping, each transaction affects at least two of these accounts Of course, it is important that a company chooses its accounts judiciously so that it can track finances at the level of granularity and detail that it wants to.

Each account in a Chart of Accounts is identified by a unique account number with each one belonging to one of the 5 account categories – asset, liability, owners' equity, revenue or expense. Table 9 shows an example of a Chart of Accounts.

| Account number | Account name / purpose |
|---|---|
| 1000 | Cash (checking account) |
| 1100 | Debtors (accounts receivable) |
| 1200 | Stock on hand (inventories) |
| 2000 | Creditors (accounts payable) |
| 2100 | Bank overdraft |
| 3000 | Capital (owners' equity) |
| 3200 | Accrued retained earnings |
| 4000 | Credit sales |
| 4100 | $5,000 |
| 5000 | Cost of goods sold |
| 5200 | Accounting fees |
| 5300 | Bank charges |
| 5400 | Rent |

*Table 9: Sample Chart of Accounts*

A Chart of Accounts is only a set of account numbers, their types and the purpose for which each account number will be used. The Chart of Accounts is just an empty structure and does not have any actual financial information in it. It has no values included in it. It is merely a design for some company to use as a basis for its actual accounting. For example, many companies can use the Chart of Accounts in Table 9 as a basis for their accounting.

In SAP, every Company Code must have a Chart of Accounts associated with it. Several company codes within a Client could adopt the same Chart of Accounts. Each Company Code within a client could also adopt a different Chart of Accounts.

***Review 5:*** *For each account mentioned in the Chart of Accounts in Table 9, identify the category to which it belongs (asset, liability, etc.). Do you see any pattern?*

***Review 6:*** *Find a friend and, in your own words, explain to them the concept of Chart of Accounts.*

SAP provides several pre-defined charts of accounts. We can also create custom charts of accounts for our own needs. When multiple company codes share a common Chart of Accounts, they all have a similar accounting structure. This facilitates easy account consolidations across company codes.

## General Ledger

Companies keep the details of accounting transactions in their General Ledger (G/L). The G/L is a collection of all accounts in the company along with the details of all transactions posted in these accounts. When we said earlier that a company code must have a Chart of Accounts, what we meant is that the

G/L of every company code must be based on a Chart of Accounts.

If a company chooses to base its G/L on the Chart of Accounts shown in Table 9, then the G/L will have all the accounts shown there and each transaction that occurred in those accounts will be listed in the G/L.

The General ledger is a report showing for each account (in the Chart of Accounts being used), the transactions that occurred for that account over a certain period of time. For example, the general ledger account for the bank account would keep track of all withdrawals from and deposits into the account. Likewise, the material stock account will keep track each instance where materials were received into stock and each instance where materials were issued from stock. The sum total of debits and credits (discussed below) in the overall general ledger must always match because of the practice of double-entry book-keeping – if not, we know that something is wrong.

***Review 7:*** *What is the relationship between the Chart of Accounts and the General Ledger?*

***Review 8:*** *If two different company codes use the same Chart of Accounts for their General Ledger, does this mean that they will always have identical transactions posted for each account? Explain.*

## Accounting Transactions

When companies maintain their General Ledger in paper form, they actually record transactions into the G/L as they carry out business. With automated business transaction processing and with ERP systems like SAP, accounting entries mostly occur seamlessly in the background as we carry out other business transactions like buying, selling and manufacturing. Of course, this is possible only if someone has properly configured things so that SAP has enough information to determine which accounts to update for each stage of a business process.

Despite accounting entries mostly being posted automatically, you might still find it useful to understand the logic of double-entry accounting postings.

Single vs. double-entry book-keeping: As we have seen already, in single-entry book-keeping we enter each transaction in only one place. In double-entry book-keeping, every transaction affects at least two different accounts, and sometimes more. In double-entry book-keeping, every account has two sides – debit and credit. The amount of each transaction is recorded equally on the debit and credit sides of different accounts. This redundancy helps to avoid some types of errors.

For an accounting transaction worth $1,000, there will be a total debit of $1,000 entered into one or more accounts and an equal amount entered as credits into one or more other accounts. The rules for debits and credits can sometimes seem quite confusing, but they need not be. We now turn our attention to these rules.

# Logic of double-entry book-keeping

Whenever there is a financial transaction, there is a shift of value from one entity to another. For example, if Adam gives Bob $1,000, then $1,000 have changed hands from Adam to Bob. Although some value has changed hands, the total value between their two accounts is still constant.

You might have already come across some rules like "debit what comes in" and "credit what goes out" and found them to be quite confusing. The main culprit in this confusion is our (mis)interpretation of the terms debit and credit in terms of their normal day-to-day usage. We tend to erroneously think of debit as a decrease, or as an outflow, and credit as an increase, or as an inflow.

The key to financial accounting heaven (if ever there can be such a thing), lies in banishing these evil misunderstandings. So, for now, simply forget any association of increase or decrease with the terms debit and credit. You have to remember just one single rule for correctly understanding debit and credit accounting postings!

The original creator of the double-entry system of bookkeeping quite arbitrarily decided that when an asset increases, we should debit the corresponding asset account. You need to remember just that single rule. You can derive all the other rules from it. Consider these examples:

- We buy a machine our fixed assets increase by the value of the machine. Applying the above rule, we debit the fixed asset account.
- Our material stocks increase (because a vendor shipped items that we ordered), then we debit the stock account.

Easy!

So, the only rule, or axiom is: “When an asset account increases in value, debit it.”

What did we mean when we said that we can infer all other rules from this one axiom? Let us see.

What would you do when an asset account decreases in value?

Suppose we sell a machine (a fixed asset) and therefore the fixed assets decrease. Think a bit before reading on.

Should we not do the reverse of what we did when an asset increased? Yes, of course! In this case, we credit the fixed assets account.

What about revenue and expense accounts? Think a bit about the relationship of these to assets and liabilities. If we can figure out where these would eventually end up on the balance sheet – as everything must (why?), then we can finagle the rules we already have to arrive at the posting rules for these as well.

So how does sales revenue affect the balance sheet? The answer lies in understanding the income statement. Note that the last line of the income statement says that the money left over after taking away all costs, interest, taxes and dividends is transferred to retained earnings on the balance sheet – which is part of owners' equity. It therefore behaves like a liability. Sales revenue will tend to increase this figure and expenses will tend to decrease this. Thus, revenue accounts can be treated similar to owners' equity and liabilities, and expense accounts can be treated the opposite – that is, like assets. That is all there is to it! Table 10 summarizes the logic of account postings.

| Account type | Increase/decrease | Action | Logic |
|---|---|---|---|
| **Asset** | Increase | Debit | Axiom |
| **Asset** | Decrease | Credit | Converse of above |
| **Liability/Owners' equity** | Increase | Credit | Converse of first rule since Liabilities and Owners' equity represent sources of funds whereas assets represent the use of funds. |
| **Liability/Owners' equity** | Decrease | Debit | Converse of above |
| **Revenue** | NA | Credit | Source of funds – treat like a liability |
| **Expense** | NA | Debit | Use of funds – treat like an asset |

*Table 10: Account posting logic*

Let us consider a few examples of manual posting of transactions:

***Example 1:*** *The business owner gives the business $2,000 as capital by transferring it to the company's bank account. Which accounts are involved here? Owners' equity and Cash are the accounts affected by this. Let us look at it from two viewpoints. Consider owners' equity – it is increasing by $2,000. By our rules, it should be credited and hence cash should be debited. Alternately, look at cash. It is an asset and is increasing. So, it should be debited according to the rule. So, Owners' equity should be credited. Both ways of reasoning lead to the same result.*

*We credit Owner's equity account for $2,000 and debit the Checking account by the same amount. Table 11 shows the entries.*

| | Debit | Credit |
|---|---|---|
| Checking account | $2,000 | |
| Owners' equity | | $2,000 |

*Table 11: Account postings for owner giving $2,000 to the business*

***Example 2:*** *The Company buys raw materials worth $300 from a vendor, and the terms of payment are*

*40% up-front (from our checking account) and 60% due in 15 days. Assume that the vendor has delivered the material. Look at the state after we have paid the 40% and are yet to pay the 60%. Which accounts does this affect?*

*Checking account, since we pay 40% or $120 up-front; Material stock, since the vendor has delivered, causing the material stock to increase; and Accounts Payable, since we still owe 60% or $180 to the vendor. What happened to each of these accounts? Cash, an asset, went down – so it (the checking account) should be credited for the $120 that it decreased by. Accounts payable, a liability went up, so it should be credited by the $180 it increased by. Material stock, an asset has gone up and hence should be debited for the entire $300. Table 12 shows the full picture.*

| | Debit | Credit |
|---|---|---|
| Checking account | | $120 |
| Accounts payable | | $180 |
| Material stock | $300 | |

*Table 12: Account postings for material purchase in Example 2.*

***Example 3:** The company spends $1,500 on advertising.*

*The affects cash (or checking account), and an expense account (advertising). The balance in the checking account went down and so we credit it. The expense account went up and so we debit it. Table 13 shows the picture.*

| | Debit | Credit |
|---|---|---|
| Checking account | | $1,500 |
| Advertising | $1,500 | |

*Table 13: Account postings for $1,5000 advertising expense*

***Example 4:** The Company sells goods worth $500. The customer pays $300 upfront and will pay the balance in 30 days. The cost of goods sold (the cost of making the goods) is $400.*

*This affects cash (asset), sales revenue (revenue) and accounts receivable (asset). Cash has increased – debit. Revenue has increased – credit. Accounts receivable has increased – debit. Table 14 shows these.*

| | Debit | Credit |
|---|---|---|
| Sales revenue | | $500 |
| Checking account | $300 | |
| Accounts receivable | $200 | |

*Table 14: Initial account postings for material sales in Example 4*

However, we are still not done here. After all, the materials the company sold were in the material stock account. After the sale, these materials are gone from there, but our earlier postings have not reflected this change. This part of the transaction affects the material stock account (asset) and the cost of goods sold account (expense). Table 15 shows this posting.

| | Debit | Credit |
|---|---|---|
| Material stock | | $400 |
| Cost of goods sold | $400 | |

*Table 15: More postings for material stock in Example 4*

## Sub-ledgers and Reconciliation Accounts

We already know that accounts receivable and accounts payable appear on the balance sheet as assets and liabilities respectively. For external reporting, maintaining these as single accounts might suffice. But does this suffice for a company's operations?

Clearly not. Knowing, for example, that we need to collect a total of $200,000 does not do much good unless we know how much each customer (debtor) owes. Similarly, knowing that we owe a total of $175,000 to various vendors does not do much good unless we know how much we owe to specific vendors.

Companies maintain general ledger accounts for accounts receivable and accounts payable and also maintain separate ledgers (called sub-ledgers) for the lower level accounts (one for each vendor and one for each customer). As the company conducts business, it posts debits and credits to these sub-ledger accounts. However, since the main accounts – the accounts receivable and accounts payable G/L accounts – just accumulate these sub-ledger accounts, the system **automatically** makes postings to these accounts as well.

We call these higher-level accounts reconciliation accounts. Thus, the accounts receivable and accounts payable balance sheet accounts are two examples of reconciliation accounts. There could be others as well – in any situation where the company maintains sub-ledgers to track individual transaction details and maintains a summary account that automatically accumulates these sub-ledger accounts, the summary account is a reconciliation account.

Can you think of any restriction that might apply to reconciliation accounts? That is, what can one do with a normal account that one cannot do with a reconciliation account?

We highlighted the word "automatically" in the previous paragraph for a good reason. Clearly, the system cannot allow us to manually post anything to a reconciliation account. We can post to the sub-ledger accounts and the system automatically posts these to the reconciliation account. SAP does not allow manual posting to reconciliation accounts. Figure 21 illustrates the concepts with an example.

**Sub-ledger accounts for each customer**

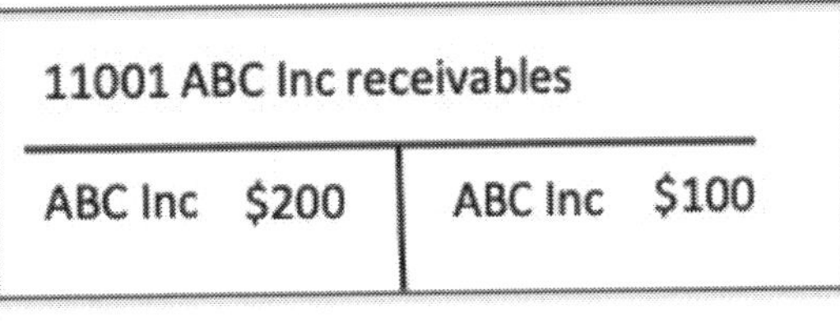

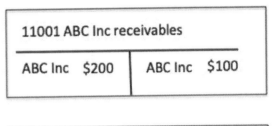

**Reconciliation account in G/L**

1100 Accounts receivable

ABC Inc $200 | ABC Inc $100
DEF Inc $350 | PQR Inc $155
PQR Inc $175

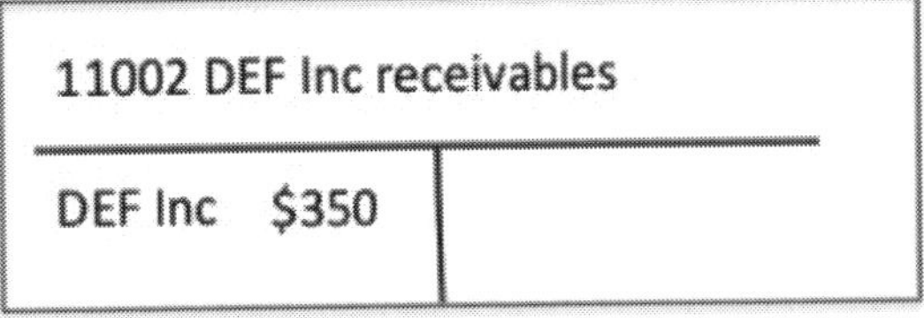


11001 PQR Inc receivables

PQR Inc $175 | PQR Inc $155

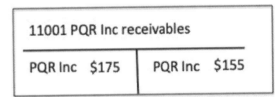

*Figure 21: The sub-ledger accounts (on the right) show that customer ABC Inc owed $200 and paid $100 of that. These have automatically been carried into the Accounts receivable reconciliation account in the Balance Sheet (on the left)*

## Depreciation

Some assets get used up within a year after being purchased – for example, raw materials from which a company makes finished products. Other assets have a long life and are used up much more gradually – For example, a machine could last 10 years or more.

Suppose a company bought a machine for $10,000 at the start of 2018. Let us assume that the machine would last five years. At the time of purchase the value of the machine would have been a part of the plant and machinery asset account. It would have also appeared as an asset on the balance sheet, if the company had generated a balance sheet soon after purchasing the machine.

Should the company have treated $10,000 as an expense (in the income statement for calculating the profit) for the year 2018?

Clearly not – since that machine would be used to make products not just in 2018, but for four more years. We should consider only a part of the value of the machine as having been used up in 2018 and hence the company should consider only a portion of the $10,000 as an expense for 2018.

However, if we look at the actual outflow of money, the company spent $10,000 in 2018. Furthermore, in the years beyond 2018, the machine will still help the company to produce materials, but the company would not have paid anything at all during that year.

Accountants handle this matter through depreciation. They would consider the value of the machine as depleting slowly over a certain number of years and allocate only the portion applicable to a particular year as an expense for that year. In the present example, the company might consider the expense for each of the five years of the life of the machine as $2,000.

Clearly, it is very difficult to figure out exactly how much value is actually used up in a certain period of time. However, for statutory reporting purposes governments set up rules to determine how much of an asset's purchase value can be charged off as an expense each year.

For example, laws could allow a company to depreciate the value of a machine over 10 years. It is possible that the machine might be used for longer than ten years, but after ten years it will no longer be treated as an asset with value.

We saw that depreciation appears as an entry in the income statement (as an expense) and affects the profits earned. Therefore, the rate at which a company depreciates impacts its financial performance (on its income statement). A large value decreases profits and a low value tends to inflate profits.

Companies can potentially use this as a way of manipulating their reported profits – hence the governmental rules.

Let us see how straight-line depreciation (a common method) works. Under this, a company depreciates an asset in equal amounts over a time span. Suppose a company depreciates a $10,000 machine over ten years using the straight-line method, then the company charges depreciation expenses of $1,000 each year.

That is, the company debits $1,000 to the depreciation expense account and credits the plant and machinery asset account $1,000 each year.

In addition to the straight-line depreciation method, accountants employ other methods as well. We will not go into the details.

***Review 9:*** *What is impact on profits if a company charges less depreciation than it should?*

We have seen that laws govern how a company can depreciate its assets. In the example above, we depreciated a $10,000 asset over a 10-year period. The laws governing depreciation do not account for the actual lifetimes of specific assets – that would make the laws very complex and difficult to enforce. However, it is possible that an asset that a company depreciates over 10 years actually lasts 15 years. By depreciating it over 10 years the company is reporting lower profits in the first 10 years than would be possible if it could depreciate it over 15 years.

If the company uses this higher depreciation to determine the cost of manufacturing (and hence the profitability) of a product that uses this machine, then it would be underestimating the profitability in the first ten years of the life of the machine.

Accurate estimates of costs can help companies considerably in making the right decisions on pricing, among other things.

However, if the company has to follow rules on depreciation, it would appear that a company cannot have an accurate estimate of its production costs. What can companies do about this?

Laws only govern external reporting and do not prevent a company from charging depreciation in whatever way it wants for internal use. Therefore, a company could follow the law for depreciation as far as external reporting goes but use a different approach to depreciation when it comes to internal decision-making.

SAP uses the concept of depreciation areas to achieve this. The same asset could belong to different depreciation areas with different policies.

To make things concrete, suppose an asset costs $10,000 and the law requires it to be depreciated in 10 years. However, for internal analysis the company might believe that the asset actually lasts 15 years. The company could keep two depreciation areas A and B, with A depreciating the asset over 10 years and B depreciating it over 15 years. *Table 16* shows the depreciation that will be charged in each of the first five years as well as the asset's value at the end of each of the first 5 years.

| | **Depreciation area A (10 years)** | | **Depreciation area B (15 years)** | |
|---|---|---|---|---|
| **Year** | **Deprcn. for year** | **Yr. end asset value** | **Deprcn. for year** | **Yr. end asset value** |
| 0 | | $10,000 | | $10,000 |
| 1 | $1,000 | $9,000 | $667 | $9,333 |
| 2 | $1,000 | $9,000 | $667 | $9,333 |
| 3 | $1,000 | $9,000 | $667 | $9,333 |
| 4 | $1,000 | $9,000 | $667 | $9,333 |
| 5 | $1,000 | $9,000 | $667 | $9,333 |

*Table 16: Depreciation areas showing how the same $10,000 can be depreciated differently in different areas*

## Review questions: Financial accounting

You can find answers on page 207. To answer questions with asterisk (*) at the end, you will need to have read the official course material.

1. What are reconciliation accounts?
2. At what level is the G/L managed?
3. What is the organization level corresponding to a legal entity in SAP?
4. Which is the smallest SAP entity that supports a full set of books?
5. Which organization element supports the creation of Balance Sheet and Income Statements that cut across company codes?
6. Which organization element is concerned with tracking of profits within a component of a company code?
7. Which organization element is concerned with tracking the performance of external market segments? *
8. How many company codes can be in a client?
9. To how many company codes can a business area be linked?
10. How many business areas can a company code be linked?
11. Where does the controlling area fit into the organizational elements of SAP?
12. How many company codes can be allocated to a controlling area?
13. What restriction applies to a company code when it is assignment to a controlling area?
14. At what level are charts of accounts maintained?
15. How many charts of accounts can a company code use? *
16. How many company codes within a client can use the same Chart of Accounts?
17. From where do G/L accounts get their definition? *
18. What are the two segments that make up a complete G/L master record? *
19. Which segment of the G/L master contains general information which describe the account? *
20. Which segment of the G/L master contains specific information about how a company chooses to use an account? *
21. ______________________ allows for "real-time integration" of G/L accounts with sub-ledger accounts.
22. The account for an individual vendor or customer would be found in the ___-ledger.
23. The Accounts Receivable G/L balance sheet account used to consolidate individual customer receivables is an example of a ______________ account.
24. The feature of the G/L that allows for postings within a document to be broken out into different categories, such as profit centers and segments is called __________ ______________. *

25. SAP customers can take advantage of light-weight management accounting functionality by using ________ __________ within FI. *
26. In SAP FI, there is a single ledger at the client level called the ________ ________. *
27. It is always possible to drill down into the line item list of an account from the balance display for a G/L account. T/F? *
28. The vendor business partner includes the following three roles: __________, __ ________, and _________ ____________.
29. The reconciliation account number for Accounts Payable in the G/L is stored in which role and which organizational level of the vendor business partner? *
30. Information about purchasing data for a vendor can be found in which role and which organizational level of the vendor business partner? *
31. The customer business partner has information in the following three roles: __________, __________, and __________

32. .

# S/4 Hana-specific Financial Accounting Overview (FI)

*NOW THAT THE PREVIOUS CHAPTER* has given you a good understanding of how financial accounting impacts your enterprise, it is time to look at how SAP S/4HANA helps support these financial accounting needs.

## Chart of accounts

As noted in the previous chapter on Financial Accounting, the Chart of Accounts is a necessary part of financial accounting. SAP S/4HANA makes available several country-specific, pre-defined Chart of Accounts for the enterprise. Recall that a Chart of Accounts is simply "a set of account numbers, their types and the purpose for which each account number will be used." A key objective of financial accounting is to satisfy the "legal" reporting requirements, via financial statements. These financial statements are legally required by the governing agencies in each country in which the enterprise does business.

However, many large enterprises have operations in several countries and the regulations in these countries can differ. For example, in the United States the Internal Revenue Service requires such enterprises to submit financial statements. These financial statements consist of the Balance Sheet reports, Income Statement reports, and in some cases, Cash Flow reports. These statements are generated from business transactions resulting in financial postings to the General Ledger. However, when it comes to financial statements, not all countries have the same requirements as the United States. As a matter of fact, each country has its own laws and regulations with which any enterprise operating in that country must comply. In some cases, an asset account in one country may be treated as a revenue account in another country. Because of this, the Chart of Accounts must be structured in a manner which complies with the laws in each country. Therefore, SAP has provided their customers with pre-defined Chart of Accounts which support the legal requirements for various countries.

## Account Types

In SAP S/4HANA, the chart of accounts is defined using account types. There are several account types, but for the purposes of this discussion and for certification, we will focus on three main account types.

- **Balance sheet accounts**: The first account type is Balance Sheet accounts. In the previous chapter, we had broken these down into asset accounts, liability accounts, and owners' equity accounts.
- **Primary cost element accounts**: The second account type in SAP S/4HANA covers Primary Cost Elements. This account type is used to keep track of normal Profit and Loss impacts. Expense and revenue postings are made to this account type and in the previous chapter, we had broken these into revenue and expense accounts. As you will see when we discuss Management Accounting, the Primary Cost Elements are used to track cost and revenue impacts within management accounting. In SAP, the Controlling or CO module deals with management accounting.
- **Secondary cost elements**: The last account type to be mentioned here is Secondary Cost Elements. Including these in Financial Accounting represents a significant change in the data model in SAP S/4HANA. Prior to S/4HANA, Secondary Cost Elements were exclusively used in management accounting or CO. Applying the simplified data model approach, secondary cost elements are now an account type in the Chart of Accounts. This means it can be reflected in both FI and CO and only one master record is required.

Traditionally, financial accounting (FI) and management accounting (CO) were quite separate, with just a single point of contact that linked expense accounts in FI to primary cost elements in CO. However, SAP has gradually been unifying FI and CO and the inclusion of Secondary cost elements right within FI itself represents a major step in this direction.

The main reason for this discussion of the Chart of Accounts and Account Types is because the account types: Primary Coast Element and Secondary Cost Element significantly impact Management Accounting, which we will address a little later.

## Universal Journal

You should also be familiar with another aspect of SAP S/4HANA, which is the simplified data model. The simplified data model provides significant advantages from an accounting perspective. One of the advantages was discussed above. In the case of Primary and Secondary Cost Elements, the simplified data model reduces the amount of master data maintenance. Another benefit is how transactional data is simplified. If we consider a transaction which has a financial accounting impact, there are many accounting characteristics involved in that transaction. For instance, a good receipt of a consumable material (expense posting) from a purchase order contains many characteristics. Below are some examples:

- Material number (Material Ledger)
- Company Code (FI)
- G/L Account numbers (FI)
- Posting Date (FI)
- Posting Amount (FI)
- Chart of Accounts (FI)
- Primary Cost element (CO)
- Profitability Segment (CO)
- Profit Center (CO)

In prior version of SAP ERP, many of the characteristics which stemmed from this transaction would have been stored in many different tables in the database. SAP has simplified that structure so both Financial and Management Accounting characteristics are now stored in a single journal, called the Universal Journal. Figure 22 shows more details about the Universal Journal.

**Universal Journal**

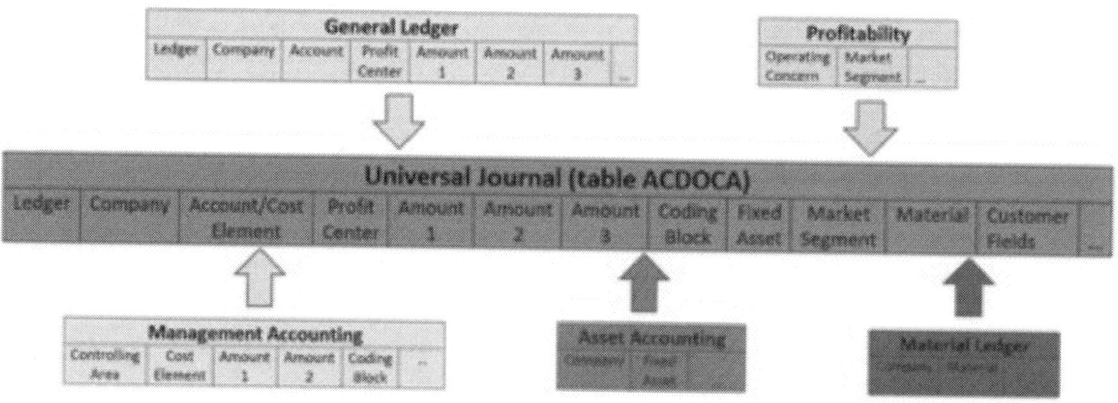


*Figure 22: Universal Journal (Image source: https://blogs.sap.com/2017/04/21/moving-to-the-universal-journal-how-does-the-new-gl-fit-in/)*

In this image, it's clear that the new data model is simplified. Financial accounting characteristics, characteristics from the Material Ledger, and management accounting (CO) characteristics are now contained in one table (ACDOCA). This simplification model allows a single view of the truth, accurate and real-time integration with management accounting, and the ability to run real-time analysis using transactional information.

## Business Partners

In SAP S/4HANA, business partners represent individuals; groups of individuals (such as a family); or organizations (such as a company). The concept of using business partners is another effort to simplify the data model in SAP S/4HANA. In prior versions of SAP ERP, master data was created separately for each vendor and each customer. In Figure 23, notice that General Data and Accounting Data are maintained for both Vendors and Customers. For vendors however, purchasing data is maintained. While for customers, sales data is maintained. In this scenario, separate master data needs to be maintained for both vendors and customers.

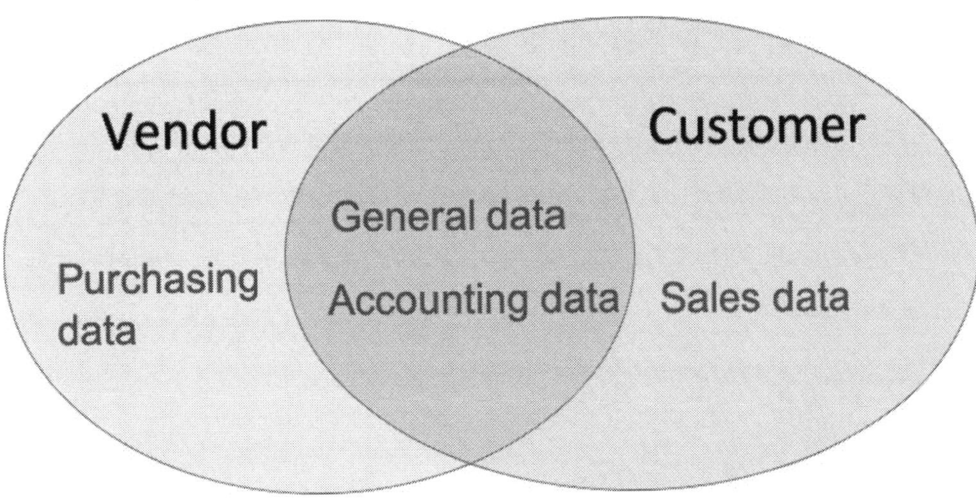


*Figure 23: Business partner data maintained in different masters prior to S4/Hana despite some commonality*

In SAP S/4HANA, SAP utilizes the "simplification list" to identify commonality across different types of data in SAP ERP. Using the above example, the simplification list would lead us to the conclusion that General Data and Accounting Data for both vendors and customers need not be maintained in separate master records. Instead, that data could be maintained once by using the concept of business partner (and business partner roles) to eliminate the need to have both vendor and customer records maintained separately. Figure 24 shows the result of using the simplification list to create a more streamlined data structure.

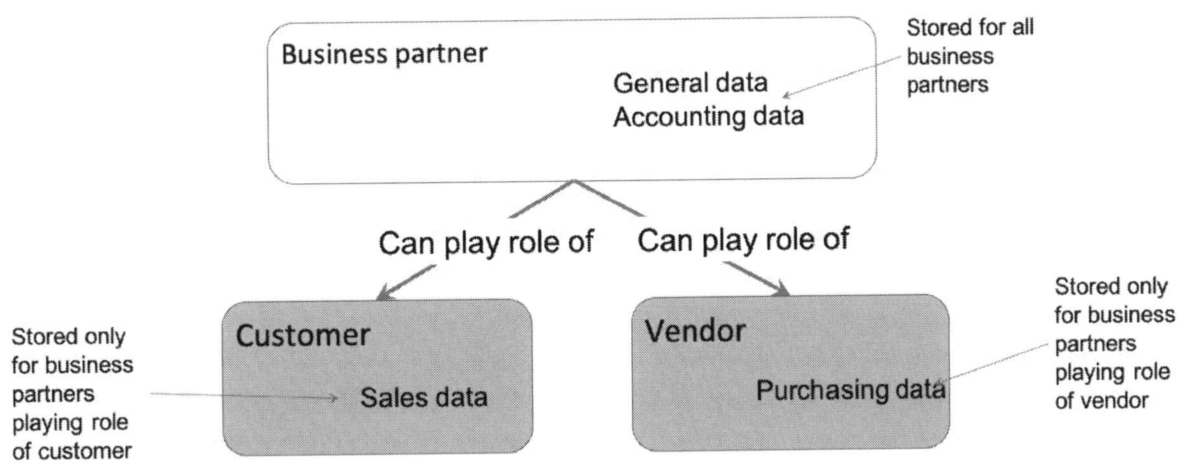


*Figure 24: Single business partner master; a business partner can play the role of vendor or customer or both and the information maintained depends on the roles played*

In this way, you can see that a single business partner can be both a vendor and customer, if needed. The data maintained is the same but modeled in a more simplified fashion. The implications this has on financial accounting is simple. If you recall from the previous chapter on financial accounting, assets and liabilities are managed in the general ledger, but are also managed individually in subledgers. The creation of the business partner essentially supports managing that business partner in a subledger account (whether that business partner be a vendor or customer). The FI role maintained at the company code level (CoCd) provides the link between that subledger account and the corresponding reconciliation account in the general ledger.

We showed the impact of the simplification list on Customer and Vendor above. The impact is even more widespread as Figure 25 shows.

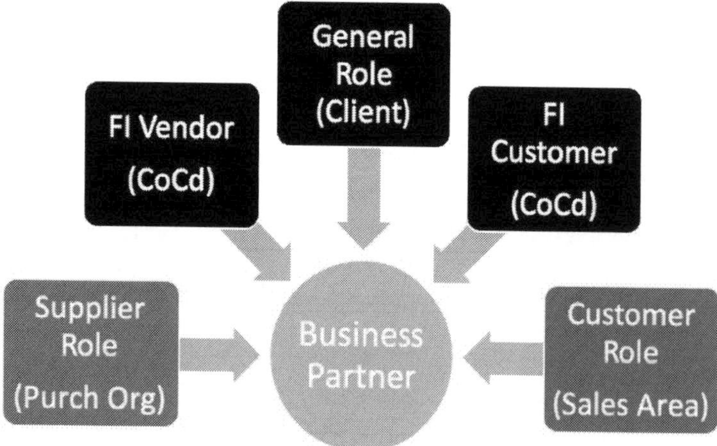


*Figure 25: Simplification list creates a more streamlined structure to unify business partner data*

# Management Accounting (CO)

*FINANCIAL ACCOUNTING* keeps track of monetary flows in an organization with the goal of external reporting according to established laws. Management Accounting also aims at tracking monetary flows but aims to use such information for making sound managerial decisions. This chapter introduces the broad ideas involved in management accounting, and specifically explains some important SAP S/4HANA concepts and terms involved. Once you grasp the contents of this chapter, you will be ready for the official materials provided by SAP. Without this background you might have some difficulties with following the lectures and using the SAP course materials.

As with prior chapters, this chapter also contains review questions which you should try and answer before proceeding. Even if you do not know an answer, you will find it useful to still try hard to provide a meaningful answer before peeking. Doing so will make it easier for you to absorb what follows. The first review question appears below. You can find suggested answers to all the review questions in this chapter on page 210.

***Review 1:*** *Explain in your own words why the information gathered for financial accounting might not be readily usable for decision-making.*

---

## Financial accounting vs. management accounting

Financial accounting aims to accurately record all the monetary flows in an organization. Being externally focused, it strives to generate compliant external reports like the balance sheet and income statement for the company as a whole.

Management Accounting provides financial and other information in a form suitable for decision-making – as opposed to producing accurate and compliant reports useful for entities outside an organization to assess its financial health.

Financial and management accounting differ in many ways. For example, financial accounting can tell us quite precisely what the profitability of the entire company is; not very surprising, because financial accounting exists for that very purpose. However, when it comes to providing an accurate picture of the profitability at finer levels of granularity, financial accounting is simply not designed for that. For example, a company would be interested in determining the profitability of each of its products, or each of its divisions or departments or at even finer levels of granularity – like the profitability of a given product in a given market, manufactured in a specific plant.

***Review 2:*** *Explain why financial accounting might not be well-equipped for the profitability computations mentioned in the previous paragraph.*

## A management accounting scenario

Let us consider the concrete example of a company that manufactures two products A and B. During a given month the company made 10,000 units of A and 6,000 units of B. The company manufactures both products in a single plant. The company uses some dedicated machinery for each product (machines used only for that product). However, the company also has some machines that both products share.

Products A and B require different materials and have dedicated manufacturing personnel. However, the same plant supervisors and foremen oversee production operations for the two products. Likewise, a single marketing department markets both products and the same sales force sells both.

The company currently sells Product A at $10 per unit and product B at $15 per unit.

***Review 3:*** *Explain how you might go about calculating the profit margin separately for the two products. Just mention the approach – you do not have enough information to come up with a number.*

Clearly, to calculate the profit margin, we need to know the revenue and all costs involved. Given the unit price and the quantity of each product we sell, we can easily compute the revenue. Big challenges lie in calculating costs. We can attribute some of the costs directly to each product.

***Review 4:*** *From the above description, which costs can we directly attribute to the individual products?*

From the description, we can attribute the following costs to each product:

- Direct labor costs (personnel dedicated to each product)
- Costs related to machinery dedicated to one product or the other
- Cost of raw materials

If $5 worth of raw materials go into the making of one unit of product A, then we can directly attribute that cost to the cost of making a unit of product A. That is, we can very easily attribute some costs directly to specific products. Management accounting refers to these as direct costs.

Certain other costs represent resources consumed in the manufacture of a product, but contribute to both products – perhaps equally, perhaps not. For example, the costs of the foremen, supervisors, top management, marketing and sales are all applicable to both products. It might not be immediately obvious as to how they contribute to the individual product costs. These represent indirect costs. To calculate the profit margin for the two products, we need to know all the costs – direct and indirect – involved in making each product.

Total unit cost of A = Direct cost per unit of A + Indirect cost per unit of A

***Review 5:*** *Choose any one of the indirect costs mentioned above (costs of the foremen, supervisors, top management, marketing and sales) and explain one way by which you can allocate the cost to the two products. We cannot specify a single correct answer but thinking about it can aid understanding.*

We might have data to indicate that, on the average, each foreman spends twice the amount of time on product B than on A. One meaningful approach to allocate the costs of foremen might be to allocate a third, or 33.33%, to product A and two-thirds, or 66.67%, to product B. There could be other meaningful approaches as well and the actual situation will determine the best approach to employ.

***Review 6:*** *Identify at least one indirect cost that the above narrative has not explicitly mentioned.*

***Review 7:*** *Identify at least two decisions that might be influenced by your calculation of the profit margins of the two products.*

***Review 8:*** *Suppose we allocate a third of the foreman's cost to product A and two thirds to product B. If it actually turns out that the foreman actually spends an equal amount of time on both products. How would this affect our cost estimates for products A and B.*

***Review 9:*** *Explain how under or over-allocating indirect costs to a particular product might affect the quality of the decisions you identified in an earlier question.*

***Review 10:*** *Suppose our company uses machine X only for product A. The company produced 10,000 units of product A during the previous year. How can we compute cost per unit of machine X per unit of product A for the previous year?*

## Cost Center and Profit Center

The concepts Cost Center and Profit Center play a very important role in management accounting.

- **Cost Center**: As the name indicates, a Cost Center is a part of an organization which incurs costs and to which costs can be allocated. For example, the accounting department of a company might be considered as a cost center. The department directly incurs costs – for example, the salaries paid to employees in the department and the cost of stationery that the department uses. Other costs although not directly incurred by the accounting department, might still be allocated to it – for example, rents paid for the office building (part of which accounting occupies).

- **Profit Center:** A part of an organization that is responsible for revenues and for costs. The paints division of a company might be a profit center. The iPod division of Apple Inc might be a profit center.

***Review 11:*** *Would it make sense to treat the accounting department of a company as a profit center? Why or why not?*

---

## Need for cost allocation

In the foregoing, we discussed the main spirit of management accounting – whereas financial accounting deals with accounting to record transactions so that we can produce statutory reports, management accounting records transactions in a way that suits business decision-making.

Many business decisions rely on accurate cost and revenue computations for various sub-units of a business, and management accounting focuses heavily on this aspect.

We have already seen that an organization can attribute some costs directly as applicable to an entity. For example, we can attribute the salaries paid to employees in the accounting department to the costs of that department.

From the foregoing discussion, we also know that units in an organization share many costs. In such cases, we have to properly divide the costs to reflect each entity's "fair share" of the cost. Management accounting uses the term allocation to refer to this process.

As an organization conducts its business, it might perform thousands of transactions each day. We already know that financial accounting uses the G/L and sub-ledgers to record all financial implications of these transactions as they occur. This is all well and good for financial accounting. What about management accounting? Financial accounting can only answer those questions that it is set up to answer. The way the G/L and sub-ledgers are set up determines how monetary transactions are recorded in specific slots. Experience has shown that we need to go beyond financial accounting to answer many important questions.

Consider some of the following questions that financial accounting might not generally be set up to address:

- What was the total cost incurred by the sales department? This includes costs directly attributable to the department and those that are allocated to it, like electricity and rent. For example, the sales department might occupy a portion of a rented building that the company occupies. The company cannot hold the sales department responsible for the rent for the entire building. Instead, it should determine the department's fair share and allocate only that amount to the sales department. Likewise, with electricity.

- What is the cost incurred by Assembly Line A during the month of December 2018? We can attribute many expenses to Line A. For example, there might be a manager whose complete salary and benefits we hold Line A responsible for. Lots of materials might be purchased specifically for Assembly Line A – for example, a special cleaning agent to clean spills. In addition, Line A might be responsible for a share of rent and electricity. Given all this, the cost of Line A comprises many costs that apply directly to it as well as several allocated costs.

One might say that the above calculations are not exactly rocket science. Conceptually, all of this is pretty simple. However, organizations incur thousands upon thousands of individual costs, many of which are shared and many of which are not. Just putting everything in the right place and computing costs correctly can still be a gargantuan task. Doing this by hand can be next to impossible for large companies. It would be far better to automate the process. Just as enterprise systems handle much of financial accounting in the background as business transactions occur, we want to set up the system and ensure that all of this management accounting (for example, cost allocation) also happens automatically in the background as organizations transact business.

The Management Accounting module of SAP (abbreviated as CO – short for Controlling) enables us to set up how management accounting is to be performed behind the scenes as a company conducts its business.

***Review 12:*** *We know that, in SAP, a client represents a conglomerate company and can have several company codes within it. Given this scenario, can management accounting cut across company code boundaries? Support your answer with examples.*

## Key SAP terms and concepts in management accounting

Management accounting in general, and SAP in particular, use specific terms. Understanding the precise meaning of these terms will take you a long way towards mastering Enterprise Systems.

Below, we discuss some important terms related to Management Accounting:

- Cost center
- Cost element

- Cost element accounting
- Settlement period
- Sender cost centers and receiver cost centers
- Primary cost element
- Secondary cost elements
- Controlling area

## Cost Center

To facilitate management accounting, whenever costs are incurred, we should immediately assign that cost to some entity. Otherwise someone will have to manually perform these tasks later in management accounting. Management accounting tracks costs by assigning them to cost centers.

Roughly speaking, for management accounting purposes, a company is divided into many cost centers and as and when costs occur, they are assigned to appropriate cost centers. As long as this process is properly configured, no one will need to go back and do this manually. For most operational transactions, we can set up the system so that applicable costs are allocated to the proper cost center.

Let us take a concrete example. Suppose there is a department called "Administration", and a cost center is created for this department so that all utility costs (among other relevant costs) in the company can be tracked in this department. Let us also assume the cost center is labeled "Administration". When utility expenses are incurred, the company will want all of these costs to go directly to the "Administration" cost center.

***Review 13:*** *List three utility costs that might be assigned to the "Administration" cost center.*

***Review 14:*** *Name three other possible cost centers in a typical organization. Do not take the easy path and go off the same theme as utilities and name other utilities. Try harder!*

The company has set up "Administration" as a cost center to keep track of utility costs and to manage them. This cost center could also be managing other types of costs, but for purposes of our demonstration, let us keep things simple and focus only on utility costs.

As utility bills come in to the company, the costs will be directly posted to this cost center. In this way, the company can centrally manage all the utility costs in one place and then allocate them at a later time to other responsible cost centers.

Utilities could account for a significant portion of the product cost and hence the company wants to manage this carefully. The following could all be relevant questions that management accounting would need to answer:

- How does what we spend compare with expenditure levels in similar companies?

- If we cut down the spending on this area by 10% how much can we save?
- If we cut down the spending on this area, can we price our product more competitively?
- What amount should we budget for the next year for utilities?

Identifying something as a cost center and tracking costs enables us to focus on the costs and also to assign responsibility for managing the cost.

Another example of a cost being assigned to a cost center might be the following: An employee might belong to a cost center. Whenever we pay salary to that employee, this cost automatically goes to the corresponding cost center.

***Review 15:*** *Having a cost center called "Administration" helps the company keep track of utility costs and manage them. Suppose a company found that it spent $1,200,000 on utilities during a specific quarter. How might this impact the profit margin that the company calculates for a particular product?*

It is important to know the total cost of utilities for the company so as to manage this cost well. Many parts of the company use these utilities – for example, the cost of electricity and water might form an important part of the unit production cost of products. To compute the unit cost of an end product, we would need to include its share of the utility costs. Thus, the cost of utilities initially accumulated in one cost center would need to be apportioned properly to entities that consumed the resources. For this purpose, companies usually set up rules to reallocate costs where needed so that costs accumulated in one cost center and be properly apportioned to other cost centers or to manufactured products. Once rules are set up, the process of cost apportionment can be automated. Without such rules, cost apportionment would need to be manual and can be a very effort intensive process.

Cost centers can be grouped together to facilitate the allocation of costs. These cost center groups are structured hierarchically to help manage and plan future costs. Figure 26 shows an example of cost centers and cost center groups.

Figure 26 shows five cost center groups (Administrative; Operations; Human Capital; Sales; Production; and Procurement). The hierarchical organization also tells us that a cost center group can contain other cost center groups. For instance, the Administrative cost center group contains both the Operations cost center group and the Human Capital cost center group. The Operations cost center group also contains three additional groups.

Within each cost center group are the individual cost centers. We see that the Administrative cost center group contains only one cost center, while the Operations group has no individual cost centers and only contains other cost center groups. The Sales cost center group on the other hand contains three cost centers.

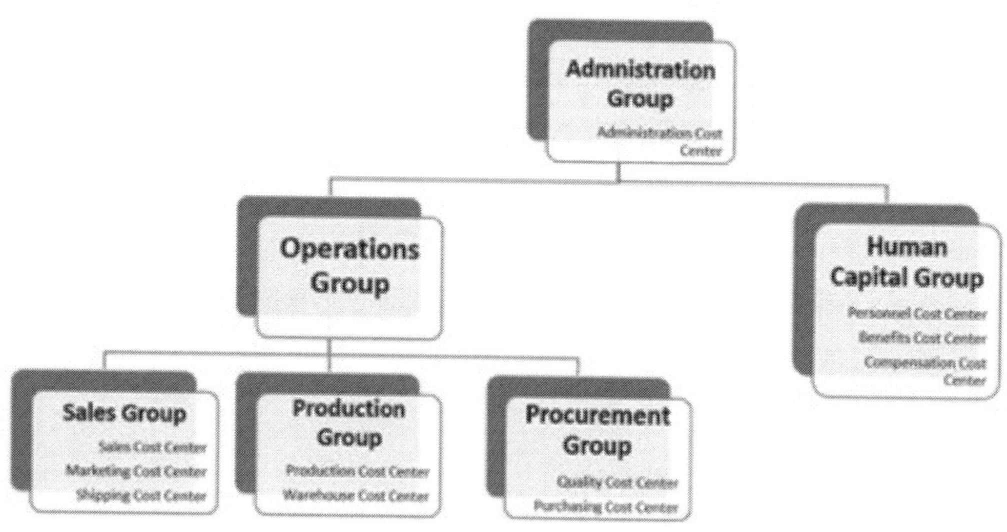


*Figure 26: Cost centers and cost center groups*

Cost center groups facilitate the allocation and planning of costs.

Let's take the example of the Utility costs. Suppose the utilities cost for a given month was $100,000 and that cost was posted directly to the Administration cost center (which belongs to the Administration cost center group). At the end of the month, the company will want to apportion those costs to those cost centers who are responsible for those costs. To keep it simple, let's also assume the allocation is based solely on fixed percentages (though this is not practical in business, it will help us understand how cost center groups support cost allocations). Assume that 80% of the utilities cost belong to the Operations group, while the remaining 20% belongs to the Human Capital group. In this scenario, $80,000 will be allocated to the Operations group and $20,000 to the Human Capital group at the end of the month. However, we can't stop there because the costs need to go to cost centers.

In the Human Capital group, suppose 50% of the costs in that group belong to the Personnel cost center; 10% to Benefits cost center; and 40% to the Compensation cost center. Doing the math, we can accurately ensure that the $10,000 of the utilities cost will go to the Personnel cost center, while $2000 and $8000 will go to the Benefits and Compensation cost centers respectively. A similar approach would apply to the Operations group. However, additional allocations would occur because of the additional level of cost center groups (Sales; Production; and Procurement).

## Cost Element

The term cost element is used to refer to a category of cost. Thus, a rent payment might be a cost element. For example, suppose the company pays rent of $3,000 in one transaction, that represents an occurrence of the cost element rent payment and can be assigned to some cost center.

Consumables purchase might be another cost element and if the company buys some consumables for use by a particular department, that is an occurrence of the cost element consumables purchase and will be assigned to some cost center corresponding to the department for which the consumable was purchased.

A cost element represents a particular type of cost which the company wants to track. The management accounting process can charge occurrences of a cost element to an appropriate cost center. In management accounting speak, individual occurrences of cost elements can be posted to cost centers. (See the discussion of primary and secondary cost account types below for a more complete discussion.)

The above examples involved the posting of cost elements to cost centers. Cost elements can also be posted to other so-called cost objects in SAP.

***Review 16:*** *Through an example, bring out the difference between a cost element and an occurrence of a cost element.*

## Cost Element Account Types

Although the notion of cost element is a part of management accounting and not strictly related to financial accounting, SAP S/4HANA has chosen to include Cost Element as an account type in Financial Accounting.

Recall from the earlier chapters on Accounting that there are various account types in a Chart of Accounts. One account type in SAP S/4HANA is Primary Cost Element. This account type is used to keep track of normal Profit and Loss impacts. This account type was previously referred to as P&L (Income Statement) account types. Expense and revenue postings are made to this account type. Primary Cost Elements are used to track cost and revenue impacts within Controlling (CO).

Another account type is Secondary Cost Element. This represents a significant change in the data model in SAP S/4HANA. Prior to S/4HANA, Secondary Cost Elements were exclusively used in CO. Applying the simplified data model approach, secondary cost elements are now an account type in the Chart of Accounts. This means that they can be used in both FI and CO and only one master record is required.

Whenever a cost is posted in CO, a cost element must be identified to track and categorize the cost. If the cost is directly associated with revenue or an expense, a primary cost element with account type "Primary Costs/Revenues" is used. In the earlier example in which we apportioned the utilities cost from the Administration cost center to the Human Capital and Operations groups, a secondary cost element with account type "Secondary Cost Element" is used when posting to these groups. A secondary cost element is required whenever a cost allocation or apportionment occurs. A cost allocation is simply a further transfer of costs from one cost object (like a cost center) to another cost object (could be a cost center, production order or any other type of cost object). Any transaction which uses a Primary or Secondary Cost Element Account Type will also be recorded in the Universal Journal (ACDOCA table).

## Primary Cost Element

We have already seen that a cost element is a category of cost, whose occurrences can be charged to a cost center. Thus, when the company incurs rent expense of $3000 for the month of December 2018 to a particular party as a single payment, Financial accounting (FI) records this to a primary cost account type. Unless the user identifies the cost object (possibly a cost center) responsible for the rent expense, the rent expense will not be posted and will not impact FI nor the management accounting (CO) module.

Management accounting then clearly needs to get hold of the expense and assign it to some cost object, perhaps a cost center, such as Sales. The expense recorded in FI has to flow from financial accounting to management accounting – as a cost.

The rent expense is first recorded in financial accounting as an expense and only becomes a cost when it enters management accounting. How does the cost flow from financial accounting to management accounting (from FI to CO)?

We already know that there are various primary cost/revenue accounts in FI to record expenses (and revenues). In SAP S/4HANA, primary cost/revenue accounts in financial accounting are examples of primary cost elements. Thus, as soon as an entry is made in FI to a primary cost account, the system automatically uses that primary cost element to transfer it as a cost for management accounting (CO) to process.

Continuing with the rent expense example, we see that a rent posting to a primary cost account in FI resulted in the use of the primary cost element rent expense. The cost was posted into (debited to) the cost center Sales.

Posting using a primary cost element into a cost center is a one-sided posting because it only resulted in a debit and no corresponding credit. This differs from postings in financial accounting which are always two-sided.

Figure 27 illustrates this posting.

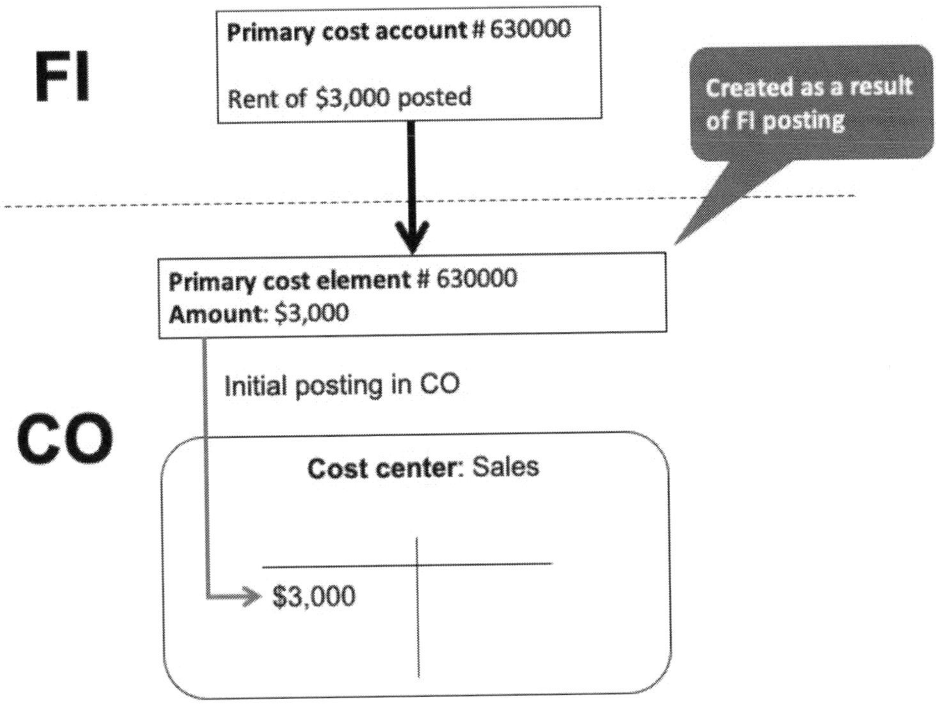


*Figure 27: Cost flow from FI to CO*

## Secondary cost element

As we discussed above, secondary cost element accounts are an account type in FI. Whenever costs are allocated (apportioned) from one cost object to another in CO, a secondary cost element is required to categorize this transfer of costs. Examples of secondary cost elements are Distributions; Assessments; Activity Allocations and Settlements. We don't need to go into each of these now. However, it's important to understand that these are all examples of cost postings from one cost object to another cost object (e.g. Cost center sending costs to a production order).

Whenever a cost allocation occurs, it results in a two-sided, balanced posting in CO. In other words, the object sending the cost (Sender) is credited by the amount of the cost, and the cost object(s) receiving the cost (Receivers) are debited. To emphasize this, let's take the example of the $3000 of rent cost that was posted to the Sales cost center. During that particular month (in this case, December 2018), the Marketing cost center actually used some of the space rented by the Sales cost center. Because of this, the Sales cost center will want to allocate the appropriate amount of the rent cost for which the Marketing cost center was responsible. Two things are going to be necessary to make this happen.

First, there has to be a mechanism to determine how much of that cost needs to be allocated. To do this, we could use the amount of square footage of space the Marketing cost center used. The Sales costs center would then know how to apportion that cost. Suppose the total space rented by the Sales cost center was 25,000 square feet and the Marketing costs center used 5,000 square feet of that space.

In this case, the Sales cost center will allocate 20% of the total rent cost for that month to the Marketing cost center.

The second thing that is required, is to define a secondary cost element to use for this allocation. For the purposes of discussion, let's define this allocation as an assessment, which is a further transfer of costs from one cost center to one or more other cost centers. In this case, the Sale cost center will distribute the $600 (20% of $3000) of rent costs to the Marketing cost center. Keep in mind, the secondary cost element is also an account type in the Chart of Accounts, which means it will also post in the General Ledger as a secondary cost. This is a significant change from previous versions of ERP. Figure 28 depicts this.

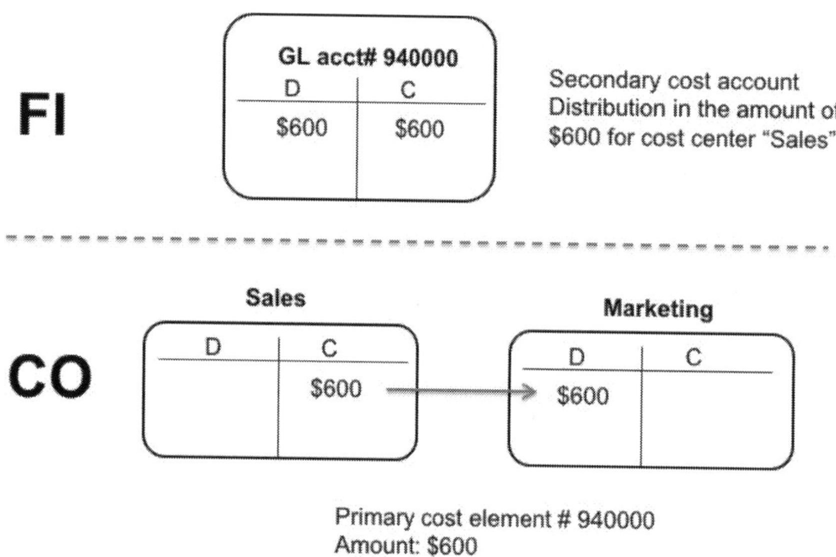


*Figure 28: Assessment posting in FI*

## Controlling Area

In SAP, management accounting can result in cost allocations that cut across company codes within a client. This could be the case when an organization would like to consolidate their costs stemming from more than one company code. For example, two company codes could incur transportation expenses and the organization would like to be able to consolidate that into a single cost for internal purposes. Or there might be a purchasing organization that does purchasing for multiple company codes. In such cases, allocation of costs might cut across company codes. For this reason, an organization level for management accounting has to have the flexibility to consolidate accounting information from more than one company code. As such, one or more company code can be assigned to a single controlling area. Therefore, the Controlling area is an organization unit for management accounting and can include multiple company codes.

However, note these two very important points:

If multiple company codes are allocated to the same controlling area, the company codes must use the same operating Chart of Accounts and fiscal year variant.

Cost movements in management accounting can only happen across company codes belonging to the same controlling area.

## Order-related cost object controlling

We have seen earlier that cost centers can collect costs for possible reallocation. In SAP, cost centers are not the only objects that can collect costs. Consider a production order with a requirement of 100 units of some product. In order to compute the unit cost of that batch of material, we would need to accumulate all costs that go towards completing that production order. To facilitate this, the production order collects costs as it progresses. For example, when materials are issued, the materials cost is added to the production order. Later some labor time might be incurred on the production order and those costs are also added to the production order, and so on. Thus, the production order acts as a cost collector and is an example of an Order-Related Cost Object.

In SAP, in addition to production orders, other orders like maintenance orders, customer service orders and internal orders (also called CO orders) can collect costs. These are also Order- Related Cost Objects. Though each of these orders is used for different processes, there are great similarities in the management accounting process that each goes through.

They all follow a standard sequence of steps from a management accounting viewpoint. Figure 29 shows the steps in the standard process that applies to all order-related costs objects. (Note: Order-related cost objects are managed using order types. Some of these order types may have additional steps required that are unique to its own process.)

During order creation, the order has not yet become a cost object. At this stage, this simply means costs cannot yet be posted to the order. However, the order is scheduled (as in the case of a production order) when resources necessary to perform work on the order become available. Thus, resources are then reserved for this order. The order may also require materials. Consider the example of a customer who brings in a defective item for repair. To repair that item, not only will resources be required, but materials are also likely to be necessary. Thus, materials are placed on reservation for the order. But what if there are no materials available? This isn't a problem for SAP S/4HANA. The user could check inventory in the system to see if the materials exist. If not, the user can simply create a purchase order for what is missing. Ultimately when the order is created, all the necessary materials and labor resources (as well as potential overhead costs) are calculated by the system. In this way, the user is now made aware of the planned costs on this order.

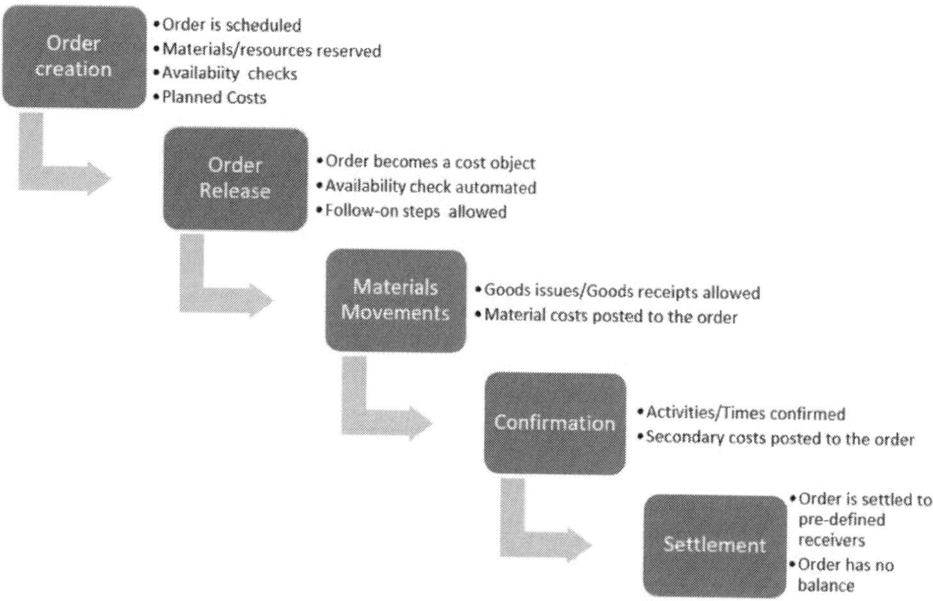


*Figure 29: Order-related cost object controlling*

The next step in order-related cost object controlling is the order release (highlighted in Figure 29). This is the most important step! If the order is not released, none of the follow-on steps can be completed. It is at this time that the order officially becomes a cost object. Actual costs can now be posted to this order and can be compared to the planned costs that were calculated in the previous step. If the user did not check material availability when the order was created, an ERP system like SAP automatically checks to see if materials are available. If they are not available (depending on the system settings) the system can block the order release until materials become available.

The step after the release of the order is generally a goods movement. The goods movement could be a goods issue from inventory to the order, or a goods receipt from a purchase order to the order. When these goods movements are posted, they are posted as expenses in financial accounting using a primary cost element account type which posts the costs to the order in management accounting. These are actual costs which again can be compared to the planned costs in the order.

Material costs are not the only costs associated with order-related cost object controlling. There are additional costs, usually resulting from work completed on the order by one or more work centers. These costs are posted to the order when work centers confirm the work they performed. They could confirm this work in various ways, but the most common methods are to confirm the amount of time they spent working on the order as well as which activities they performed. These costs are considered secondary costs because they are not a result of direct expenses posted in financial accounting. Instead, they are costs that are allocated to the order from another cost object in management accounting. Recall that secondary cost elements are used to allocate such costs. This is how labor costs are traditionally recorded in the production order.

Finally, the order will go through the settlement step. Here, the costs collected in the order are normally settled to a predefined receiver. A receiver is an object that is ultimately responsible for the costs in the order. In management accounting, an order-related cost object can settle its costs to financial accounting general ledger accounts. Other receivers might be cost centers, projects, other orders, or profitability analysis. In the end, the order is settled so there are no remaining costs. In other words, the order has no balance on the debit or credit sides; its debit and credit entries balance out.

## S4/HANA enhancements to FI-CO integration

As we have discussed in Chapter 4, S4/HANA has introduced a much greater level of integration between FI and CO than was the case in prior versions of ERP.

### Universal journal

As we saw in Chapter 4, a cornerstone of the enhanced integration comes in the form of the Universal Journal. Figure 30 shows the Universal Journal again.

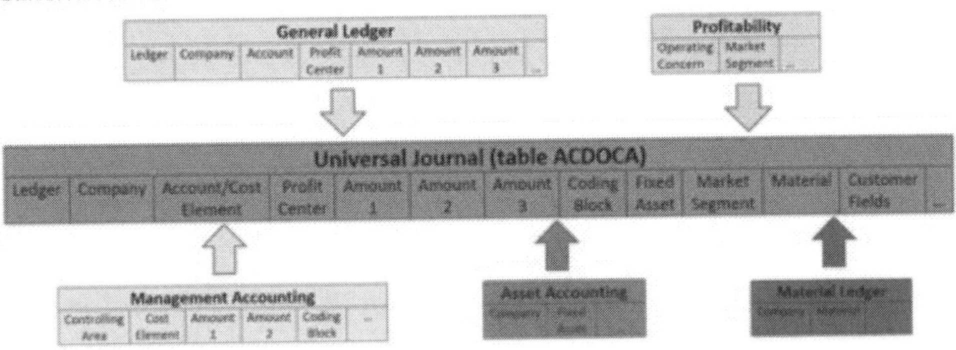


Figure 30: Universal journal in S4/HANA

There are many aspects of management accounting that need to be addressed. And we will get to those in the next chapter. But for the time-being, we will briefly address the key integration concepts between SAP FI (financial accounting) and SAP CO (management accounting).

The Universal Journal is a single view of truth from an accounting perspective. Both FI and CO postings write to the same journal and the accounting impacts are stored centrally in this table. Transactions which have financial accounting impacts will still result in the creation of a Financial Accounting document which tracks that transaction. Transactions which have a management accounting impact will still result in the creation of a Controlling document which tracks that transaction. The main difference in SAP S/4HANA from previous ERP versions is that the data used to generate these documents now stem from a single table, the ACDOCA table (Universal Journal).

## Primary and Secondary Cost Elements

Earlier we identified Primary and Secondary Cost Elements as Account Types in FI. This means that there is no longer a need to maintain Primary and Secondary Cost Element master records in CO. We only require the primary and secondary accounts in the General Ledger. When a transaction occurs which posts to a primary cost element account in FI, it is automatically tracked in CO.

Let's use a simple example to demonstrate this. Suppose the marketing department rents storage space to house their promotional materials. Each month that department pays $500 rent from a cash account (balance sheet) to cover the rental expense (primary cost). This simple transaction needs to be managed in both FI and CO. Table 17 shows the resultant FI postings.

| G/L account (account type) | Debit | Credit |
|---|---|---|
| Cash (Balance sheet) | | $500 |
| Rent expense (primary cost) | $500 | |

*Table 17: Connecting primary cost element accounts in FI to CO*

*Table 17* shows a balances G/L posting. This information is also written to the Universal Journal (ACDOCA table).

Additionally, from a management accounting view, it's important to track the $500 expense as a cost. The marketing department is responsible for this expense and we want to make sure that is also recorded accurately. Looking at Figure 30 once again, notice there are many fields in the Universal Journal. The accounts (Balance Sheet and Primary Cost) are contained in the journal as well as the source for this expense posting (in this case, the marketing department).

The result of this transaction would be the creation of a Financial Account (FI) Document and a Controlling (CO) Document. The FI Document would look very similar to the initial posting in FI. Table 18 shows this.

| CO Doc # | Date | Cost object | Amount | Cost element |
|---|---|---|---|---|
| ######### | ##/##/#### | Marketing dept | $500 | Rent expense (#) |

*Table 18: CO document view of the FI posting in Table 17*

Let's take this example one step further. Let's also suppose that the HR Department shared 20% of the storage space with the Marketing Department and that this cost needs to be allocated from the Marketing Department to the HR Department. Cost allocations use Secondary Cost Elements. Therefore, a simple cost allocation transaction will be used to credit the Marketing Department $100, while debiting the HR Department $100. This will be accomplished using a Secondary Cost Element. As we noted earlier, secondary cost element is an account type in the General Ledger and a GL account would exist for such a transaction. Thus, a CO document will be generated showing the impact on each of these departments from a management accounting perspective. And a FI document will also be generated showing the posting to the General Ledger. This occurs because the Universal Journal contains all of the necessary information to make this happen.

## Review questions: Management accounting

(You can find answers on page 212. To answer questions that have an asterisk (*) at the end, you will need to have read the official SAP course material.)

1. Which of the following questions might relate to the Overhead Cost Controlling component of CO? (two) *
   A. What is the unit cost of Product A?
   B. How much did we spend on utilities in July 2018?
   C. How should we allocate the costs of our IT department?
   D. Did Profit Center X meet its target profit?
2. Which of the following questions might relate to the Product Cost Accounting component of CO? (two) *
   A. What is the unit cost of Product A?
   B. How much did we spend on utilities in July 2018?
   C. What was the total cost of production order Y?
   D. Did Profit Center X meet its target profit?
3. Which of the following questions might relate to the Profitability Analysis component of CO? (one) *
   A. Did Profit Center X meet its target profit?
   B. How profitable was company code 1000 in the Northern Region?
   C. How much did we spend on utilities in July 2018?
   D. How much did production order Y cost as a whole?
   E. How much did project X cost?
4. Name a cost that might flow from the noted SAP module to CO. Also indicate the component within CO where it might be used. (five)
   A. FI (general)
   B. FI-AA (Asset Accounting)
   C. HCM (Human Capital Management)

D. MM (Materials Management)

E. PP (Production planning and execution)

F. SD (Sales and distribution)

5. Indicate one way in which CO might have an impact on FI.
6. In which organizational element will you find Overhead Cost Controlling? *
7. In which organizational element will you find Product Cost Accounting CO-PCA? *
8. One controlling area can have multiple company codes assigned to it. T/F?
9. One company code can belong to multiple controlling areas. T/F?
10. A Client (in the SAP sense) has many Controlling Areas with each containing multiple cost centers. Cost centers can allocate costs between Controlling Areas. T/F?
11. Scenario: Two company codes (1000 and 2000) belong to the same controlling area. Account 100000 in company code 1000 is an expense account and account 200000 in company code 2000 is an asset account. What other facts can you infer from these two facts?
12. Explain the mechanism used to transfer accounting information from FI to CO.
13. What type of cost elements exist as account types in FI?
14. Which master data in CO is used to track where costs are incurred within the enterprise?
15. How are cost centers structured in SAP?
16. What do the cost center groups enable?
17. The unit price of an activity in Activity Based Costing is determined by the combination of _________ ___________ and ___________ ___________. *
18. A company has determined that rental costs will be allocated based on square footage used by various departments. The square footage is fixed across time periods. This is an example of a ______Type Statistical Key Figure. *
19. You are preparing an assessment in SAP ERP Management Accounting. Which type of cost element is used to perform an assessment? (one) *

    A. Primary

    B. Secondary

    C. Revenue

    D. Cost object

20. In SAP S/4HANA, expenses in FI are tracked using which account type? (one)

    A. Primary cost account

    B. Secondary cost account

    C. Balance Sheet account

    D. Sub-ledger account

21. A company accumulates costs associated with its cafeteria in a cost center and allocates this cost to other cost centers at the end of each month. What is this process broadly called?
22. A company accumulates costs for a training event in an internal order and then allocates this cost to other cost centers at the end of the month. What is this process broadly called?
23. What is the difference between CO postings to primary cost elements and to secondary cost elements in CO?
24. What two entries must be made for a journal posting in FI to properly post in CO?
25. What is the purpose of a periodic allocation?
26. Which of the following is not an example of periodic allocation? (one) *
    A. Direct activity allocation
    B. Assessment
    C. Distribution
    D. Periodic reposting
    E. Template allocation
27. For which of the following scenarios would you suggest using an Internal Order? (three) *
    A. The company is going to produce finished goods and wants to have a mechanism to accumulate production costs.
    B. The company is organizing a promotional seminar and needs to track all costs incurred for this purpose.
    C. The company is buying a new machine and wants an object to which to charge the cost of the machine as well as future costs incurred on the machine.
    D. The company is constructing a new parking lot and wants to accumulate the costs incurred.
28. When does settlement occur for internal orders? *
29. Which of the following cannot be a receiver when the costs of an internal order are settled? (One) *
    A. Profit center
    B. Cost center
    C. Project
    D. Asset
    E. Profitability segment
30. What is the difference between a true cost object and a statistical object? *
31. What is the purpose of a statistical cost object? *
32. Which of the following are examples of characteristics used in profitability segments? (three) *
    A. Sales region

B. Cost of goods sold

C. Sales revenue

D. Product

E. Customer

33. What is the effect on the material master when the material standard cost estimate is marked? *

34. What is the effect on the material master of releasing a material standard cost estimate

# Procurement business process (MM)

*THIS CHAPTER DEALS* with purchasing various items for use by the company in carrying out its business. The main external entities with which this process interacts are vendors. This chapter provides a high-level overview of the topic so as to prepare you to be able to read the SAP course materials. The chapter does not get into too much detail as those can be found in the SAP course materials. In SAP, procurement is part of the Materials Management or MM module.

---

## Process overview

Whether or not you have prior exposure to purchasing processes within an organization, you might benefit at this point by listing the steps that you think should make up the process. As far as possible, try and list these steps chronologically.

Obviously, business processes vary from industry to industry and even from company to company. In fact, even a single company could employ a few variations. In this module, we will discuss the basic purchasing process in SAP S/4HANA. As you might already have guessed, SAP allows for many configuration options to enable a company to tailor the system to suit its specific needs. Figure 7 from page 15 discussed the process briefly. We reproduce it here for convenience in Figure 31, and amplify the earlier discussion.

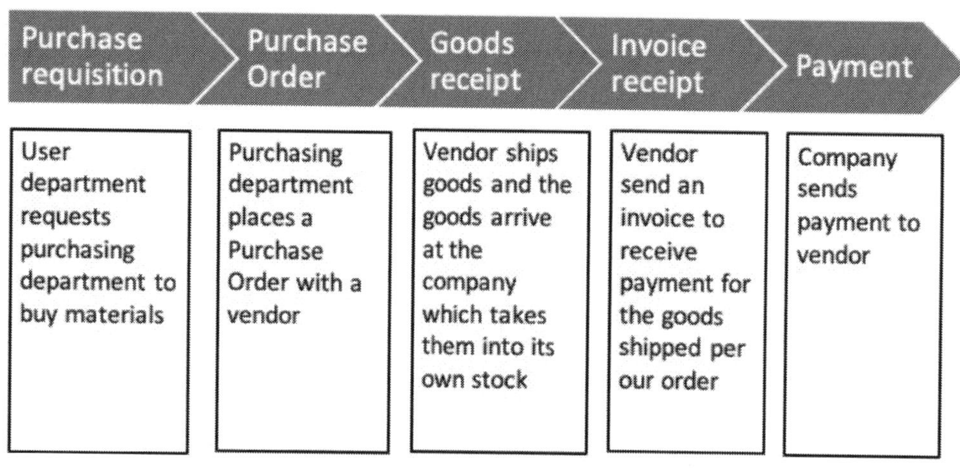


*Figure 31: Procurement business process outline*

We now look at each step in the procurement business process.

1. Purchase requisition: Initially some department or process identifies that something needs to be purchased. This results in a Purchase Requisition.
2. Source of supply: The company then needs to find a source of supply. This can happen in one of many ways:
   - Select existing vendor: The company might have many existing vendors who can supply the item. In this case, the company can use performance history and select one from among its existing vendors.
   - Existing agreement or contract: Often companies have standing agreements or contracts with a vendor for agreed quantities and prices. In this case, the company could simply order against an existing agreement or contract. SAP refers to such standing arrangements as Outline Agreements or Contracts.
   - Bidding process: Sometimes a company might choose to invite bids and select a vendor based on the bidding process. In this case, the purchasing company could send out a Request for Proposal (RFP) or a Request for Quotation (RFQ) to each of several vendors and select a vendor based on their responses. SAP provides capabilities for issuing and managing RFQ/RFP.
3. Purchase order: After completion of the previous step, the company has identified a vendor (or other source of supply) with whom to place the order. At this point, the purchasing department creates a Purchase Order and sends it to the chosen vendor.
4. Goods receipt: Based on the Purchase Order, the vendor ships the goods. When the goods arrive, the company performs a goods receipt. The goods receipt process represents the steps to physically receive the goods and then put them into storage. Of course, in an integrated

ERP system like SAP S/4HANA, just recording that the goods are in storage alone will not suffice. Think for a minute about what else an integrated system might need to do while receiving goods.

- Verification: The first step in receiving goods would be to verify that the shipment is in fact related to something that the company ordered. We therefore need to verify that the items supplied were in fact ordered, and note the quantity supplied. Thus, the goods receipt process will need to refer to the purchase order for verification.
- Material document: SAP and other ERP systems generally create a document to record the fact that a business transaction took place. When goods are received, SAP creates a material document with information about the items received, the quantities received, and the storage location where the items were stored.
- Put away in warehouse: Not only do we have to record that materials were received, but we also have to physically store them in a warehouse. SAP clearly distinguishes between Inventory Management and Warehouse Management. Inventory Management deals with keeping track of how much of each item we have in storage in various storage locations. It deals with tracking quantities of items and also their value. Warehouse Management deals with the actual placement of items on storage and retrieval from storage shelves. It deals with knowing precisely where the items are and also with how to optimally put away and fetch multiple items from the shelves. You might have had the opportunity to see massive warehouses by the side of highways. Sometimes these warehouses span half a mile or more. Warehouses use forklift trucks and other mechanical equipment to handle material and they have to manage their use of energy and manpower. Suppose the warehouse manager ordered a forklift operator to make a trip each time a piece of material was to be put into storage or retrieved from storage, the warehouse would be woefully inefficient. Typically, warehouse operations will bunch together many requests for materials and then use some optimizing algorithm to figure out the most efficient way to pick up all of the materials. For example, they might minimize the distance traveled to pick up all the items. When goods are received, the goods receipt process needs to make the warehouse aware that there is some material to be put away on the shelves. This will enable the warehouse people to plan and operate efficiently. Thus, the purchasing process needs to interface with warehousing. We will discuss Warehouse Management in more detail later on in this book. Receiving the goods (which we most likely have

not yet have paid for), causes our current assets to increase. Thus, the process will also interface with Financial Accounting.

5. Invoice receipt: Having delivered the goods, the vendor will then send the purchasing company an invoice. The purchasing company then performs invoice verification to make sure that the invoice is in fact for something that was ordered and something that the vendor actually shipped in the correct quantity. This step is sometimes called three-point invoice verification (or three-way match) – purchase order, goods receipt and invoice. Sometimes, for simplicity, companies might not always perform a three-point verification.
6. Vendor payment: Once the invoice is verified, accounting can pay the vendor, satisfying the liability and completing the Procure to Pay process.

## Organizational Levels

The purchasing business process touches many organizational levels.

Figure 32 shows some – but not all – of the organization levels involved. These four organizational levels occur in all logistics modules in SAP S/4HANA – Materials Management (MM), Sales and Distribution (SD), Production (PP) and Enterprise Asset Management (EAM).

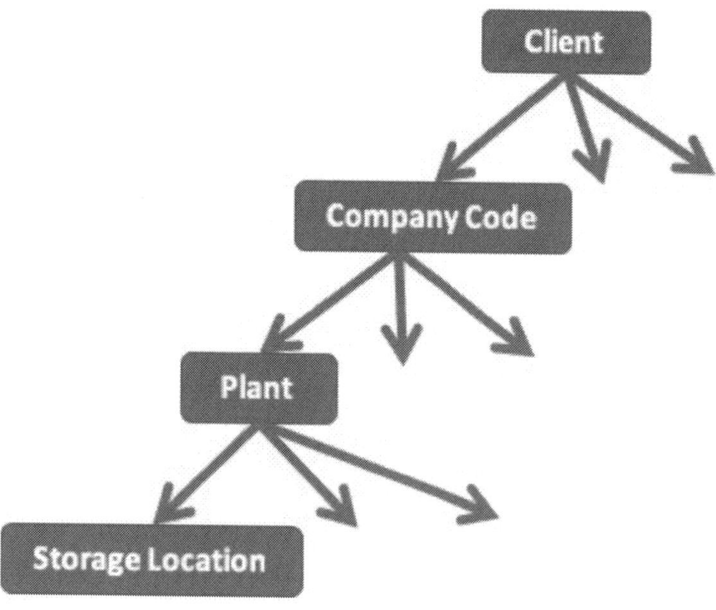


*Figure 32: Organization levels in Procurement (MM)*

We already know about two organizational levels related to MM – client and company code.

A company code can have many plants. (Note that plants in SAP are not always production plants. Plants could also be locations from which services are provided.) In a consulting organization, an office from which it provides services could be treated as a plant. For example, the New York city office of a consulting company could be configured as a plant in SAP.

In SAP, materials are managed at the plant level. A plant can have many storage locations. A storage location is a location where stocks are maintained. Thus, we might have 10,000 units of a particular material in a company code, but these might be kept in several different storage locations across different plants, all of which belong to the same company code.

To understand how this works from a material valuation perspective, the company code is the organizational level where the value of materials impacts the Balance Sheet. However, a company may want more detailed knowledge of the value of inventory for each plant. A Material Ledger (ML) allows the company to keep track of valuation of materials in inventory at each plant as a sub-ledger account. SAP has made the Material Ledger obligatory in S/4HANA. The ML has advantages beyond keeping valuation of materials in sub-ledger accounts. The ML also supports the ability to calculate actual costs of materials during goods movements.

Purchasing organizations in SAP S/4HANA allow a company to strategically manage the purchase process. A purchasing organization is the organizational level where data regarding terms and conditions relevant to purchasing are stored. The terms and conditions may be negotiated by many different individuals in the company. It's important to note that purchasing organizations do not represent the "people" who perform the negotiations. (Terminological note: In SAP, actual purchasing work is done by Purchasing Groups – groups of people. Purchasing organizations are the organization levels where negotiated terms with vendors are stored.) A purchasing organization can thus serve several company codes.

Alternately we could have a purchasing organization that stores the negotiated terms and conditions for vendors for a single company code or for even just a single plant within a company code. Figure 33 shows the three possibilities.

Purchasing group on the other hand, refers to a set of people who actually carry out purchasing related activities. These activities mainly involve the sourcing decisions and creation of purchase orders. A purchasing group can represent an individual or a group of individuals who perform these activities.

## Master data

In SAP S/4HANA, the procurement process is supported by master data. Some of the master data required include Material master, Vendor master, Purchasing Info-records, and Conditions master data. We introduce the basic ideas behind these; the SAP certification course materials discuss these in greater depth.

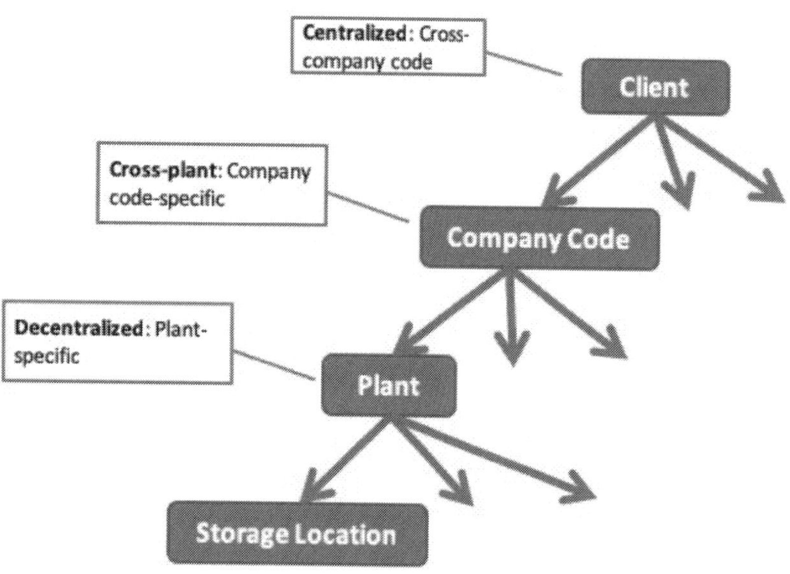


*Figure 33: Three possible locations for purchasing organizations*

## Material master data

Materials account for a significant proportion of purchasing needs in a company. As such, material master data is required to support the purchasing process. All master data must be associated with one or more organizational levels. To ensure that a material master record exists only once in the database for any given material, basic information about each material is stored at the Client level. This includes things like the material name, material number, and dimensions of the material (such as weight and size).

Generally speaking, each material is used at the plant level to support operational activities, such as purchasing and different plants might need to store different information for the same material. To support this requirement, SAP allows us to maintain some material master information at the plant level. This includes such things as purchasing information; how the material will be stored in inventory; how the material is valued; and how the material is costed (among other things). Figure 34 illustrates this.

## Vendor master data

Information about vendors also provides important support for the procurement process and is kept in the vendor mater. Like material master data, vendor master data is also maintained at various organizational levels. Recall from the SAP S/4HANA Introduction chapter, that vendors are maintained as Business Partners in SAP S/4HANA. Figure 35 recaps the idea of business partners and their roles.

To support the procurement process, a Business Partner with the functioning characteristics of a vendor must be maintained.

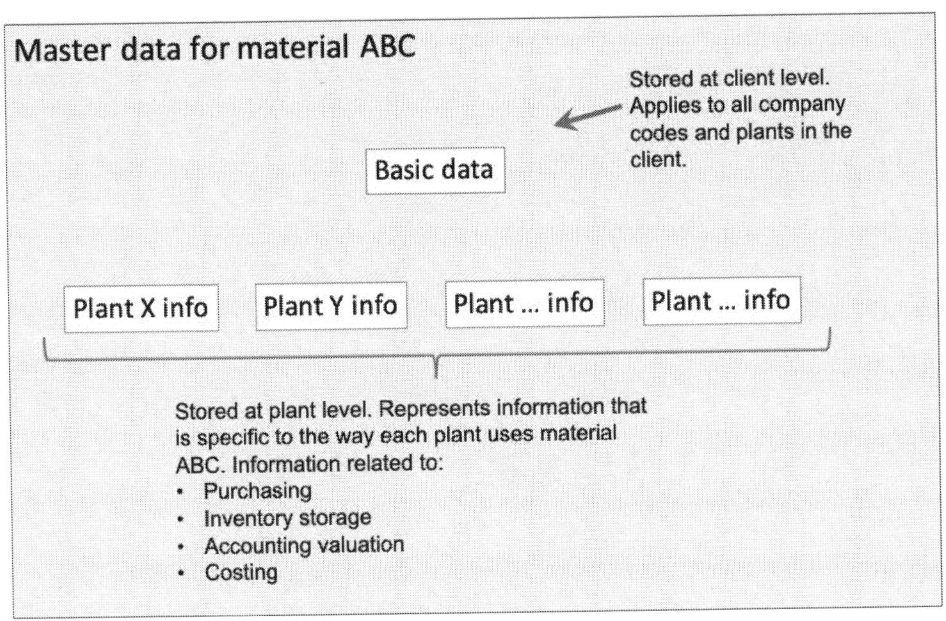


*Figure 34: Material master – levels at which different types of information are stored*

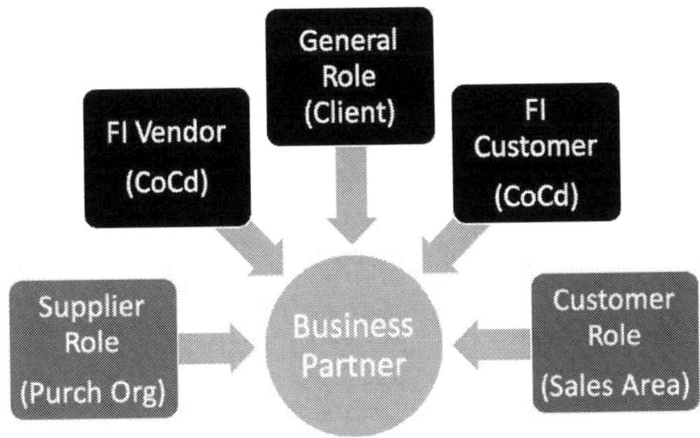


*Figure 35: Business partners*

Figure 35 shows the various roles (at different organizational levels) that must be maintained for any Business Partner for purchasing. The following points are worth noting:

Like the material master, there is some general data that is maintained at the Client level to ensure this business partner exists only once in the database.

However, for the purposes of purchasing, the vendor serves as a creditor (meaning we will ultimately have a liability in Financial Accounting to the vendor when we are invoiced for purchases). For this reason, we must maintain Financial Accounting (FI) information for this vendor at the Company Code level. (Note: Each Company Code will need to have its own unique data for each vendor.)

In addition to the FI information, terms and conditions required for purchasing are negotiated with each vendor in the Supplier Role. Recall from the discussion above regarding organizational levels, that terms and conditions are information stored at the Purchase Organizational level.

Figure 35 helps reinforce the necessary information to maintain for a vendor as well as which organizational levels will contain this information.

## Inventory management vs. Warehouse management

Inventory management is the process of keeping track of how many units of each material we have in each storage location. It is concerned with quantities of materials in the storage locations.

Do not confuse inventory management with warehouse management. Whereas inventory management is concerned with how much of each material we have on hand at each storage location, warehouse management is concerned with physically managing the storage and movement of materials in storage.

Warehouse management is concerned with things like "Which bin in which shelf in which aisle contains how much of what material? What is the most effective way for us to store a set of items or to pick up a set of items from the warehouse?"

The steps associated with the physical management of materials are collectively referred to as Logistics Execution. We discuss Warehouse Management in a separate chapter.

## Procuring for Stock or for consumption

A company can buy materials whose usage can be looked at in two different ways.

Procuring for stock: A company can purchase materials which it will then place in stock, to be used sometime later as needed. This method involves multiple goods movements. For example, when the material is received, a Goods Receipt must be posted to place the material into stock at some storage location. Later, when it is needed for use, the company must perform a Goods Issue to remove that material from stock.

Procuring for consumption: Companies can also purchase materials that will not be placed in stock and will instead be consumed immediately.

We discuss these below.

### Procuring for stock

Let us suppose that a company buys 10,000 units of a particular raw material (say material X) and places it in stock. At this time, these materials have not yet been used for anything and hence the cost of these cannot yet be allocated to any cost center or other cost object. That is, when materials have been purchased and placed in stock for later use, they exist in the form of current assets that have not yet been expensed. Since no department or business process has yet consumed the material, the company has not yet incurred any expense – from a financial accounting viewpoint.

In the previous sentence, we used the term expense from a financial accounting perspective and not in its general sense. Of course, when the company purchased the material, it paid the vendor and one might say that the amount paid was an "expense" incurred by the company. However, from a financial accounting perspective, something is an expense only when it affects the income statement. Recall that in the income statement, we show the income and expenses incurred during a time period in order to compute the profit or loss for that period. The cost of a material becomes an expense only when the material is actually used in some way, for example for manufacturing a finished product. In the present situation, the 10,000 units of material X have not yet been used and hence the company has not incurred any expense on these units of the material yet.

At some later point in time, the company might need to use the material X that is held in stock to make some finished products. For example, let us assume that the company is about to initiate the production process and needs to use 500 units of material X for this. The company will create a Production Order. To execute the Production Order, a goods issue of 500 units of material X from stock would be required. These 500 units are issued against Production Order – therefore the production order is now responsible for the cost of these materials. It is only now that the company has incurred the cost for 500 units of material X. The cost of the material will be included in the cost of finished goods produced for this Production Order. (Recall from the Management Accounting chapter that all cost postings in CO require a primary cost element account and a cost object. In this case, the production order serves as the cost object, collecting the material costs.)

The key point is that when the material was originally purchased, we knew that the material would eventually be used, but had no idea exactly which object(s) would bear the cost. That becomes known only when some objects come along and consume the material – like the above production order did. It also required an additional goods movement (goods issue) to ensure the cost is posted accurately.

The above illustrates purchasing for stock. In summary, when materials are purchased for stock, their cost is not allocated to anyone or anything at the time of goods receipt for that purchase. These materials just form part of the current assets and only impact the balance sheet of the company when the purchase process is executed. They have not yet become expenses for the company – that is, they have still not had an impact on the income statement of the company. That will happen when they are consumed. When the materials are consumed later, an additional goods movement will then be required. Figure 36 illustrates these ideas.

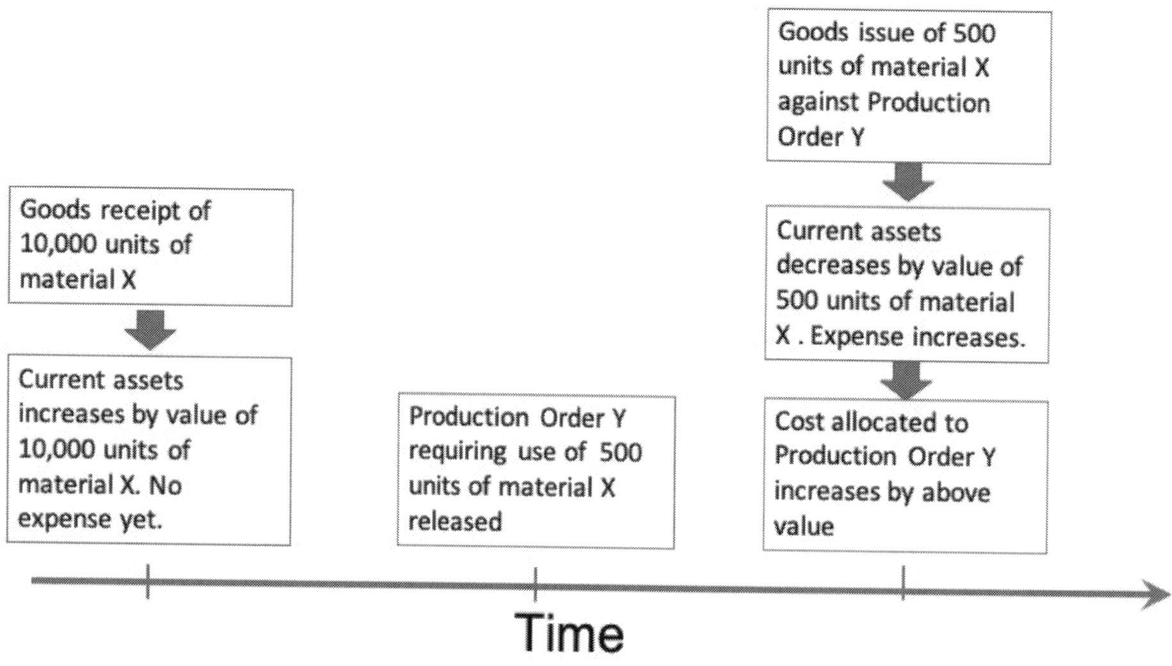


*Figure 36: Procuring for stock*

## Procuring for consumption

This happens when materials are purchased for a specific use and the cost of the material is immediately allocated to some cost object – for example, a cost center or a production order. When the material for such a purchase arrives, it is not placed in inventory for later use but is instead treated as consumed directly. This does not require a subsequent goods movement. It is handled immediately at the time of goods receipt.

Whether a material is being procured for stock or for consumption is determined at the time of purchase (that is, when the purchase order or purchase requisition is created). If a material is being purchased for consumption, then at the time of purchase, the company must determine which object will be responsible for the cost of the items. In such cases, the cost of the material is directly treated as an expenditure at the time of goods receipt, and hence the value of the material does not increase current assets. SAP refers to the cost object as an account assignment object. The account assignment object is required in the purchasing document for a material whenever the purchase of a material is for consumption.

Let us take a concrete example. Let us suppose that the company needs to buy the 500 units of material Z specifically for a production order P. In this case, the material will not be received into inventory and will not become part of the company's assets. Instead, at the time of goods receipt, 500 units of material Z will be consumed (expensed) and the cost will be posted directly to production order P.

To make this happen, the purchasing document (let's assume in this case we are referring to the purchase order (PO)), must contain the production order as the account assignment object. When the 500 units of material X are received during the Goods Receipt step, the material will be expensed, and the cost will be posted directly to the production order. In this case, there is no need for a subsequent goods movement to expense the material because it is not being issued out of inventory. Figure 37 illustrates this.

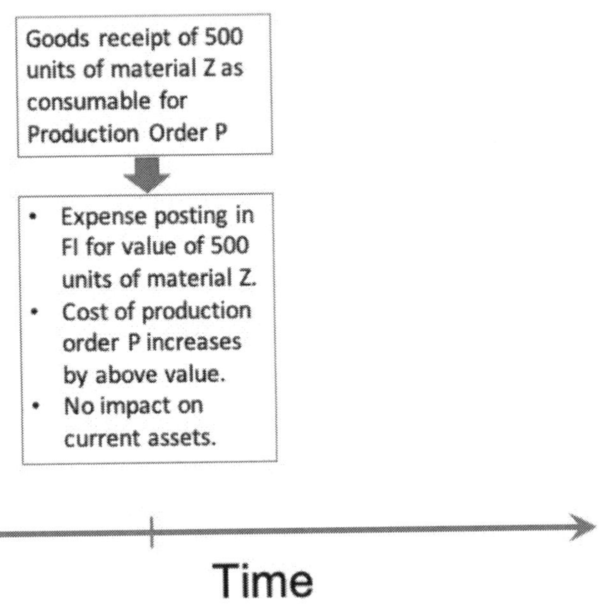


*Figure 37: Procuring for consumption*

## Value-based and quantity-based inventory management

Whether we are procuring for stock or for consumption, we must still consider the impact on Inventory Management. Both situations impact inventory management in different ways. Inventory management in SAP deals with keeping track of materials.

In value-based inventory management, we track the quantities and the monetary value of materials – typically those that form part of the assets of a company. In quantity-based inventory management, we track only the quantities of the concerned materials and do not keep track of their monetary value. Regarding the case of material Z being purchased as a consumable for the production order, the material would not be subject to either value-based inventory management or quantity-based inventory management. This is because the materials will neither be counted in inventory nor valued in inventory as it is put into immediate use by the production order.

However, in the first example, material X was procured as a stock item. In that case, we keep track of both the value maintained in inventory as well as the quantity of material X in inventory. SAP S/4HANA tracks value-based inventory with an FI document and quantity-based inventory is tracked with a material document.

In some cases, a company will want to expense a material (a consumable) which is procured while also wanting to keep track of the quantity in inventory. This is common for materials like office supplies, such as printer paper. When a department in the company orders and receives the printer paper for a PO, the company will want to post this as an expenditure to supplies expense account, as well as posting the cost to the department directly responsible. Therefore, an account assignment object is required. In this case, we would use the cost center as the account assignment object. This would be the cost center to which this department belongs. In such an example, when the printer paper is received, it will be expensed, and the cost will be posted to the cost center. We would also be able to keep track of the quantity of that paper in inventory. Because the printer paper was consumed, there is no value-based inventory. However, the ability to manage the quantity of the printer paper in inventory will make it subject to quantity-based inventory management.

In SAP S/4HANA, individual materials might be subject to either form of inventory management (value-based inventory management and/or quantity-based inventory management) or not subject to inventory management at all.

The key difference between procuring for stock and for consumption is that the latter requires that we specify an account assignment object at the time we create a purchase order.

Another example of an account assignment object is an asset – like a piece of machinery. Suppose we are buying spare parts for a specific piece of equipment – say a truck. In this example, the cost of the spare part does not hit the income statement immediately but will do so when depreciation is charged for the asset (truck) at some future point in time. Other examples of account assignment objects are project and internal order.

The distinction between procuring for stock and for consumption has another implication. When an invoice for an item that is purchased for consumption arrives, any small price difference regarding the amount can be charged to the appropriate account assignment object (like cost center). Therefore, the process potentially interfaces with management accounting (CO).

## Goods Movements

You've read references above to various goods movements in the procurement process. When we procure materials, we receive materials and place them in stock in some storage location. Goods receipt is an important step because it populates a storage location with the material that was not there earlier. Receipt of goods into a storage location is an example of a goods movement.

SAP recognizes several types of goods movements. Each movement is assigned a number to indicate what type of movement it is. The movement type determines how the accounting postings are made and how to process that material.

Goods can be received into different stock types. Three examples of stock types are: unrestricted use stock, stock in quality inspection and blocked stock.

When the stock type is unrestricted use stock, the corresponding materials are ready for use and can be issued to users.

For some materials, the company policy might be to first inspect the materials and only then use them. In such cases, the material will first be received into stock in quality inspection.

Sometimes goods might be received into blocked stock.

In most cases, the goods in all three these examples are valuated. That is, the value of these goods is part of the current assets of the company. These three examples of stock types noted above are associated with movement type 101.

We can distinguish between goods movements that are actually physical movements and some which are considered movements but involve no physical movement of the goods. Suppose we receive 200 units of some raw material into unrestricted use stock and place them in some storage location. However, later we come across information to the effect that goods supplied by the concerned vendor have defects. We now decide that we should inspect those materials before using them.

Thus, we must re-categorize those materials as being in quality inspection and not in unrestricted use stock. This re-categorization may not involve any actual physical movement. The materials may remain in the same place, but we now record them as being part of quality inspection stock. This re-categorization is another form of a goods movement although it involves no physical movement.

Generally, goods movements involving physical movements are called stock transfers and those that do not involve physical movement are called transfer postings. We will describe this in greater depth in a later chapter.

## Review questions: Procurement

(You can find answers on page 216. To be able to answer questions marked with an asterisk(*), you should have read the official SAP course material.)

1. Which of the following represent organization levels at which stock levels can be viewed? (four) *

   A. Storage location

   B. Client

   C. Business area

   D. Company code

E. Plant

2. Which of the following represent valid assignments of the purchasing organization? (three)

   A. Cross client

   B. Cross company code

   C. Cross plant

   D. Dedicated to a single plant

   E. Cross storage location

3. A storage location may be assigned to how many plants?

4. How many storage locations can be assigned to a single plant?

5. A plant may be assigned to how many company codes?

6. How many plants can be assigned to a company code?

7. Can more than one plant be assigned the same number?

8. What combination is required to uniquely identify a storage location?

9. Which of the following represent levels at which material master data is defined? (three) *

   A. Plant

   B. Client

   C. Company code

   D. Purchasing organization

   E. Storage location

10. Which of the following represent the roles of the vendor business partner? (three) *

    A. Reconciliation role

    B. General role

    C. FI Vendor role

    D. Supplier role

11. Which of the following represent organizational levels at which the vendor business partner is defined? (three)

    A. Plant

    B. Client

    C. Company code

    D. Purchasing organization

    E. Storage location

12. Which master data contains information about the combination of a material and a vendor?

13. Which of the following is not part of the standard SAP procurement process? (one)

    A. Supply source determination

   B. Goods issue

   C. Purchase order monitoring

   D. Invoice verification

   E. Goods receipt

14. Which of the following is not a valid scenario in SAP procurement? (one) *

   A. Procuring a stock item with a material master record

   B. Procuring an item without a material master record for consumption

   C. Procuring an item with a material master record for consumption

   D. Procuring a stock item without a material master record

15. Which of the following represent ways by which a purchase requisition can be created in SAP? (four) *

   A. Via SAP SRM

   B. Via SAP CRM

   C. Via SAP SCM

   D. Manually

   E. Automatically via MRP

   F. From a purchase order

16. For what reason would one maintain a material master record for a material that is being managed in inventory on a quantity base, but not a value base? *

17. When purchasing material for which there is no material master, how does the material description get populated in the purchasing document (PR or PO)? *

18. Which of the following purchasing scenarios requires an account assignment object? An account assignment object is mandatory for procuring: (two) *

   A. Any material that is subject to value-based inventory management

   B. Any material that is not subject to value-based inventory management

   C. Any material without a material master record

   D. Any material for stock which will later be consumed for production of finished goods

19. Which of the following are examples of valid account assignment categories? (four) *

   A. Cost center

   B. Profit center

   C. Vendor

   D. Project

   E. Asset

   F. Order

20. What is the difference between an account assignment category and an account assignment object?

21. How does the procurement of a stock item differ from that of a consumable?

22. What type of a purchase order is used when materials are purchased from another plant? *

23. While checking the status of a purchase order, SAP supports status checking for the entire orders as well as individual items in the order. T/F? *

24. Which of the following is not part of a purchase order? (one) *

    A. Header

    B. Item overview

    C. Schedule lines

    D. Item detail

25. Which item category is used for vendor owned inventory? This is inventory that is ordered and received but is still owned by the vendor until it is used. (one) *

    A. Standard

    B. Subcontracting

    C. Consignment

    D. Third party

    E. Stock transfer

26. Which of the following is not an effect of a goods receipt of materials for a PO? (one) *

    A. Creation of a material document

    B. Posting to a vendor account

    C. Creation of an accounting document

    D. Update of the purchase order

27. A company wants to select a specific stock type for a material in a PO. How is this set? *

28. When material is received into stock type: quality inspection, will the value of stock increase before it clears inspection? *

29. The Stock overview is said to be a static view. What does this mean? *

30. A material was in a storage location, awaiting quality inspection. After it was inspected, it was changed to unrestricted use stock. Is this goods movement an example of a stock transfer or a transfer posting?

31. Will a stock transfer of a material from one storage location to another within the same plant have any financial impact? *

32. All goods movements result in the creation of material documents. T/F?

33. If warehouse management is active, how does a goods receipt impact warehouse management?

34. Does a goods receipt for a PO impact the material master? *

35. What is the impact of a goods receipt if QM is active? *

36. What step completes the logistics portion of the procurement process?

37. Under what conditions would an invoice-posting result in the update of the moving average price in the materials master record?

# Material Planning

*THIS CHAPTER INTRODUCES* the material planning business process as relevant for the SAP TS410 certification examination. It introduces key terms and provides background knowledge that will prepare readers for SAP's course material. The Material Planning business process deals with the integrated planning of the procurement of raw materials used in manufacturing finished products. Think for a moment about the various things that the process of planning the procurement of raw material must take into consideration (see Figure 38: Things that material planning needs to ):

- Production plans for the relevant planning horizon.
- Material stocks at various locations.
- Safety stocks of various materials.
- Procurement lot sizes for various materials.
- Finalized or firmed up production orders that will soon become available in stock.
- Purchase orders and other means of procurement that are already in the pipeline and against which the company will receive materials
- Confirmed sales orders for made-to-order items (that is items that the company does not produce for stock and instead only manufactures against firm orders).

Figure 38 illustrates this.

*Figure 38: Things that material planning needs to consider*

We can see that unless the process takes all the above into account, the result might not be as good as it could be. Even moderate sized companies deal with many finished goods, each of which consumes many raw materials. Furthermore, numerous purchase orders could be in various stages of fulfillment and several production orders could be in a firmed state.

The process includes additional complicating factors that the above list does not show. Given all these, planning for materials could be a very complicated process consuming much time and effort. The Material Planning process serves to integrate and automate this complicated activity.

## Organization Levels

Material Planning involves the following organization levels:

- **Client**: Client is a single instance of SAP used in all modules and business processes. (see Figure 39)
- **Company Code**: Representing a legal entity from a Financial Accounting perspective
- **Plant**: In SAP, materials are managed at the plant level and thus plants play a critical role in material planning.
- **Storage Location**: Materials are physically stored in various storage locations and stocks are also tracked primarily by storage location. Thus, storage locations also play an important role

in material planning (see Figure 40)

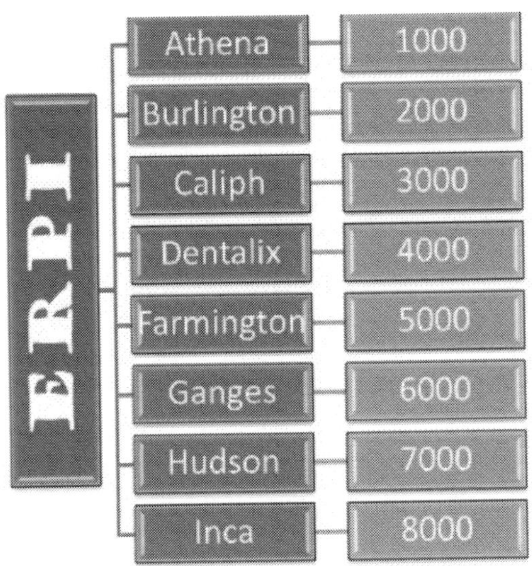


*Figure 39: Client and company codes*

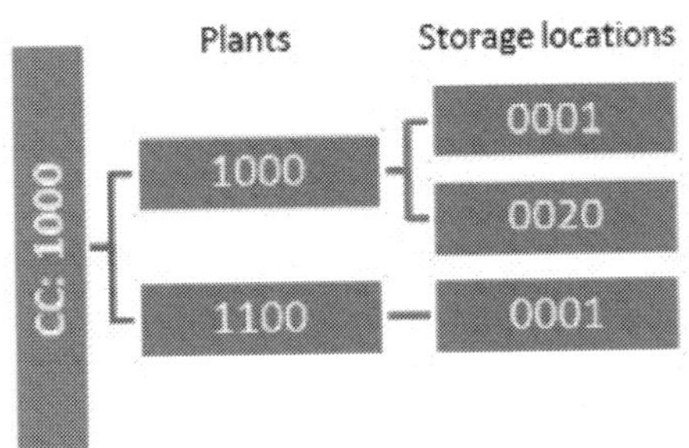


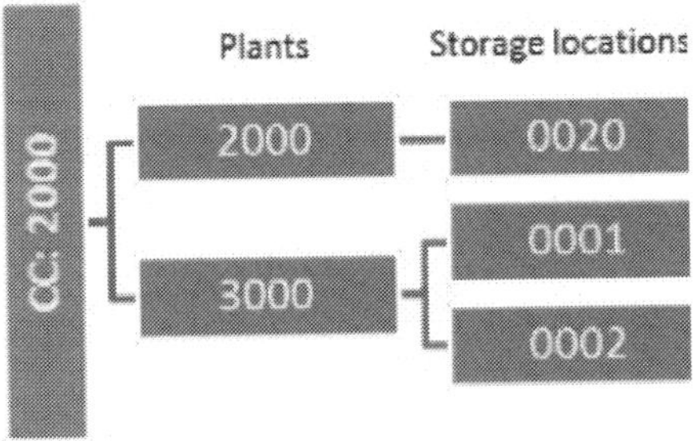


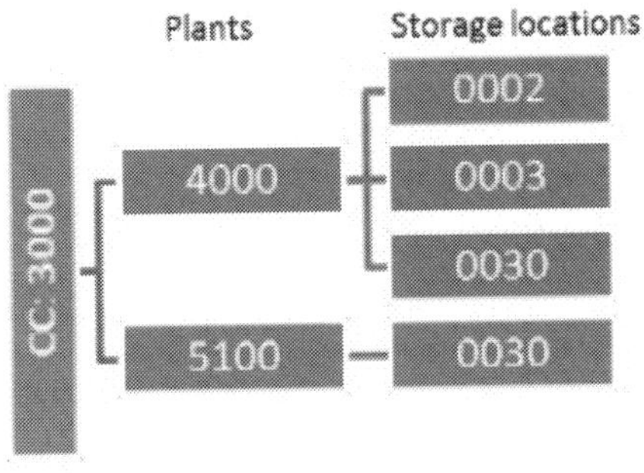


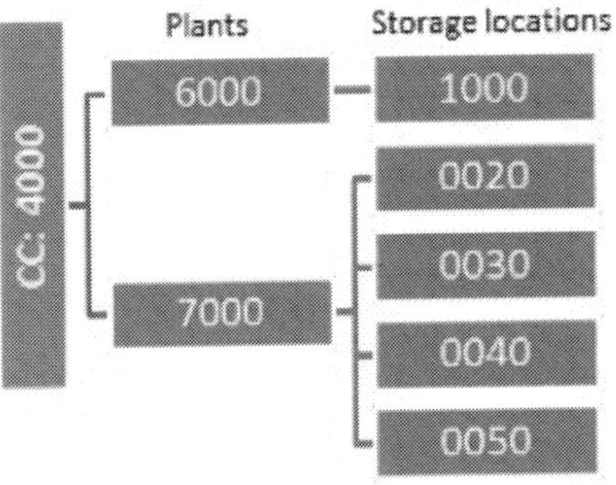


*Figure 40: Company codes, plants and storage locations*

## Master data

Business processes in SAP S/4HANA make use of various items of master data. The material planning business process uses the following which are maintained for each Plant:

- **Material Master**: Contains information about each material – including material number, name, units of measurement, and such.

- **Bill of Materials or BOM**: For every product, its BOM specifies what components and how much of each goes into the product. A BOM does not just specify what raw materials go into each finished product. It actually specifies the complete hierarchy of sub-assemblies and raw materials that make up each finished product. From the BOM, one can figure out exactly how much of each material is needed to make a certain number of units (or quantity) of a product.
- **Routing**: Routings specify the steps in the production process for a finished product. For each step, the routing specifies the work center where the step will be performed, the time it takes to set up the machine, the time it takes to process a single piece and so on. Why is the routing important for material planning? It looks like routings are more concerned with the actual process of production rather than for material planning. After all, so far as material planning is concerned, what does it matter where an operation is performed or how long it takes? It does matter, because in material planning, we are concerned not just with how much of a material is needed, but also with when it is needed. Not all materials might be needed when the process starts. If a material is not needed until the fourth step in a routing, it's possible that step might not start until a week or more after the first step starts. In that case, procurement can be planned accordingly.

## Production Strategies

Production strategies define the various approaches that are available to a company when planning and running production. There are many forms of production strategies, but for simplification purposes, we will only address a few of these.

At the very outset, let us establish a couple of basic strategies. • In a make-to-stock scenario, a company makes finished products and stores them as finished goods stock. Then the company sells finished products from inventory as customers place sales orders. • In a make-to-order scenario, a company first receives sales orders from customers and only then manufactures finished goods to fulfill the sales orders already received. Sales orders are not fulfilled from inventory.

What are the pros and cons of each strategy? In make-to-stock, a company takes on greater risk because it is producing in advance. What if some of the manufactured products do not sell? There is scope for finished goods to go to waste. In make-to-order a company takes on no risk of a finished product going unsold, but the downside is that its delivery lead time will be greater since it will produce only after receiving the order. A competitor who can ship quicker could have an advantage.

In this book we assume that a company could be using a mix of the two approaches. Perhaps for some of the products the company could use make-to-stock and for others, use make-to-order. Companies also use a hybrid option that serves to get the best of both worlds. This is sometimes called subassembly planning. In subassembly planning companies might produce sub-assemblies (one or more components required to produce the finished product) to stock, making only the final assembly required. This option often allows a company to reduce inventory of finished goods, while also reducing the lead time of delivery to the customer.

At its core, the material planning business process aims to make materials available in time for production processes to be completed on schedule to fill planned sales. To make this happen, the material planning process is often repeated at regular time intervals. We will discuss this planning process next.

## Material Planning (MRP)

In this book we will look at a simple outline of the process to emphasize the key aspects. The SAP course materials go into greater detail. Once you understand the simple sketch of the process, you should be in a good position to take on the additional details in the official course material.

Suppose a company does material planning once every month for all its materials (a simplification of reality, no doubt, because companies could have different planning cycles for different materials and for different plants). At the start of each month, the company might plan ahead for the following three months. Although, at the start of January, the company would have planned its materials through the end of March, we have to remember that the company would have made its plans based on various forecasts and estimates. At the start of February, things would hardly have gone exactly according to plan and thus the material plan done at the start of January would need to be modified for February and March. When the company plans its materials again at the start of February, it can correct for the deviations from previous plans.

The material planning process (MRP) plans for materials for manufacturing and must therefore be driven by planned production activities. (Note: MRP can also be used to plan for materials for other processes, beyond manufacturing.) Production plans, in turn, must be driven by estimates of sales – for products and sub-assemblies that the company makes for stock, and by actual sales orders for products that the company makes to order.

The sales forecasts referenced above can be done in a variety of ways. It's not important right now to describe each method, but you should be aware of some influencing factors as well as some basic planning tools.

It's been said that the best predictor of the future is the past. Keeping this in mind, sales forecasts are best when based on historical data. There are a couple of basic tools for recording the sales forecasts. One approach is the use of a Sales and Operations Plan (SOP). The SOP is a traditional tool used in SAP ERP and it still available in the earliest versions of SAP S/4HANA. Ultimately, it appears that the SOP will be replaced with the SAP Integrated Business Planning (IBP) tool. SAP IBP is similar to the SOP; however, it contains more optimization models and some additional functionality. Both tools work well when forecasting based on historical data. However, there are times when historical data is not available and other means are necessary. SAP SOP and SAP IBP also offer capabilities to plan without historical data.

Once a forecast has been established, the material planning process has two high level steps that we outline below and describe in slightly greater detail later (see Figure 41).

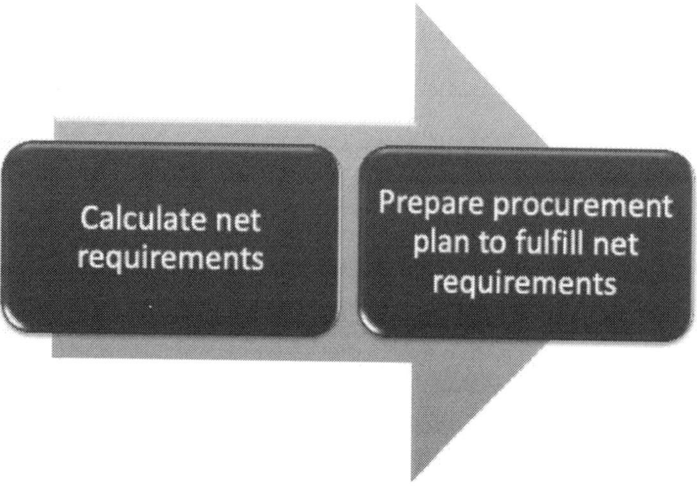


*Figure 41: High level steps in MRP*

- **Calculating net requirements**: In this step, MRP determines the material shortfall for each day of the planning horizon, taking into consideration all requirements (see Figure 42).
- **Preparing procurement proposals**: In this step, MRP prepares a plan for how to fill the shortfall. Since the material planning process does integrated planning, it starts out with the shortfall in finished goods and works backward using the BOM to calculate the requirements and shortfall of all sub-assemblies and raw materials. Filling the shortfall could therefore, involve purchasing raw materials as well as producing sub-assemblies and finished goods. (see Figure 43)

Once MRP has determined the net requirements, it will identify how to fill those requirements. Here we must consider the different types of materials that a company would deal with (finished goods, raw materials and semi-finished goods). Furthermore, it is possible that a company would buy some of the materials from vendors and produce some of the materials (especially finished goods and semi-finished goods) in-house. Often though, companies can flexibly produce some goods in-house as well as to buy the same materials from vendors when needed.

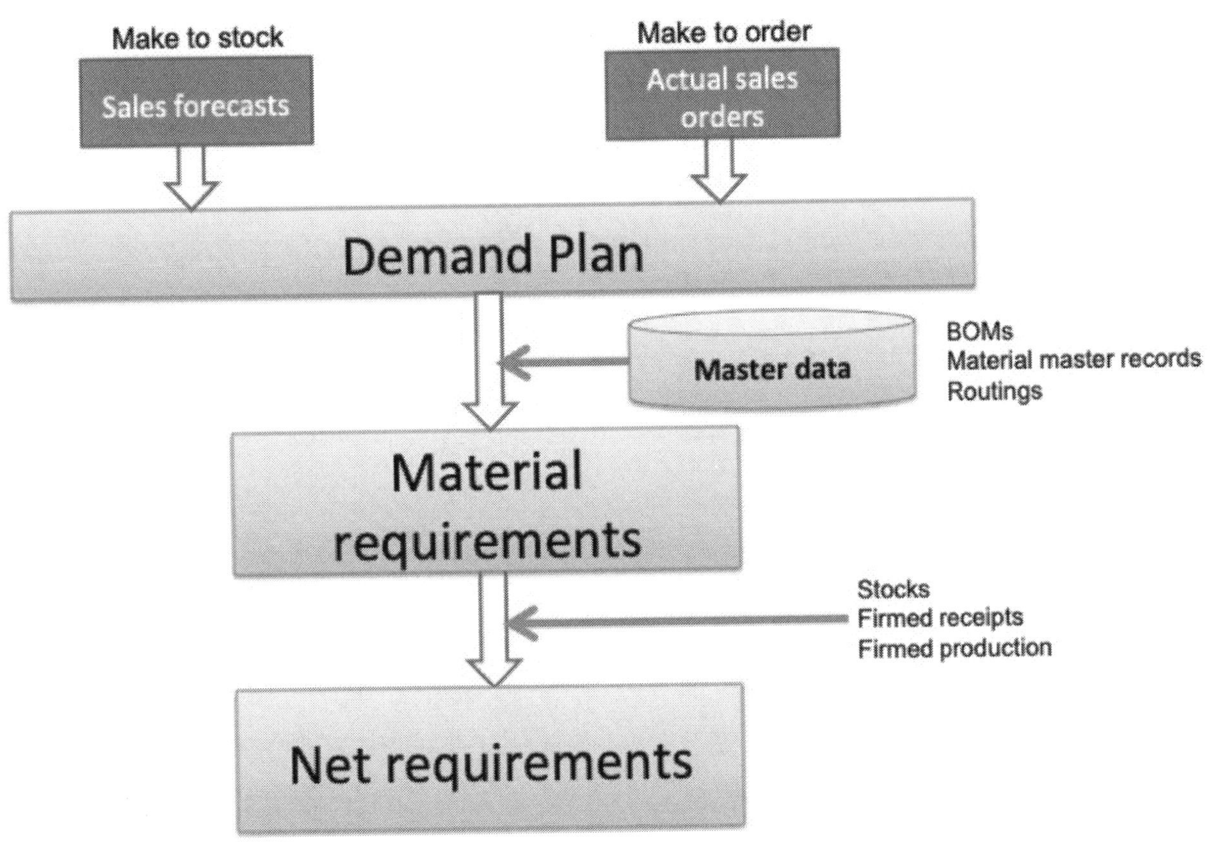


*Figure 42: Calculating net requirements*

For materials that are only bought from vendors and never made in-house, MRP often generates purchase requisitions. (Note: Other options are explained later and in the SAP course materials.) These purchase requisitions would be created in such a way that they consider when a material is needed, purchasing lot sizes and other considerations like safety stock. The purchasing processes are then employed to convert the purchase requisitions into purchase orders.

Similarly, for materials that the company only makes in-house, MRP creates planned orders. The manufacturing processes are then used convert these planned orders into production orders.

For materials that a company can make in-house and purchases from vendors, the process generates planned orders. Later, when the time comes, the company could decide to convert the planned orders into either purchase requisitions or into production orders.

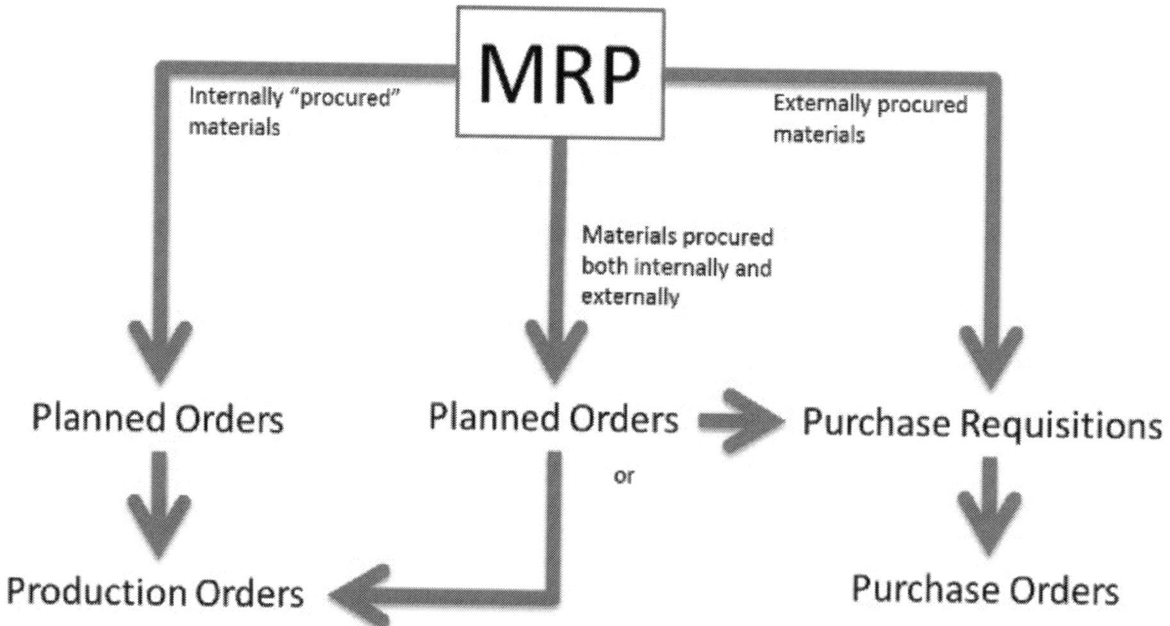


*Figure 43: Creating procurement proposals*

## MRP Live

As you can well imagine, the planning of materials can be rather complex. The scope can also be quite overwhelming if this planning were to be done the old-fashioned way (using spreadsheets). In prior versions of SAP ERP, the MRP run was very capacity intensive and demanding of the system itself. As such, MRP runs were performed at times when they had minimal impact on system performance. Often the MRP run would take place overnight or even run only once per week.

SAP S/4HANA has enabled significant improvements to handle the demands of the MRP run. Because of these improvements, SAP in S/4HANA refers to the new MRP run as MRP Live. Some of the advantages of MRP Live are listed below:

- Faster run times
- Ability to run MRP more frequently
- Ability to plan materials across several plants
- Better processing capabilities, meaning less manual input
- Real-time insight

The SAP course materials go into more detail regarding MRP Live. But for now, consider the term MRP Live to mean you can run MRP as often as needed to get a "live" view of your material requirements.

## MRP Type

Thus far we have generally assumed that MRP does material planning for all items based on BOMs.

This need not always be the case. Companies might plan for some materials based on BOMs – that is first consider how many finished products or sub-assemblies need to be made and then explode the BOM to calculate the quantities of raw materials needed. However, planning for all materials need not be done this way. For some materials that are inexpensive, such an elaborate process might not be worthwhile – for example, small nails, generic screws, small generic fasteners and glue.

Other materials might actually not go into the finished product at all even though they might be used in the manufacturing process – for example, cleaning supplies and rag cloth. For such items, rather than planning based strictly on BOM, companies use consumption-based planning. How the planning for a material is to be done is stored in the material master in a field called its MRP Type. Broadly, the MRP Type can be either "MRP" or "consumption-based planning".

For materials with MRP type "MRP", the process utilizes BOM explosion to determine quantities needed of such materials. For materials with one of the consumption-based planning MRP types, the process determines the quantity needed based on their consumption pattern rather than on BOM explosion. Typically, this enables companies to automate the process and reduce processing costs. This also enables companies to focus on costly and critical materials while preventing less important materials from taking up valuable time. There are many types of methods for consumption-based planning. Some examples appear below:

- **Reorder point planning – VB**: In Reorder point planning (see Figure 44), companies determine the following for the material: safety stock, reorder point and reorder quantity or lot size. Companies keep using these materials until the stock reaches the reorder point. At this stage the company reorders the material and the quantity ordered is the reorder quantity or lot size. Because of the time pattern of how the material stock looks, this is also called the saw-tooth model of inventory management.
- **Forecast based planning – VV**: In this, companies independently forecast the consumption of the material and act accordingly.
- **Time based planning – R1**: In this, companies simply procure a certain quantity at regular intervals.

## MRP Run

As mentioned earlier, the MRP run has traditionally been very demanding on the system. The MRP run could involve the planning of many materials with many levels of requirements. With the introduction of SAP S/4HANA, the processing demands have been greatly reduced. Because of this, there are now only two (2) MRP Processing Keys for the MRP run. The MRP Processing Keys essentially defined the scope of the MRP run. Today, with SAP S/4HANA, planners have the flexibility of choosing between NETCH and NEUPL Processing Keys.

NETCH is called "Net Change" and is the processing key used for planning materials that have undergone changes since the last MRP run. As an example, suppose an aluminum component was used in the BOM of a product, but was recently replaced with a titanium version of the same component. Since the material changed, it needs to be re-planned.

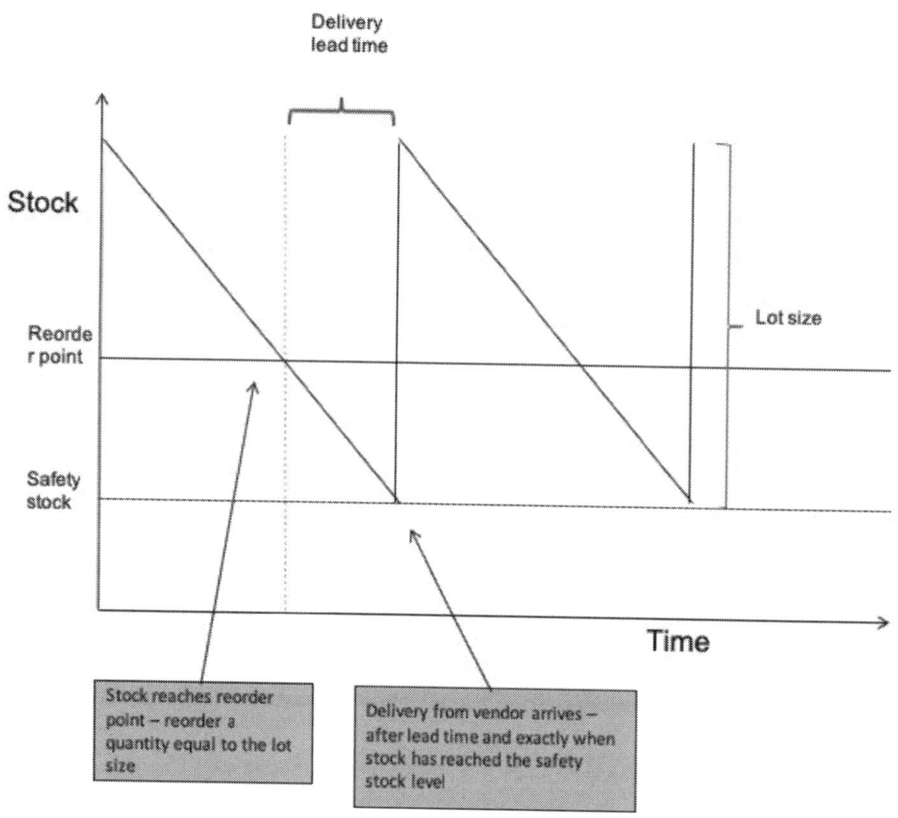


*Figure 44: Reorder point planning*

When the MRP run is performed using NETCH (assuming no other materials changed), the MRP run will only re-plan the component that changed and leave previously planned materials as they were. This approach greatly reduces the scope of planning.

On the other hand, NEUPL is called "Regenerative Planning" and is the processing key used to plan ALL materials, regardless of whether any changes occurred. As you can tell, the scope using this processing key is extensive.

When performing the MRP run, the planner will choose the Processing Key among other things. If we revisit Figure 43, some materials are procured externally. In the case of external procurement, we see in the figure that MRP can generate a procurement proposal in the form of a Planned Order or a Purchase Requisition. (You will discover in the SAP course materials, there is a third option for external procurement, not discussed here.) The question becomes, how does MRP know what option to choose for materials procured externally? The answer is simple. The planner decides this during the MRP run.

Along with choosing the Processing Key, the planner has additional Control Parameter settings. These settings define the output for external procurement during the MRP run. As you can see in the image, MRP can generate a Planned Order or a Purchase Requisition. The selections of the Control Parameters in the MRP run are set based on how the planner decides to procure the materials.

## Integration with SAP APO

SAP APO (Advanced Planning Optimizer) was part of what was formerly considered the SAP Supply Chain Management application in the Business Suite. In SAP S/4HANA, the Business Suite no longer exists in its previous form, but is incorporated as Lines of Business (LOB's). Thus, SAP APO is still available as part of SAP S/4HANA.

In SAP S/4HANA, planning with APO is called Advanced Planning. Since this is an optimized tool, it is done only for finite planning, which assumes capacity is relatively constant. With known values, SAP can plan in a more detailed fashion. Advanced planning leverages Production Planning/Detailed Scheduling (PP/DS) in SAP APO. Some advantages of PP/DS include:

- Optimized scheduling with exact times to the minute
- Seamless integration in S/4HANA using the Core Interface (CIF)
- Alerting
- Reduction in set up costs and production delays
- The SAP course materials provide more insight into the integration or the MRP run with SAP APO.

## Review questions: Material planning

(You can find answers on page 220. To answer questions that end with an asterisk (*), you will need to have read the official SAP course material.

1. At which organizational level is material planning generally performed? (one)

    A. Client

    B. Company code

    C. Plant

    D. Storage location

2. Which of the following represent master data required in Materials Planning? (three)

    A. Materials

    B. Work centers

C. Routings

D. Bill of materials

3. Which of the following represent required views in the material master record for Material Planning? (one) *

A. MRP

B. Work scheduling

C. Accounting

D. Forecasting

E. Quality management

4. Explain how each of the following fields in the material master is used: *

MRP Type:

Procurement type:

Strategy group:

5. When creating a material master record, you assign it a material type. Which of the following are valid material types? (three) *

A. In house production

B. Raw material

C. Finished good

D. Externally procured

E. Operating supplies

6. What does the material type determine? (two) *

A. What views are displayed for maintaining the material

B. How the material number is assigned

C. The strategy group assigned to the material

D. The MRP Type for the material

7. All BOM master records in SAP are single-level. T/F?

8. What is the difference between the header quantity and the component quantities in the BOM?

9. In SAP it is possible for a material to have multiple BOMs. These are referred to as versions. Explain BOM versions. *

10. What does the BOM usage field in the BOM header determine? *

11. Which of the following represent valid item categories in a BOM? (three) *

A. In house production

B. External procurement

C. Stock item

D. Non-stock item

E. Variable-size item

12. Can a consumable material be included as a component in a BOM? *

13. In SAP ECC, planning is managed using a Sales and Operations Planning (SOP) table. In SAP S/4HANA, the SOP is being replaced with which process? (one)

    A. COPA planning

    B. Production Planning

    C. Integrated Business Planning (IBP)

    D. MRP Planning

14. What is a product group?

15. The lowest level of a product group hierarchy contains ________ ____________. *

16. With respect to requirements in MRP, which of the following statements are true? (two)

    A. Planned independent requirements represent customer orders

    B. Customer independent requirements are based on forecasts and plans

    C. Planned independent requirements can be based on forecasts and plans

    D. Customer independent requirements are sales orders

    E. Dependent requirements can be based directly on forecasts and plans

17. Demand management results in the creation of independent requirements. What does MRP create to meet these independent requirements? (one)

    A. Planned orders

    B. Purchase requisitions

    C. Production orders

    D. Schedule lines

18. To plan procurement proposals, MRP performs a supply v demand calculation known as the Net Requirement Calculation. Which of the following make up the demand side of that calculation? (one)

    A. Purchase orders

    B. Safety stock

    C. Firmed planned orders

    D. Confirmed purchase requisitions

19. The MRP type is used to define how materials are planned. Some materials are planned based on independent requirements, other forms of planning are based on ___________.

20. Which of the following are valid procurement proposals generated by MRP? (three)

    A. Sales orders

    B. Planned orders

    C. Purchase requisitions

    D. Schedule lines

    E. Purchase orders

21. MRP Live is part of SAP S/4HANA. Which of the following is not a feature of MRP Live? (one)
    A. Faster run times
    B. Planning at individual plants
    C. More frequent MRP runs possible
    D. Real time insight
22. Which of the following control parameters determines the scope of the MRP run in SAP S/4HANA? (one)
    A. Processing Key
    B. Purchase Requisitions
    C. Planned Orders
    D. Schedule Lines
23. Which of the following processing keys is no longer needed in SAP S/4HANA? (one)
    A. NEUPL
    B. NETCH
    C. NETPL
24. What is the main difference between the stock/requirements list and the MRP list?

# Manufacturing

*THIS CHAPTER INTRODUCES* the manufacturing execution business process as relevant for the SAP TS410 certification examination. It introduces key terms and provides background knowledge that will enable users to read and understand SAP's course material. The chapter does not aim to duplicate content from the official SAP course materials. Instead it describes the broad framework in an easily understandable form and lays the foundation for students to delve deeper into the detailed course materials.

The Manufacturing Execution business process covers all the steps and interactions involved in producing finished products from raw materials and sub-assemblies. The official certification course material uses many technical terms. Without clearly understanding the context and relating the terms to reality, the official course material might appear much more complicated than necessary.

After all, the manufacturing process uses some raw materials to produce finished goods. To do this, it uses certain facilities, labor and other resources. All this is, of course, happening in the context of a demand plan that has determined the quantities of finished products to be produced at various times. While the details of this can get complex on the shop floor, we only need to grasp the big picture – which is not at all complex. So, as you read this chapter and SAP's official certification course material, focus your energies on clearly understanding the big picture and relate the various terms that the course material uses to the real-world.

In the real world, many different types of production processes have evolved.

- **Manufacturing based on Production Orders** arguably represents the simplest process wherein we want to make some finished products using some raw materials and we ask the manufacturing department to produce x pieces of a product. In small organizations this asking could be just that – verbally asking. However, larger organizations need to do things more formally to avoid waste and inefficiency. They follow formal processes and track and control the processes through various documents. They initiate the production process by creating a formal document. In SAP, we initiate most processes by creating some kind of Order, and a Production Order formally initiates production.

- **Repetitive Manufacturing** deals with the situation where materials continuously flow through an assembly line.
- **Process Manufacturing** is concerned with process industries where the end products are not discrete products. Here typically fluids (or gases) flow through the process.

Each type of manufacturing presents different issues and challenges. This chapter covers only manufacturing based on Production Orders.

## Master Data

A few important pieces of master data used in manufacturing are:

- **Material Master** – Used to get appropriate information about the materials used as relevant to manufacturing.
- **Bill of Materials** – Specifies what materials are needed and in what quantities to make other materials.
- **Work Center** – Provides the capacity needed to perform work. A work center could be a machine, a group of machines, a person or a group of people.
- **Routing** – Steps or operations to make a product, and the specification of each operation, including the time required and the work center needed for the operation.
- **PRT** – Production Resources Tools. Some operations will require the use of special equipment (other than the work center itself). These could be special jigs and fixtures or specialized measuring instruments and so on.

## Process Overview

As mentioned earlier, a Production Order formally starts the process. However, in SAP, a formal order is often not the first step in a process. SAP always provides the functionality of using an informal step before the formal one. For production, the use of a Planned Order represents this informal step. It usually (but not always) precedes a production order. A Planned Order does not formally authorize production. None of the formal steps for manufacturing can be accomplished simply based on a Planned

Order. It simply represents a preliminary planning step.

The Planned Order remains an informal document with no actual impact until someone or some automated step converts it into a Production Order (see Figure 45). This allows the organization to commit resources to it – resources like machine time, labor, and materials. However, actual work on the Production Order cannot begin until it is released. Releasing a Production order authorizes subsequent activities to take place; for example, only after release can materials be issued against the production order. Recall from order-related cost object controlling that only after release does the production order becomes a cost object.

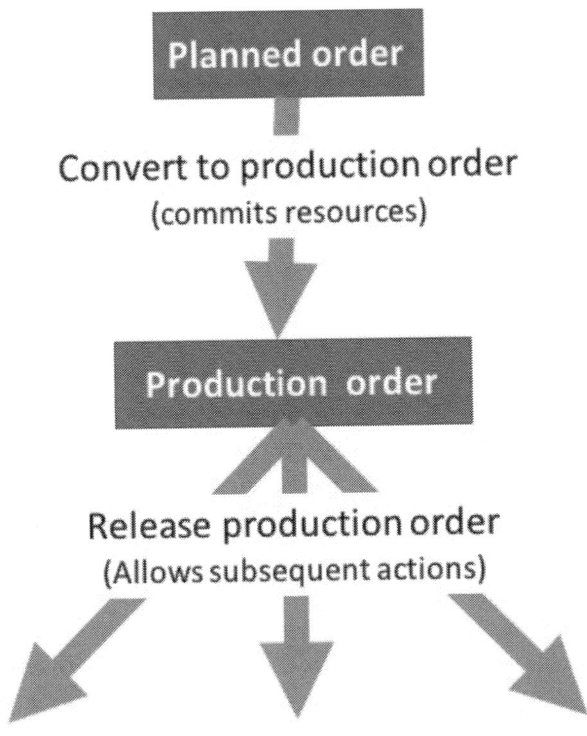


*Figure 45: Converting planned order to a production order reserves resources and releasing a production order, makes subsequent operations possible*

Common sense tells us that certain things must be in place before converting Planned Orders into Production Orders and before releasing Production Orders. Think a little bit about what must be in place before we should attempt to perform these steps. When a Planned Order is converted into a Production Order, various other business processes will assume that this order will now be executed. For example, materials management will assume that some amount of material will be consumed. Capacity planners will assume that this order will take up some machine time and labor and so on. Thus, converting a planned order has real consequences and can result in inefficiency if not done carefully. Before converting a Planned Order into a Production Order and before releasing a Production Order, we must ensure that the materials and resources needed for the order (machine capacities, labor, PRT, etc. at the work centers) are available. This process is called the Availability Check. Of course, the steps can be completed even if the Availability Check fails – there is room for judgment – but the system alerts us of any non-availability (see Figure 46).

As it relates to materials held in inventory, the production department would also want to assure themselves that all available materials held in inventory are reserved for the production order. Failing to reserve those materials could result in the materials being used elsewhere in the enterprise, making what was once available, now unavailable. This would certainly cause unnecessary delays in the production process. Likewise, the available resources at work centers need to be reserved for the production order so when the time comes, they aren't allocated for things other than the production order. Again, this would result in delays in the production process.

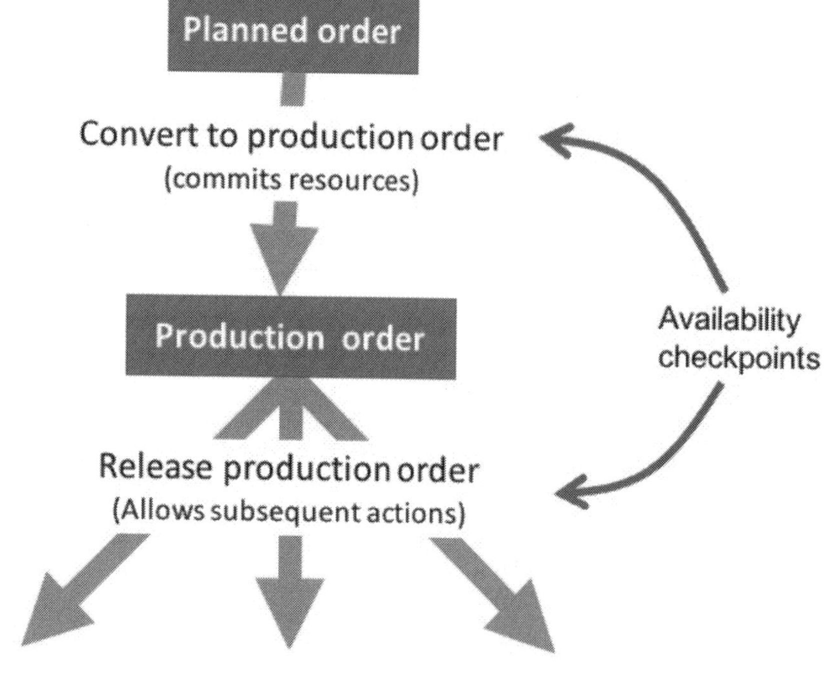


*Figure 46: Availability checkpoints in the manufacturing execution process*

Having learned how the Production Order is initiated, let us go further. A released production order has kinetic energy and can cause actions to take place. Materials necessary for completing the production can now be issued from inventory; Work Center Capacities that were allocated, can now be used; any special tools (called Production Resources Tools or PRTs) can also be issued. When a production order is released, the system can also print any documents needed for the work to be done on the shop – for example, any drawings, instructions and other shop documents can be printed. In cases where numerically controlled machines or robotic machines are being used, we might need to upload appropriate programs as well to these machines (see Figure 47).

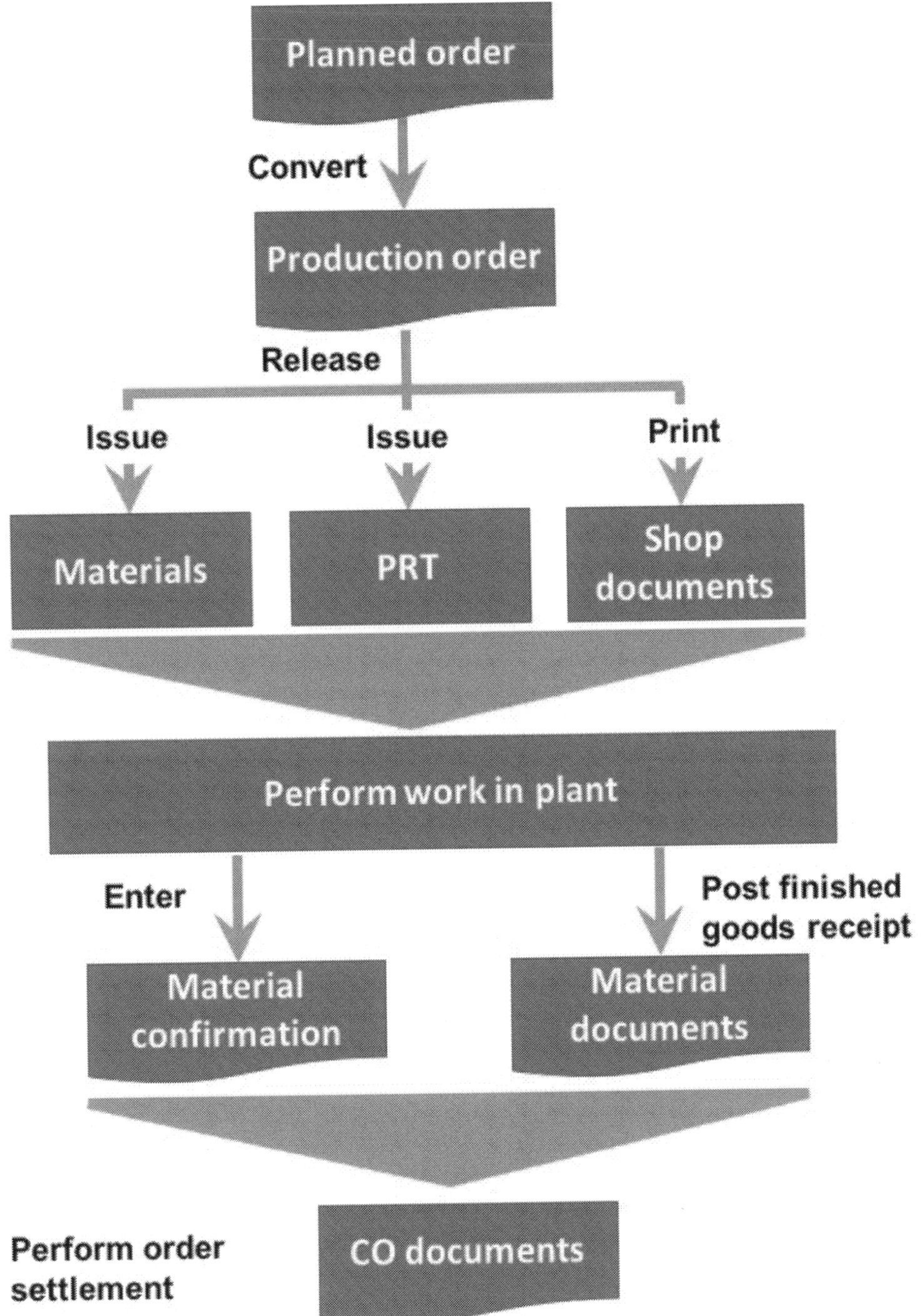


*Figure 47: Manufacturing execution process*

Once all the materials needed to complete the order are issued, work can begin – assuming the required capacities like machine time and labor hours are still available.

At this point in the process, the work centers previously assigned to the operations begin their work on the production order. To record the completion of work on the production order, workers at the work centers enter confirmations. To make it concrete, suppose we issued a production order to make 50 chairs.

The concerned people receive the issued materials needed and go off to work on the chairs. When they finish making these chairs, they will enter an Order Confirmation in the system indicating how many were produced, how much time the process took, how many pieces did not pass quality checks, and so on. The information from these confirmations also provide management with knowledge concerning efficiencies and costs. When the products have been confirmed, the quantity of the Finished materials are to be placed in finished goods stock. Thus, a goods receipt is posted, affecting inventory management and accounting. Upon completion of this step, the newly produced finished goods show up in the financial books as assets in finished goods stock. Before this they appeared as work in progress inventory.

After the goods receipt posting, everything seems complete as far as the manufacturing process is concerned – after all we have finished producing the goods and handed them over to inventory. However, the business process has additional steps remaining. The production order has been happily consuming resources – using up materials, machines, labor and so on. Prudent management accounting would require that the cost of using all these direct and indirect resources be properly allocated. Technically, these costs have been allocated to the production order during the manufacturing execution process. After all, a production order follows the order-related cost object controlling steps. When the goods receipt step described above is completed, the value of the product that was placed into inventory is offset by taking that same value out of the production order. What remains is considered a variance.

The calculation of the variance state above is very important from an accounting perspective. Accountants are responsible for making sure all cost are properly assigned at the end of the month. This is typically referred to as month end closing. Recall from the Management Accounting chapter, some costs collected on cost objects (including variances in production orders) are generally settled during the settlement period. The settlement period is also likely to coincide with month end closing. At this time, the production order's variance will be settled. Figure 47 above shows this step as Order Settlement.

## Interfaces with other SAP Modules

The SAP TS410 course emphasizes integration, that is, the interconnections across modules. After all, enterprise is the operative word in an enterprise system like S/4HANA, and such systems aim to increase efficiency and effectiveness by integrating various business processes.

Let us look at the various ways in which Manufacturing Execution (PP) integrates with other modules:

Materials management (MM): Clearly, when PP consumes materials and PRTs, and when MM issues materials or receives finished products, PP interfaces with MM. From the materials planning unit, we also saw that MRP might create Planned Orders or Purchase Requisitions which are used in the MM

Procurement process.

Management Accounting (CO): As mentioned in our discussions above, we are going to revisit order-related cost object controlling. Virtually the entire process described above follows the order-related cost object controlling steps. Figure 48 shows a side-by-side comparison of an image we saw in the Management Accounting chapter and the image of the production process from Figure 47. It also shows the parallels between the two processes.

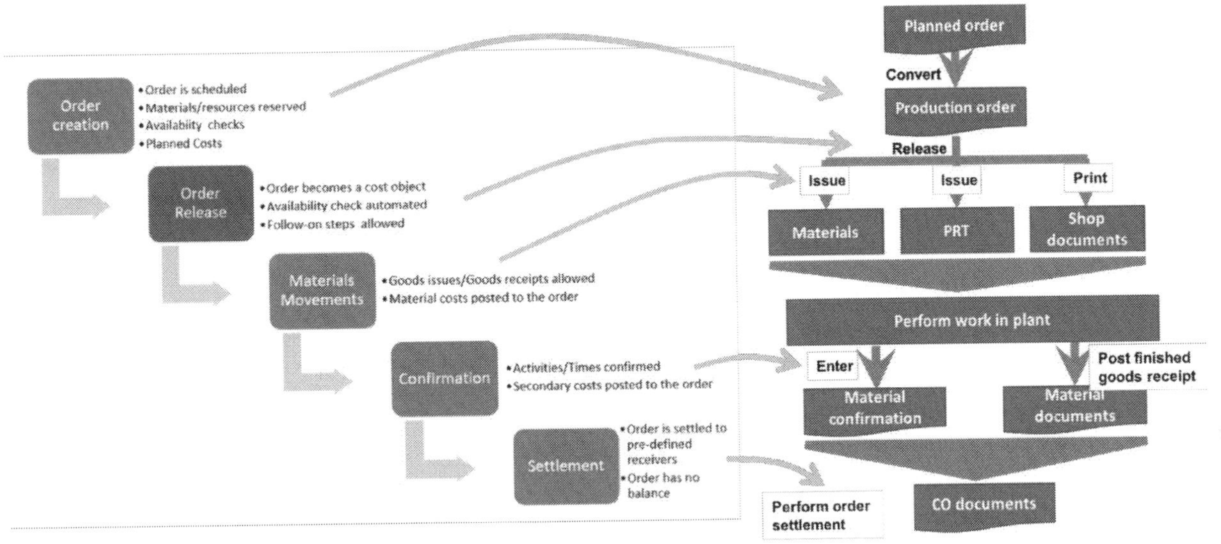


*Figure 48: Order-related cost object controlling and manufacturing execution processes viewed side by side with gray arrows to highlight the connections*

There are parallels in these two images because they are essentially the same. Converting a planned order to a production order in PP is the equivalent of the order creation in order-related cost object controlling. Notice the subsequent steps in both are the release of the order; the goods issue (goods movement) of materials to the production order; confirmation of the materials produced, and the work performed; and finally, the settlement activities.

If you are able to draw the parallels identified here, that will go a long way in understanding many of the concepts you will see in the TS410 certification course.

## Other Salient Points

- **Origin of production orders**: Most often, production orders result from planned orders being converted. However, we can also directly create production orders. order release can also be automated.
- **Automating goods issue inventory postings**: For efficiency, SAP provides the option to automate good issue postings. Thus, when a Production Order is released, the corresponding goods issues could be posted without requiring an additional manual step.

- **Backflush goods issue postings**: In the interest of efficiency, some companies do not post the issue of certain materials separately. A good example is a repetitive manufacturing process like the manufacturing of automobiles. Suppose a company produces 40 units of a specific model of car during a certain time period. When order confirmations are entered for these, they clearly know that 160 tires of a certain kind must have been used. Thus, they can post goods issue for that quantity automatically. This saves time and effort. This form of automation is more common with repetitive and process manufacturing.
- **Material usage**: In the Procurement chapter, we noted that when materials are purchased for stock, the cost of such materials is not immediately reflected as expenses. These materials simply go into the raw materials stock and affect only balance sheet accounts. During manufacturing execution, when raw materials are issued against a released production order, these materials are finally accounted for as expenses. The production order is responsible for the cost of the materials it uses. This is necessary for accurate product costing. This is why order-related cost object controlling is so important.
- **Order confirmation options**: We had earlier mentioned that confirmation of a production order occurs when the order completes. There are alternatives. SAP allows for many more options for finer tracking if needed. For a production order, we can enable tracking at the level of each operation. Which means that confirmations can be entered as soon as an operation is complete. In fact, confirmation is even possible at specific points within an operation.
- **Automating goods receipt inventory postings**: As with automating goods issue inventory postings, SAP also provides the option to automate goods receipt inventory postings for finished goods when an order confirmation is entered.

---

## Review questions: Manufacturing

(You can find answers on page 224. To answer questions that end with an asterisk (*), you will need to have read the official SAP course material.)

1. At which organizational level are costs managed in a production order? (one) *
   A. Client
   B. Controlling area
   C. Company Code
   D. Plant
2. During the manufacturing execution process, which steps include a material availability check?

3. When a production order is created, costs are planned, and the order is scheduled. Which master data is responsible for the scheduling of the order? (two) *

    A. Material

    B. BOM

    C. Routing

    D. Work center

4. When a production order is created, materials are reserved. Which master data is responsible for these reservations? (one)

    A. Material

    B. BOM

    C. Routing

    D. Work center

5. A production order can be confirmed before the release of the order. (T/F)

6. What procurement type would you suggest in the material master for finished goods?

7. What are task lists and what are the different types of task lists in SAP? *

8. What are PRTs and what type of data are they?

9. What field in a work center master record links the work center with a CO object? *

10. Which of the following represent categories of data stored in the work center master record? (three) *

    A. Actual cost determination

    B. Scheduling

    C. Costing

    D. Capacity planning

11. What combination in the work center master record is used to define activity prices?

12. Operations in the routing include time elements. What is an example of a fixed time assigned to an operation? *

13. Operations in the routing include time elements. What is an example of a variable time assigned to an operation? *

14. BOM components not assigned to an operation in a routing default to which operation? *

15. In addition to BOM components, name other master data that can be assigned to an operation. *

16. Master data in manufacturing support various logistics steps. Which master data in manufacturing also integrates directly with SAP HCM?

17. Which of the following steps in the manufacturing process can be automated? (two)

A. Order creation
B. Order release
C. Material staging
D. Material withdrawal posting
E. Order archiving

18. Which of the following can be directly assigned to operations on a production order? (three)
    A. Materials
    B. Cost center
    C. PRT
    D. Trigger points
    E. Profit center
19. Which step in the manufacturing execution process will result in the initial financial impact?
20. At which step in the manufacturing execution process will labor costs post to the production order?
21. In what status must the production be before a goods issue can be posted for the order?
22. In which steps of the manufacturing execution process do availability checks occur?
23. What are the inventory impacts of posting a goods issue to a production order?
24. Which of the following accounts are impacted when a goods issue occurs against a production order? (two)
    A. Stock/inventory
    B. Product
    C. Overhead
    D. Consumption expense
25. The production order is updated when goods are issued against a released production order. T/F?
26. When goods are issued to a production order, does the SAP system create a Controlling document?
27. What two options exist for confirming production?
28. Can goods movements be automated during the manufacturing process?
29. Explain the process of backflush and the automated goods issue posting during backflush.
30. Materials from a production order are received into a storage location/plant combination assigned to a warehouse number. What automation occurs in warehouse management because of this goods receipt?
31. Which accounts are updated when goods are received against a production order?

32. When a production order is settled, what mechanism determines the receiver(s) of the settlement?
33. In the manufacturing process, which step follows the goods receipt? (one)
    A. Release
    B. Confirmation
    C. Variance Calculation
    D. Settlement

E.

# Sales order processing (SD)

*THIS CHAPTER INTRODUCES* the Sales Order Processing (also referred to as the Order to Cash) business process as relevant for the SAP TS410 certification examination. This business process encompasses all the steps starting from pre-sales activities all the way to the generation of a billing document which results in the customer being invoiced. Processing the customer's payment occurs in the financial accounting (FI) module. Although this is probably easy to understand because of our general familiarity with the process, it would still be a good idea for you to read this chapter before proceeding to the SAP certification course materials. The Order to Cash business process covers all the steps and interactions involved in pre-sales activities up to and including invoicing the customer. The process comprises the following main steps:

- Pre-sales
- Sales Order
- Outbound Delivery
- Post Goods Issue
- Billing the Customer
- Payment processing

## Pre-sales activities

Although a Sales Order represents the formal document that triggers the subsequent steps in the sales process, the selling process does not have to begin with a Sales Order, although it can. In its simplest form, pre-sales could involve a prospective or existing customer making an inquiry. For example, a customer might inquire about specific products' availability, possible delivery dates and prices. The company might respond to the customer with details and a Sales Inquiry results. A customer could then decide to proceed with placing an order -- a formal Sales Order.

A Sales Inquiry is one kind of pre-sales activity. SAP supports other pre-sales activities as well, like a company bidding on a customer's Request for Proposal (RFP) or having standard agreements (like contracts) with customers for providing materials under agreed upon terms and conditions. We will look at these later.

## Sales Order

A Sales Order represents a formal, legally binding document. It is a document containing items the customer has ordered from our company. SAP provides means by which pre-sales documents – like Sales Inquiries can be directly converted into Sales Orders – avoiding the need to re-enter much of the same information again. Figure 49 shows an example of a sales order.

**ABC Inc** **Sales order no: 2013-ZZ-98734**

Date: March 3, 2013 Sold to: Top Woodworks

| No | Material | Description | Qty | Unit price | Total |
|---|---|---|---|---|---|
| 1 | AZ23412 | Banded saw-brush | 2 | $10.93 | $21.86 |
| | | 1 unit to be delivered on March 30, 2013 | | | |
| | | 1 unit to be delivered on April 15, 2013 | | | |
| 2 | BQ98645 | Leopard miller | 30 | $45.00 | $1350.00 |
| | | 20 units to be delivered on April 20, 2013 | | | |
| | | 2 units to be delivered on May 1, 2013 | | | |
| | | 8 units to be delivered on May 5, 2013 | | | |
| 3 | AM32345 | Psychedelic saw | 10 | $32.90 | $329.00 |
| | | 10 units to be delivered on March 30, 2013 | | | |

*Figure 49: A Sales Order*

While creating a Sales Inquiry or Sales Order, SAP makes available complete support for determining the applicable price for each material ordered. SAP uses the term "condition" when dealing with price determination and you will soon see why.

Seemingly simple, determining the price applicable for a product on a sales order can be very complex. For instance, we could have specific prices for a customer for a particular material – like customer X gets product Y at $5 per unit, whereas customer Y pays $5.25 per unit. Rather than stating a specific dollar amount, the above two conditions could specify discounts (percentages or dollar values). Alternately, we could be offering a promotion on a particular product during specific dates. The promotion could again be a specific dollar price or a dollar or percentage discount. Numerous other possibilities exist. A price could be based on the geographic region where a sale occurs or could be based on total dollar value of sales order and so on. Price often represents a very important tool used by companies and hence calls for utmost flexibility. Broadly speaking, the price applicable on a sales order for a particular product is determined by various conditions as illustrated above. This is why SAP uses the term condition when referring to prices, discounts, and surcharges. While creating a sales order or sales inquiry, SAP also makes available features to determine the delivery dates for items on a sales order. Delivery dates can be determined not just based on available stocks, but also based on production orders – for finished goods, on purchase orders – for trading goods, or based on customer needs. (Recall that finished goods are products that a company makes and sells whereas trading goods are goods that a company just buys and sells.)

## Structure of a sales order

A sales order has an order header, a set of sales order items and, for each sales order item, possibly one or more schedule lines. Figure 50 shows a sales order with its individual components highlighted.

Figure 50 shows the following:

- **Sales Order Header**: A sales order contains one order header with information that is common to the entire order (information like order number, customer number, and order date).
- **Sales Order Items**: A sales order can have several sales order items – but must have at least one.
- **Schedule Lines**: Each order item can have one or more schedule lines to indicate the delivery dates for various quantities of the material ordered on the order item. It is possible for all the units ordered on an item to be required on the same date (single schedule line), or for the total quantity to be broken up across several delivery dates (multiple schedule lines).

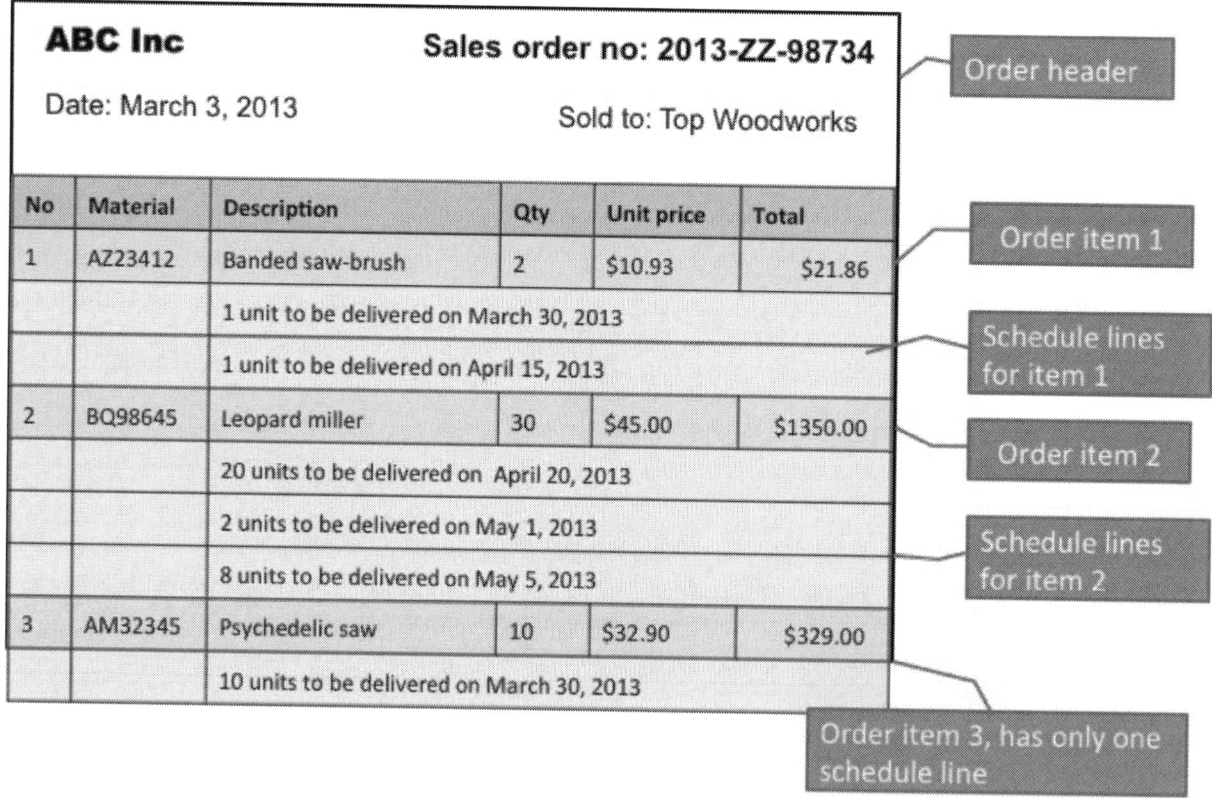

**ABC Inc** — **Sales order no: 2013-ZZ-98734**

Date: March 3, 2013 — Sold to: Top Woodworks

| No | Material | Description | Qty | Unit price | Total |
|---|---|---|---|---|---|
| 1 | AZ23412 | Banded saw-brush | 2 | $10.93 | $21.86 |
| | | 1 unit to be delivered on March 30, 2013 | | | |
| | | 1 unit to be delivered on April 15, 2013 | | | |
| 2 | BQ98645 | Leopard miller | 30 | $45.00 | $1350.00 |
| | | 20 units to be delivered on April 20, 2013 | | | |
| | | 2 units to be delivered on May 1, 2013 | | | |
| | | 8 units to be delivered on May 5, 2013 | | | |
| 3 | AM32345 | Psychedelic saw | 10 | $32.90 | $329.00 |
| | | 10 units to be delivered on March 30, 2013 | | | |



Figure 50: Structure of a sales order

While creating a sales order, it's important to consider the risks involved in allowing credit sales -- that is, providing a customer with goods up front and then invoicing the customer for payment as opposed to requiring payment up front from the customer before shipping the goods. This risk is managed as part of Financial Supply Chain Management in SAP S/4 HANA. This risk must be managed to ensure continued cash flow for the company. Because of this, the system needs to offer the capability to ensure customers do not exceed their credit limits. SAP will track this and automatically block a sales order if the order will cause the customer's credit limit to be exceeded. As noted, SAP provides this functionality as part of its Financial Supply Chain Management (FSCM) component. SAP can track credit utilization and limits for each customer.

## Outbound Delivery

SAP uses the term Outbound Delivery in a way that might not be immediately clear, but you will do well to understand precisely what the term represents. The term Outbound Delivery sounds like it refers to an activity. However, in SAP, the term actually represents a document that signals the start of the shipping process for items in a sales order. The schedule lines in the line items of the sales order determine the number of outbound delivery documents required. If you refer again to the sales order example shown in Figure 50, you'll see that several outbound delivery documents would be required.

As demonstrated in Figure 50, the first schedule line for the first item (Banded saw-brush) and the schedule line for the last item (Psychedelic saw) have the same delivery date. Therefore, a single outbound delivery document can be created for both schedule lines and they can be shipped together. The remaining schedule lines will require separate outbound delivery documents because they all have different delivery dates.

Thus, the Outbound Delivery step is managed with the outbound delivery document. By creating this document, the shipping process is initiated. We highlight this point because SAP course materials generally assume that readers understand this. Much confusion arises from a misunderstanding that the term "outbound delivery document" refers to a process.

## Post Goods Issue

Once the Outbound Delivery document has initiated the shipment process, this enables warehouse operations to be carried out. The required materials can be physically removed from the warehouse and readied for shipment. Removing items from the warehouse represents a purely physical operation. Though the materials might have moved physically, they are still in the company's possession and comprise part of the current assets of the company. This physical movement in the warehouse is referred to as picking. (See the Inventory and Warehouse Management chapter for reference).

The Post Goods Issue step formally removes the materials from stock and they are no longer part of the current assets of the company. At the end of this step, the quantity on hand of the material goes down, current assets decrease, and the goods are technically in transit to the customer from that point on. This is the first step in the order to cash process that has an impact on financial accounting.

As a matter of fact, have you noticed that in the Procure to Pay and in the Manufacturing Execution processes, the first financial accounting impact occurred with the first goods movement? In the Order to Cash and Manufacturing execution processes, the first goods movement is a goods issue, resulting in a reduction of stock. In the case of the Procure to Pay process, we performed a goods receipt, resulting in an increase in stock.

While we might think that the customer owes us money at this point, that is incorrect – the customer will owe us money only after we have invoiced the customer.

## Billing the customer

Once we have posted the goods issue, we can create a Billing Document which is a company-internal document signifying the fact that the goods have been shipped and have become the customer's property. At this point, the customer owes us money for the goods that we shipped. The billing document results in the creation of the customer invoice, which is an external document to be sent to the customer. This step also results in the realization of revenue in financial accounting as well as a receivable from the customer.

The conditions and terms in the customer invoice dictate when the customer payment is due, and the monetary value owed. The terms, Billing Document, and Invoice are sometimes used interchangeably, but the former is an internal document and the latter is sent to the customer.

## Post Customer Payment

This step is carried out in financial accounting. Once the customer receives our invoice, the customer will most likely send us a payment. Accounting receives the payment and applies it to the customer's account, reducing the receivable by the amount received.

## Organization Levels

Figure 51 shows some of the organization levels that Sales and Distribution (SD) shares with several other logistics modules.

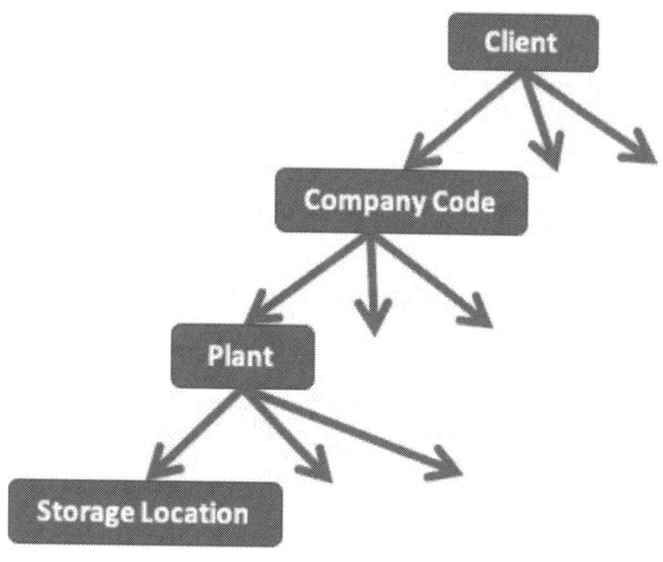


*Figure 51: Organization levels in Sales Order Processing (SD)*

Along with the logistics organizational levels shown in Figure 51, SD has its own dedicated organization levels as well.

- **Sales Organization**: A company code could have many Sales Organizations. Each Sales Organization can belong to exactly one company code. A Sales Organization is responsible for the distribution of goods and services, negotiating the terms and conditions of sale and for issues arising out of the sale of a product – like product liability. All SD documents are created in a Sales Organization and it is also the highest summarization level for sales reports.
- **Distribution channel**: This represents the means to reach customers. Examples would be retail, wholesale and Internet.

- **Division**: A division usually represents a product line.

It is possible to combine Sales Organization, Distribution Channel and Division in many ways; each such unique combination that is defined is called a Sales Area.

## Material Master Data

Clearly, material master data support the sales process. We saw from our presentation of the material master record in the procurement process, that material master records are maintained in views. the Basic Data view is at the Client level. Most other views are maintained at the Plant level for whichever plants use a material. To support the sales process, Sales views must also be maintained. The Sales views are also maintained at the Plant level and also at the Sales Organization and Distribution Channel levels. Figure 52 diagrammatically depicts the above information.

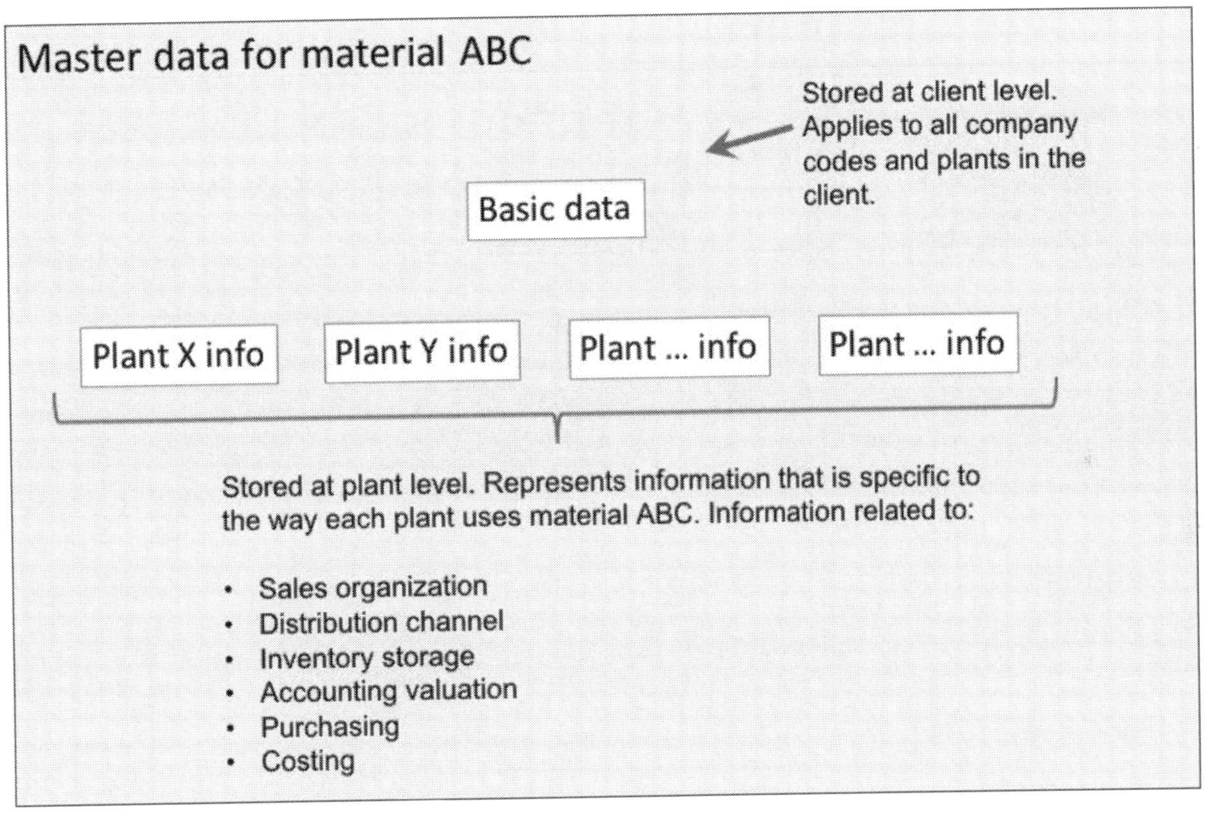


*Figure 52: Material master showing information maintained at the plant level as well as information maintained at levels dedicated to sales order processing (SD)*

## Customer master data

Customers are another important piece of master data that supports the sales process. Like materials, customer master data is also maintained at various organizational levels. Recall from the SAP S/4HANA Introduction chapter, that customers are maintained as Business Partners in SAP S/4HANA. To support the procurement process, a Business Partner with the functioning characteristics of a customer must be maintained. Figure 53 reproduces the image we used when we first introduced Business Partners.

Figure 53 shows the various roles (at organizational levels) that must be maintained for the Business Partner for sales. Like the material master, there is some general data that is maintained at the Client level to ensure this business partner exists only once in the database. However, for the purposes of sales, the customer serves as a debitor (meaning we will ultimately realize a receivable as an asset in Financial Accounting from the customer when we invoice them for sales). For this reason, we must maintain Financial Accounting (FI) information for this customer at the Company Code level. (Note: Each Company Code will need to have its own unique data for each customer.)

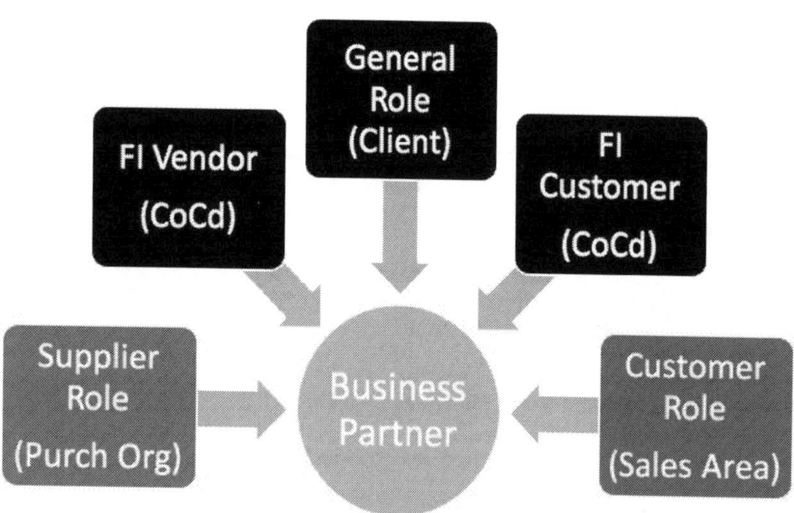


*Figure 53: Business partners*

In addition to the FI information, terms and conditions required for sales are negotiated with each customer in the Customer Role. Recall from the discussion above regarding organizational levels that information on terms and conditions is stored at the Sales Organizational level.

## Other master data

The SD module requires additional master data to support the sales process. These other master data are addressed in the TS410 certification materials. Those will be addressed in your certification class.

## Other Salient Points

- **Availability Check**: While creating a sales order, delivery dates have to be specified. To promise delivery dates, SAP ensures that materials are available. The screen for sales orders has features to perform a material availability check before assigning delivery dates. While performing the availability check, the system can consider not only stocks on hand, but also anticipated stocks based on production and procurement schedules. In this sense, this is a dynamic availability check.

- **Forward and Backward calculations**: If the customer has specified required delivery dates for an item, SAP first calculates backward from the customer's dates and applies the various lead times (manufacturing lead time, shipping lead time, etc.,) to determine if the customer's delivery requirement can be met. If so, it assigns the date. If the date cannot be met, the system calculates forward from the current date and determines the earliest possible shipping date.
- **Relationships between sales order items, schedule lines, outbound deliveries, billing documents and payments**: From the foregoing, it is clear that a single sales order could have several sales order items. In addition, a single sales order item can contain more than one schedule line. Thus, each sales order item can have more than one outbound delivery. For example, if a sales order item is for 10 units, we can break it into multiple shipments, thus requiring multiple outbound deliveries. Under certain conditions, it is also possible to combine more than one sales order into a single outbound delivery. Can you guess what might be required that would allow for this? We might choose to create a single billing document for an outbound delivery or create multiple billing documents. One customer payment might cover a single billing document or cover several of these. Similarly, a single billing document might be cleared by multiple customer payments as well. All of these represent practical situations and SAP supports these common scenarios.

## Review questions: Sales order processing

(You can find answers on page 228. To answer questions that end with an asterisk (*), you should have read the official SAP course material.)

1. Which of the following define a sales area? (three)
    A. Division
    B. Sales organization
    C. Sales Group
    D. Distribution channel
    E. Plant
2. Which of the following organization levels are unique to Sales and Distribution? (two)
    A. Shipping point

B. Sales Order

C. Sales organization

D. Sales location

E. Product Group

3. How many sales organizations can be assigned to a single company code?

4. To how many company codes can a sales organization be assigned?

5. Which of the following are examples of distribution channels? (two)

A. Internet sales

B. Wholesale sales

C. Distribution center

D. Shipping point

E. Loading dock

6. What does the Division represent in Sales and Distribution?

7. Which of the following statements about sales areas are true? (two)

A. One division can be part of only one sales area

B. A single sales organization could exist in several different sales areas

C. A division can be used in defining several different sales areas

D. The same combination of sales organization, distribution channel and division can occur in multiple sales areas

8. How many sales areas can a plant be associated with?

9. Are sales areas automatically defined based on combinations of existing sales organizations, distribution channels and divisions?

10. What is the role of the plant in SD?

11. How would you describe the relationship between plants and shipping points?

12. Which component in SAP S/4 HANA determines a customer's creditworthiness when a sales order is created? (one)

A. Quality Management

B. Management Accounting

C. Financial Accounting

D. Financial Supply Chain Management

13. Which steps in the sales order process directly impacts a customer's available credit? (two)

A. Order creation

B. Goods Issue

C. Billing

D. Payment

14. Which step in the standard sales order process represents the first financial accounting impact? (one)

    A. Creation of the sales order

    B. Creation of the outbound delivery

    C. Goods Issue

    D. Billing

15. Which of the following represent master data relevant to a sales order? (three) *

    A. Plant master

    B. Customer master

    C. Output master

    D. Condition master

    E. Price master

16. Which of the following represent mandatory partner functions in the customer master record? (two) *

    A. Sold to party

    B. Contact persons

    C. Ship to party

    D. Billing party

    E. Forwarding agent

17. Which role of the customer master record contains the partner functions?

18. Which role of the customer master record contains the G/L reconciliation account for receivables?

19. What master data determines how documents are communicated or sent to various parties? *

20. Which of the following are examples of condition master data? (four)

    A. Material Price

    B. Customer/Material Price

    C. Discount

    D. Payment terms

    E. Surcharges

21. Which of the following represents the sequence of steps in the standard sales order process? (one)

    A. Sales order> Inquiry> Billing> Payment

    B. Inquiry> Sales order>Delivery> Billing> Payment

    C. Inquiry> Sales order> Billing> Delivery>Payment

    D. Sales order> Delivery> Payment> Inquiry

22. A sales order can be created by referencing which documents? (two) *

    A. Sales Inquiry

    B. Purchase order

    C. Quotation

    D. RFQ

23. The structure of a sales order document includes which of the following? (three)

    A. Header

    B. Billing

    C. Line items

    D. Schedule lines

24. Which of the following is required to create a sales order? (three) *

    A. Sales group

    B. Sales area

    C. Customer

    D. Required delivery date

    E. Customer material number

25. Which of the following represent flexibility in terms of how sales orders are created? (two) *

    A. A purchase order can be the reference document for a sales order

    B. Can be created independently of any other sales document

    C. Multiple pre-sales documents can be combined into one sales order

    D. Can be based on prior scheduling agreements

26. Which partner functions appear in the header of a sales order? (two)

    A. Sold-to party

    B. Payer

    C. Ship-to party

    D. Bill-to party

27. Which of the following scenarios would require separate schedule lines for a single line item on a sales order? (one)

A. Customer orders 500 units of a material and wants them to be delivered in two separate shipments

B. Customer orders two different materials in the order and specifies a different delivery date for each material

C. Customer places two separate sales orders with separate delivery dates, and one item on each order.

D. The customer wants all the pieces of the materials on each order to be delivered on the date specified in the respective orders.

28. While placing a sales order, the system determined that the requested date for a material could not be met. What kind of scheduling is used to make this determination?

29. In the above scenario, what kind of scheduling might the system use to propose a new delivery date?

30. The _____________ ____ can be used to find out required fields are missing when creating a sales order. *

31. Sales orders are considered _________ _________ requirements in MRP. *

32. Under what conditions can multiple sales orders be combined into a single delivery document? (three)

   A. The delivery dates are the same

   B. Sold-to party is the same

   C. Ship-to party is the same

   D. Plant is the same

   E. Shipping point is the same

33. Which of the following documents contain schedule lines? (one)

   A. Billing documents

   B. Invoices

   C. Sales orders

   D. Outbound deliveries

   E. Inbound deliveries

34. Picking lists are used to support which logistics process? (one)

   A. Warehouse management

   B. Shipping

   C. Billing

   D. Order processing

35. Under what conditions would a transfer requirement be created for an outbound delivery? *

36. You are in the process shipping an item against a sales order. You have created an outbound delivery and look at the stock/requirements list. In a different session, you proceed to a post goods issue for the outbound delivery. When you go back and refresh the stock/requirements list, what changes will occur? *

37. Which G/L accounts are affected when a goods issue is posted against for an outbound delivery?

38. Which accounts are affected when a billing document is generated for a delivery?

39. Which feature displays all the related documents generated during the sales order process and allows the user to navigate to anyone of these documents? *

40. Which of the following modules has direct integration with Sales and Distribution? (three)

    A. Materials management

    B. Warehouse management

    C. Manufacturing execution

    D. Material planning

# Inventory and Warehouse Management

*THIS CHAPTER INTRODUCES* Inventory and Warehouse Management concepts as relevant for the SAP TS410 certification examination. Inventory Management deals with keeping track of stock quantities of materials. Warehouse Management is responsible for physically putting away materials into storage and retrieving them from storage. Another term often used to describe the functionality of warehouse management is Logistics Execution. As with the other chapters, you will benefit from reading this document before proceeding to SAP's certification course materials.

Any ERP system must enable a company to keep track of its materials. How much do we have on hand of each material? More specifically, we need this information for each storage location and not just the aggregate figure. Knowing quantities alone does not suffice – we also need to know their values as well. It is also essential for a company to have a mechanism in place to keep track of movements of stock.

In addition to keeping track of quantities of materials, organizations also need to efficiently handle the physical logistics of moving materials into and out of storage as well as keep them in physical locations in such a way as to promote efficiency. In this module we look at the following topics:

- **Types of goods movements**: SAP defines several types of goods movements, not all of them involving physical movement of goods. The obvious types of movements involve good receipts, putting materials into stock and goods issues, taking materials out of stock for some use. (see Figure 54) Good receipts mostly (but not always) occur when the company receives shipments from vendors and when the manufacturing process produced finished goods that will be taken into stock. Goods issues often occur when raw materials and semi-finished goods are issued for manufacturing against released production orders. They also occur when finished goods are to be shipped out to a customer to fulfill a Sales Order. Remember that the words “receipt”, and “issue” are written from the perspective of inventory. So, when we say goods receipt we are talking about inventory receiving goods and when we talk about goods issues we are referring to goods being issued from inventory. Apart from the above two obvious types of goods movements, we have transfer postings, which are technically considered goods movements, but do not involve any physical movement of material. We will look at goods movements in greater detail soon.

- **Options for goods movements**: An ERP system must be able to carefully track goods movements. Goods are often moved from one storage location to another. When this happens, a good issue occurs at the sending storage location and a goods receipt occurs at the receiving storage location. Under some conditions, for efficiency, SAP allows, (but does not force), these two postings to be performed in a single step. Goods movements can occur between two storage locations of a single plant, or between storage locations belonging to different plants or even across company codes.
- **Stock Transport Order:** When moving goods across different plants, SAP provides two options. The first is to use goods issues and receipts. the second approach is to use a Stock Transport Order, which is a form of an internal purchase order. Recall that a normal purchase order is something that a company sends to its suppliers and those suppliers deliver goods based on the purchase order. In the case of a Stock Transport Order, the supplier is not a vendor, but another plant within the enterprise. Thus, it is the same as a purchase order, except that it is an internal document and does not get fulfilled by a vendor. Instead the materials are sourced from a plant within the enterprise. We will soon see the conditions under which a stock transport order makes sense.
- **Warehouse management:** We can easily get confused between the two terms: Inventory Management and Warehouse Management. The former deals simply with keeping track of stock quantities. Thus, Inventory Management keeps track of how much of each material is in a storage. Inventory management also periodically reconciles book inventory and actual physical stocks. Inventory management has nothing to do with the physical processes of putting away material into storage areas and removing them from storage areas. Warehouse Management deals with the physical logistics involved in efficiently retrieving materials from

and putting away into warehouses. Again, the physical logistics mentioned here are often referred to as Logistics Execution in SAP. Warehouse Management also keeps track of precisely where a material is within the warehouse – which shelf, in which aisle and in which area (see Figure 55).

- **Physical inventory procedure**: Periodically companies have to match their book inventory with actual physical inventory because differences could arise due to material shrinkage (evaporation, for example) or from pilferage or theft. Physical inventory is important to ensure accurate financial information as well as accurate inventory quantities for MRP calculations.

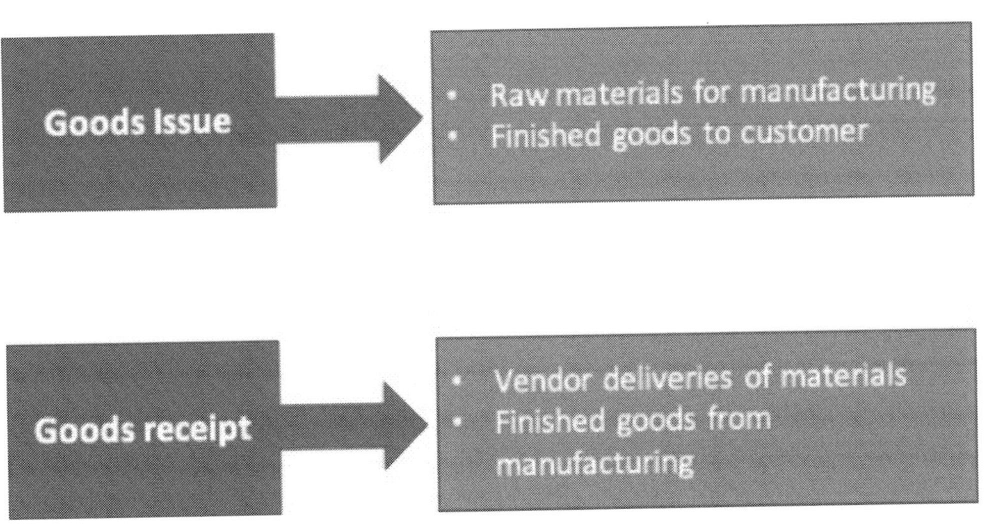


*Figure 54: Goods issue and goods receipt*

## Types of goods movements

As we have already mentioned, goods issues and goods receipts comprise the two obvious types of goods movements involving the addition of material into stock and issuing of material from stock. We already know that SAP creates a document to record the occurrence of any business event. The document creation also applies to goods movements. SAP generates material documents to document all goods movements. For example, if 500 units of a material is issued for manufacturing, SAP creates a material document recording the details of this goods issue. In SAP, physical goods movements between storage locations are considered as stock transfers. Figure 56 shows the different types of stock transfer.

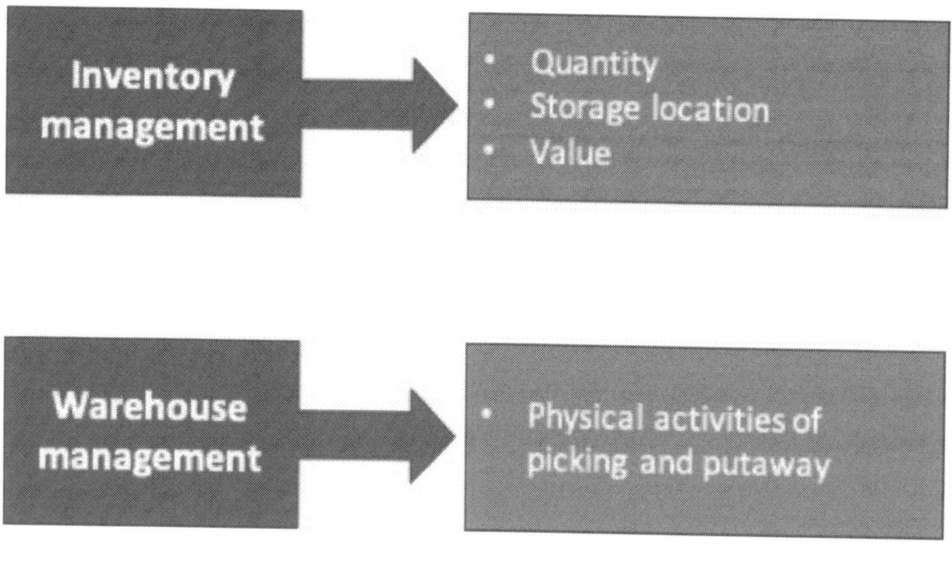


*Figure 55: Inventory management vs. warehouse management*

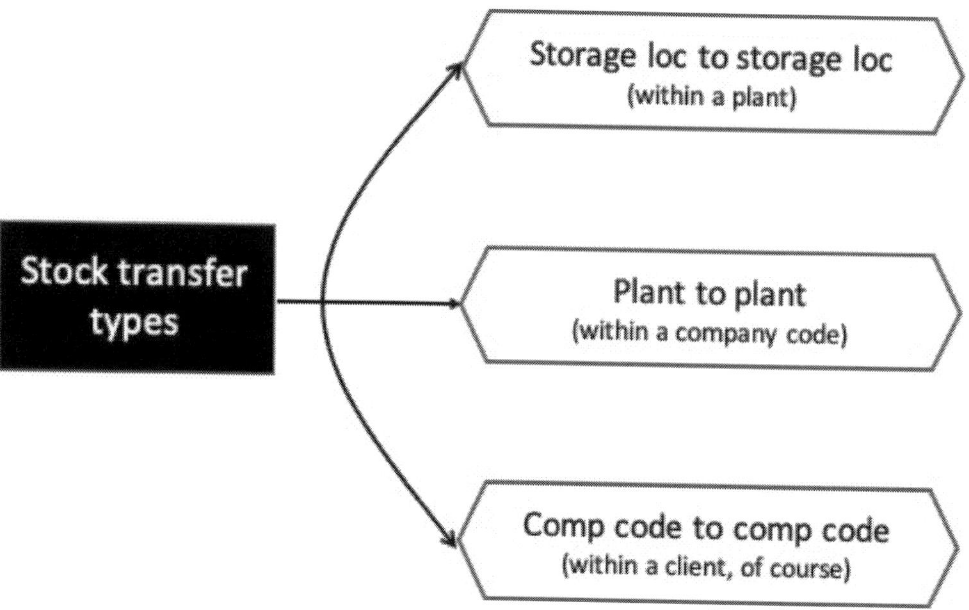


*Figure 56: Types of stock transfer*

SAP also allows for some types of movements which do not represent actual physical movement of goods. The goods remain exactly where they were but acquire a different designation. The most common way in which this occurs is when some material, originally designated as unrestricted use stock is now designated as goods in quality inspection. The goods have not moved physically, but SAP considers this as a goods movement. This is an example of a transfer posting. Keep in mind, even though this may not result in the material being physically moved, a material document will still be generated to track this transaction.

The SAP TS410 course materials will reference other examples of transfer postings. Be sure to check out the following types of transfer postings (see Figure 57):

- stock to stock
- material to material
- consignment to warehouse

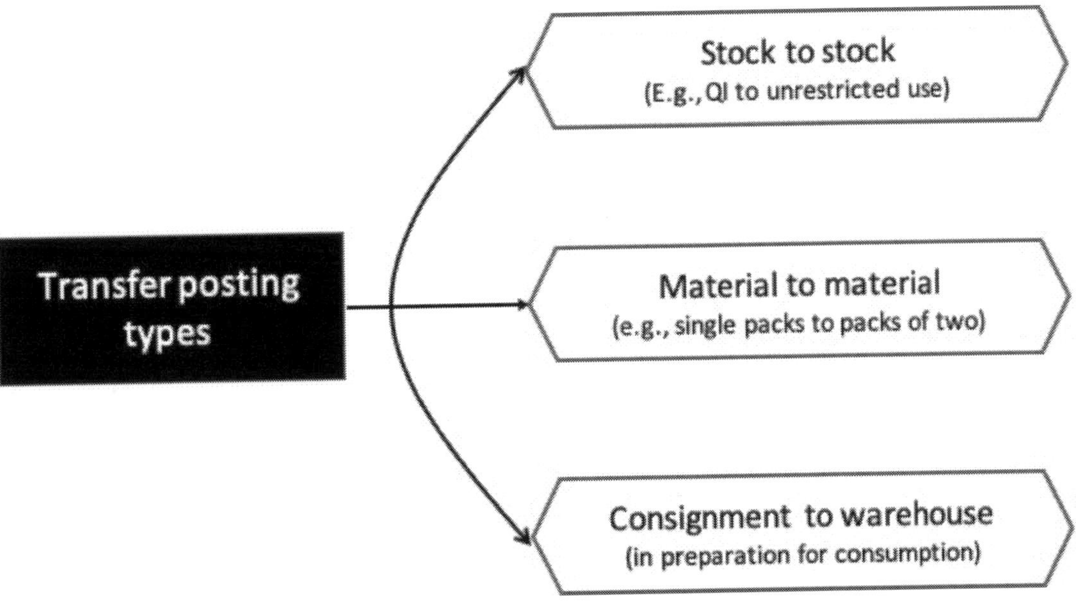


*Figure 57: Types of transfer posting*

## Options for goods movements

As we saw earlier, SAP creates a material document to record any goods movement that occurs. Every physical goods movement need not result in a material document. For efficiency, under some conditions, SAP allows a single material document to document multiple movements. For example, the issue and the subsequent receipt could both be recorded in a single document when these two goods movements occur using a single transaction. The goods issue and goods receipt are thus handled in the single transaction. However, physically, the materials would be taken out of inventory and placed into inventory as two separate tasks. SAP classifies this as a one-step stock transfer. (Hint: Every goods movement transaction results in a material document. If the transfer posting is completed in one transaction, SAP will only generate one material document. If the transfer posting is completed in two separate transactions, SAP will generate separate material documents for each transaction.)

Goods movements often generate an accounting document (there are occasions when this is not the case). For example, receipts of goods from a vendor will generate both a material document to record the goods receipt but will also generate an accounting document. Because this goods receipt resulted in an increase of current assets, financial accounting is impacted which is recorded in an accounting document. Similarly, goods issue for a customer also generate both a material and an accounting document, because quantity of material and its value are both affected.

Using movement types, SAP categorizes the purpose of goods movements. Movement types are represented with three-digit numbers. Each movement type indicates precisely what kind of movement took place. For example, the movement type 311 indicates movement of unrestricted use stock at one storage location to unrestricted use at another storage location. Movement type 101 is used for a goods receipt related from an order, like a purchase order to receive goods into stock. Movement type 103 is used for non-valuated goods receipt, which is one of those special cases when a material document is created but does not result in the creation of an accounting document. (For purposes of certification, it's not likely that you will need to memorize the movement type numbers).

You should be aware of another special form of a goods movement which does not result in the creation of an accounting document. We already know now that when goods move from one location to another, SAP will generate material documents to record these flows so that the location and quantity of the material can be tracked. In most cases, SAP generates an accounting document to track the change in valuation resulting from the goods movement. However, an accounting document would not be needed if the goods movement involves the movement of materials between storage locations within the same plant. Since material valuation is normally maintained at the plant level, no change in valuation results from the physical movement of materials between storage locations within a plant. Thus, no accounting document is generated.

As noted, when materials are valuated at the plant level, a goods movement would not affect the current assets position and thus no accounting document would be necessary. Under certain circumstances, companies value goods differently within the same plant (split valuation). If stocks move from one storage location to another within the same plant, and the company employs different valuation for the material in the different storage locations – split valuation – SAP will generate an accounting document.

In the case of a goods movement between company codes, SAP will generate at least one material document and will always generate two accounting documents to reflect the change in valuation of assets in both company codes. As an example, when a goods issue occurs in the originating company code and a goods receipt occurs in the receiving company code, the current assets of both company codes are affected. Therefore, accounting documents are generated in both company codes.

We've discussed in some length various types of goods movements, including stock transfers. Stock transfers can be executed using more than one method. The certification course discusses one-step and two-step goods movements. As mentioned earlier, in some situations, SAP allows us to make two postings – goods issue and goods receipt – with just a single material transaction for efficiency. This is considered a one-step stock transfer. If the goods issue and goods receipt are posted in separate transactions, then this is referred to as a two-step stock transfer. Be sure to understand these concepts from the SAP TS410 course materials.

## Stock Transport Order

A company can move goods between plants (either within the same company code or across company codes), through the usual process of a goods issue at the sending end, and a goods receipt at the receiving end. However, sometimes when we need to track the transfer more closely, SAP allows the use of a special kind of order called a Stock Transport Order (which is like a company-internal purchase order). From the procurement chapter you will recall that SAP allows us to track purchase orders. At any stage, we can see how much material has been delivered against a PO, how much has been invoiced and how much has been paid. SAP updates these statuses in the PO as the company records goods receipts, invoice receipts, and makes payments. Stock Transport Orders behave almost exactly like standard purchase orders, except Stock Transport Orders are internal documents where the source of the materials is another plant instead of a vendor.

As the receiving plant receives goods against a Stock Transport Order, SAP updates the status of a Stock Transport Order just as it would the status of a purchase order, thus enabling tracking. When the status of a goods movement needs to be tracked closely, Stock Transport Orders turn out to be a good choice. Other advantages also exist and are discussed in the SAP TS410 certification course.

## Warehouse Management

Warehouse management deals with the physical logistics of removing materials from stock (picking) and placing them into stock (putaway). You must pay careful attention to the difference between inventory management and warehouse management. The former is concerned only with tracking the quantity of material stock at various storage locations and with periodic reconciliation of physical inventory with book inventory.

Of course, the two are closely linked and SAP achieves the linkage by allowing us to enable warehouse management for storage locations. Not all storage locations need to be warehouse management-enabled. Some may be and others may not be – based on how a company wants to handle this. Some storage locations might be small and not require any warehouse management at all. For example, a storage location could be just a room for storing a few hundred items and hence not need any warehouse management at all. Other storage locations might be huge facilities with several square kilometers of space and could need extensive warehouse management to function efficiently. We could also have special storage needs like refrigerated/freezer storage which have special requirements, thus a need for warehouse management processes.

We already know that material stocks are tracked at the level of storage location. That is, for each material that is tracked, SAP keeps track of the quantity of the material per storage location. However, as we already know, inventory management is not concerned with the physical handling of materials -- which is the domain of warehouse management. In SAP, storage locations form the link between inventory and warehouse management. It is not necessary that every material for which we perform inventory management must also come under the purview of warehouse management. To take an extreme example, a diamond mine would hardly be using warehouse management to keep track of its diamonds -- the quantities and weights invoked would be too small to present any serious logistic challenges. However, there would be other materials needing warehouse management.

In SAP, we talk about a storage location being used with or without warehouse management. Continuing the diamond example, the storage locations where diamonds are stored would not be under warehouse management.

Each storage locations that is under warehouse management has a Warehouse Number associated with it. One warehouse number could be associated with several storage locations, but each storage location can be associated with at most one warehouse number.

A storage location number in SAP does not uniquely identify a storage location. It is the combination of the plant number and storage location number that is unique. A warehouse number is therefore actually linked to a plant number/storage location number combination. Figure 58 illustrates these ideas.

Figure 58 highlights certain important points:

- **Unique identifiers for storage locations**: Storage location numbers can be duplicated across plants, but the combination of plant number and storage number has to be unique. In other words, a single plant cannot have storage locations with duplicated numbers under it.
- **Relationship between warehouse numbers and storage locations**: Warehouse number 001 is linked to two storage locations from the same plant (Plant 1000). Warehouse number 002 illustrates the point that a single warehouse number can be linked to storage locations from multiple plants (Plants 1000 and 1100). More generally, one warehouse number can be associated with several storage locations, but a single storage location can never be associated with more than one warehouse number.
- **Storage locations not under warehouse management**: Storage locations that are not linked to any warehouse number are not under warehouse management. In Figure 58, storage location 40 in plant 1100 and storage location 30 in plant 1200 are not under warehouse management as they are not linked to any warehouse numbers.

- **Triggering warehouse operations**: Goods movements related to storage locations that are under warehouse management (that is, storage location/plant combinations linked to a warehouse number) can generate transfer requests, which trigger warehouse operations. Goods movements related to storage locations that are not under warehouse management do not trigger transfer requests.

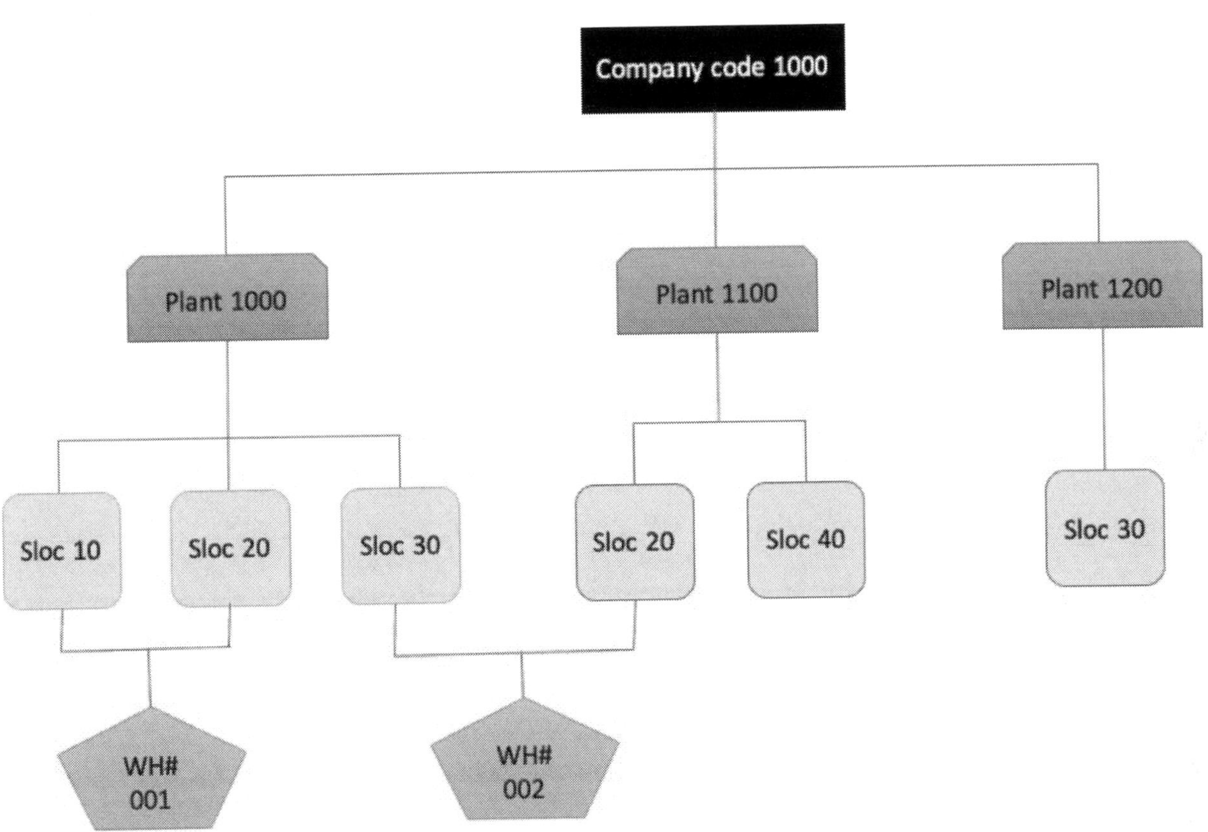


*Figure 58: Linking inventory and warehouse management*

Recall that in SAP, some form of an order controls almost every operation – such as a purchase order, sales order, production order, stock transport order or maintenance order (to be discussed in a later chapter).

A Transfer Order is used to initiates warehouse operations. When a goods issue or goods receipt occurs in a storage location that is under warehouse management, SAP requires a Transfer Order to signal to warehouse management that it has some work to do.

With huge warehouses, retrieving materials from and putting materials into the warehouse should not be done haphazardly. Working haphazardly would be very inefficient and costly. Instead, warehouse management systems are designed to perform these operations as efficiently as possible using mathematical techniques. However, to plan warehouse operations, warehouses need advance information about the expected material movements. Outbound delivery documents and Inbound delivery documents are created in SAP ERP and are used to manage goods movements as well as to help manage the warehouse management (WM) planning process. We have already seen Outbound delivery documents in the Order to Cash business process. After a Sales Order is saved, we initiate the shipment process by first creating an Outbound delivery document for each shipment in the sales order. If the materials in an outbound delivery are in a storage location that is under warehouse management, then this would initiate the warehouse management picking of the item from the shelves.

Similarly, Inbound delivery documents occur when a planned goods receipt is set to occur. Although the certification course does not specifically cover Inbound delivery documents, they can be used to initiate planned goods receipts. For example, suppose we are moving goods from one plant to another, we could then create an outbound delivery to initiate the process from the issuing location and could also create an inbound delivery document to signal an impending goods receipt at the receiving location which then enables warehouse management to plan for the putaway.

Often Purchase orders are handled without a delivery document. Thus, warehouse management operations might be required for material movements that occur without any associated delivery documents. (Later in the Extended Warehouse Management discussion we explain conditions when delivery documents are required).

When a goods issue or receipt occurs, we need to perform inventory management operations – updating the quantity of materials – as well as warehouse management operations – picking or put away. In what order should these operations be performed?

Figure 59 illustrates the sequencing for SAP Warehouse Management (WM). When a goods movement is performed against a delivery document (inbound or outbound), warehouse operations are performed first; otherwise inventory management operations are performed first. In Figure 59, ovals represent warehouse operations and rectangles represent inventory management operations.

In cases where the Goods Receipt or Goods Issue occurs first, SAP automatically creates a Transfer Requirement. The Transfer Order for the warehouse workers is then created with reference to this Transfer Requirement.

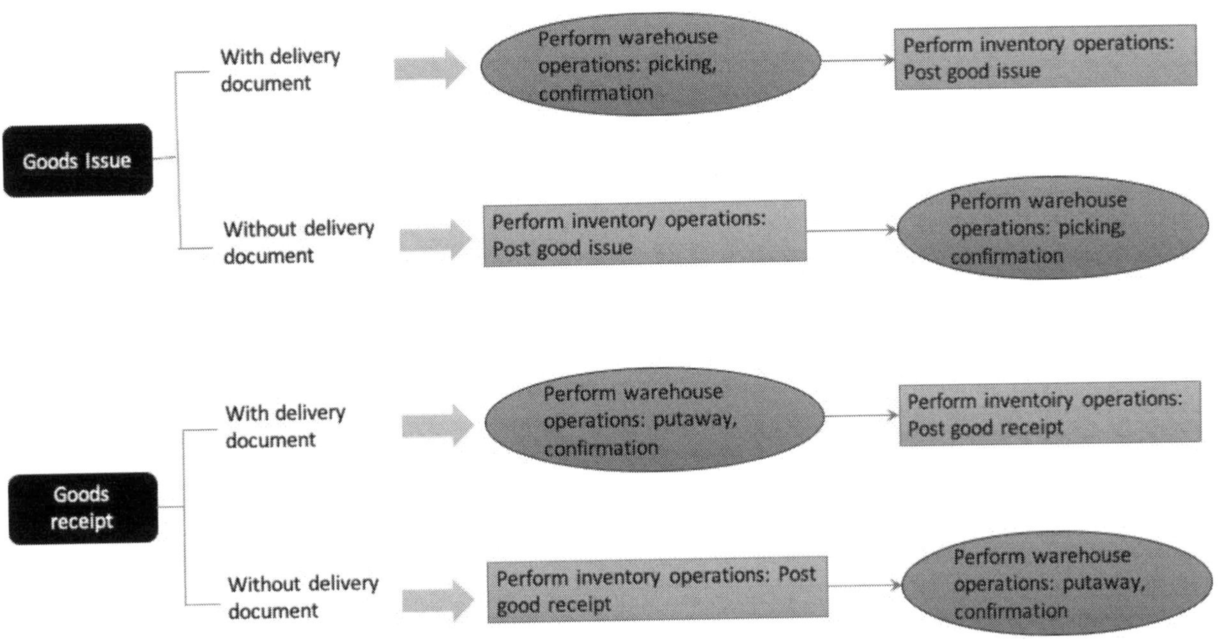


*Figure 59: Determining whether inventory or warehouse operations occur first*

# Extended Warehouse Management (EWM)

Extended Warehouse Management (EWM) is designed to manage more complex warehouse management and supply chain scenarios. In short, EWM has all of the capabilities of WM, but includes additional functionality, providing more transparency into a company's warehouse management activities. Your SAP course materials provide more detail on EWM, but for now we list some of the additional features of EWM below:

- Yard management
- Cross-docking
- Labor management
- Wave management
- Slotting

SAP EWM is not new in SAP S/4HANA. The option to use SAP EWM has been available for some time, but it was run as a separate application from SAP ERP and SAP WM. It's important to note that SAP EWM was not intended to replace WM. It was designed to provide capabilities not inherent in SAP WM. Figure 60 shows the connections between standard warehouse management (WM) and Extended Warehouse Management (EWM).

Like SAP WM, SAP EWM utilizes a Warehouse Number to manage the warehouse activities. Whereas SAP WM uses three-digit warehouse numbers, SAP EWM uses four-digit warehouse numbers.

From a technical standpoint, SAP WM and SAP EWM are very complex systems which must be very responsive to changing demands. Thus, these systems are very computer resource intensive. Historically, SAP has recommended these systems run on a separate server from the ERP system. This is referred to as decentralized warehouse management. This means the WM system is physically separated from the ERP system.

SAP also allowed for the WM system to run on the same machine as the ERP system. This design is referred to as centralized warehouse management.

Though it is possible for SAP WM to run as a centralized warehouse management system, prior to SAP S/4HANA, SAP EWM was always managed as a decentralized warehouse management system for performance reasons. A very important detail concerning a decentralized warehouse management system is the requirement of outbound and inbound delivery documents. A decentralized warehouse management system MUST use outbound and inbound delivery documents to manage the processes. In SAP S/4HANA, SAP EWM can be embedded and can be run on the same server as S/4HANA. This means S/4HANA offers the option of running EWM in a centralized environment without a performance penalty. Whether or not EWM is run centralized or decentralized often depends on the demands on the enterprise warehouse processes. Regardless of how the customer chooses to deploy EWM, delivery documents are still mandatory!

Your SAP course materials will provide more detail regarding centralized versus decentralized warehouse management systems. You'll also learn about additional technologies that support warehouse management activities.

## Review questions: Inventory and Warehouse Management

(You can find answers on page 234. To answer questions for which an asterisk (*) appears at the end, you should have read the official SAP course materials.)

1. In which of the following scenarios would a goods receipt be required? (two)
    A. Arrival of materials from a purchase order
    B. Materials from inventory are needed for a production order
    C. Finished product for a production order need to be put away in the warehouse
    D. Materials for a sales order need to be shipped to a customer

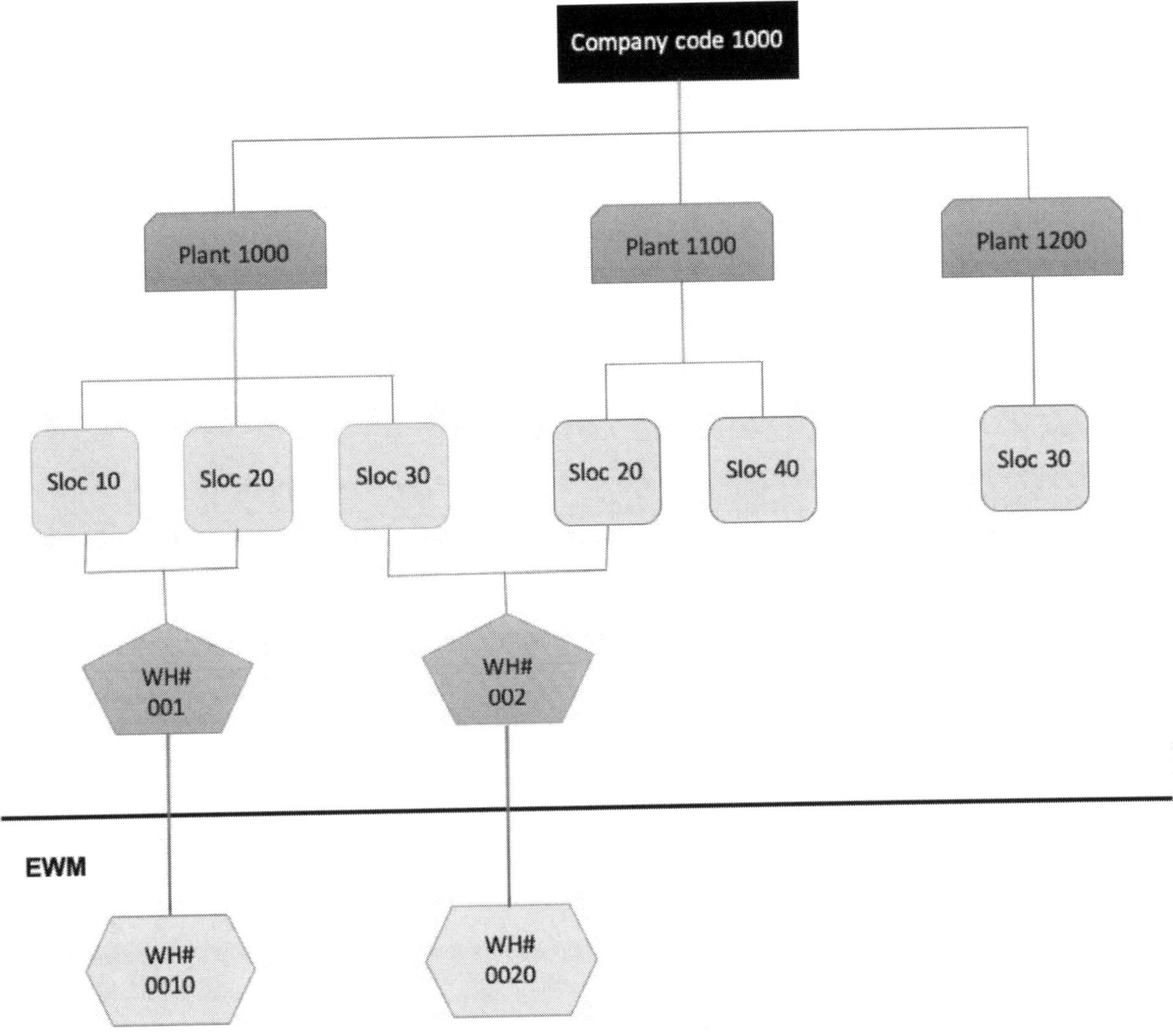


*Figure 60: Relationship between standard warehouse management (WM) and extended warehouse management (EWM)*

2. In which of the following scenarios would a goods issue be required? (two)
    A. Arrival of materials from a purchase order
    B. Materials from inventory are needed for a production order
    C. Finished product for a production order need to be put away in the warehouse
    D. Materials for a sales order need to be shipped to a customer
3. In which of the following scenarios would a transfer posting be required? (two)
    A. The warehouse confirms a transfer order for an inbound delivery
    B. Materials on consignment are now needed
    C. Stock is moved from one plant to another within the same company code
    D. A material in stock type, "Quality Inspection" is now cleared for use
4. Which of the following are true about one and two step stock transfers? (two) *
    A. One step stock transfer result in the creation of two material documents

B. One step transfer result in the creation of one material document with two-line items

C. Two step stock transfer results in the creation of two material documents with two line items on each

D. Two step stock transfer results in the creation of two material documents each with one line item

5. What is an advantage of a two-step stock transfer procedure over a one-step procedure?
6. After the first step of a two-step procedure, at which location can the material be found?
7. If valuation occurs during a two-step procedure, at which step does the valuation take place? *
8. Will an accounting document be generated for a stock transfer?
9. If valuation takes place during a stock transfer, when is the accounting document generated?
10. Under what conditions will an accounting document be created for storage location-to-storage location stock transfer?
11. During a one-step storage location-to-storage location stock transfer, the material can be issued from any stock type and received into any stock type. (T/F)
12. Which of the following scenarios is correct for a storage location-to-storage location stock transfer? (one) *

    A. A material in unrestricted stock from the origin can be moved to stock in QI at the destination

    B. A material in unrestricted stock from the origin can be moved to blocked stock at the destination

    C. A material in unrestricted stock from the origin can be moved to unrestricted stock at the destination

    D. A material in QI stock at the origin can be moved into QI stock at the destination
13. Describe the financial accounting impacts of a company code-to-company code stock transfer.
14. Suppose you are planning to move stock from one plant to another and would like to include additional costs such as freight charges associated with this move. What form of stock transfer would be best? What other benefits does this approach provide over the alternative approaches?
15. When an STO is used for the purposes of a stock transfer, what is the restriction on the issuing plant and where do the materials appear after the posting of the goods issue?
16. How is inventory management integrated with warehouse management?
17. Is a goods issue posting part of inventory management or warehouse management?
18. Is the execution of a transfer order part of inventory management or warehouse management?
19. Which field in a goods movement transaction defines the purpose of the goods movement?
20. With respect to warehouse management which of the following statements is correct? (one)

    A. Multiple plant/storage location combinations can be assigned to a single warehouse number

B. All the storage locations assigned to a warehouse number must have the same storage location number

C. Different storage locations of a given plant cannot be allocated to different warehouse numbers

D. If one storage location of a plant is allocated to a warehouse number, then all storage locations in that plant must be allocated to warehouse numbers, but not necessarily the same one

21. Which document is required to perform logistics execution steps in warehouse management?

22. Which document is required to perform warehouse tasks in extended warehouse management?

23. What is the structure of the warehouse number in warehouse management?

24. Which of the following is not an additional feature of extended warehouse management? (one)

A. Bin management

B. Yard management

C. Cross-docking

D. Wave management

E. Slotting

25. Describe the difference between centralized warehouse management and decentralized warehouse management.

# Enterprise Asset Management

*THIS CHAPTER INTRODUCES* Enterprise Asset Management concepts as relevant for the SAP TS410 certification examination. Enterprise Asset Management – formerly referred to as Plant Maintenance – deals with servicing the physical assets of a company and remains completely internal to a company. These physical assets include plant and machinery used for manufacturing, as well as other assets that may require maintenance.

This topic deals with both preventive maintenance and breakdown maintenance. Preventive maintenance refers to the routine maintenance of an asset (to prevent failure) – similar to when we change motor oil in our cars regularly, even in the absence of a tangible malfunction. A machine does not need to fail or break down for preventive maintenance to occur. Companies perform Breakdown Maintenance – as the name clearly suggests – when a machine fails. This unit covers the SAP business processes involved in breakdown maintenance. As with the other chapters in this book, you might benefit from reading this chapter before proceeding with the SAP TS410 course materials.

Proper care and maintenance of physical assets, commonly referred to as Enterprise Asset Management (EAM), plays an important role in the success of organizations, particularly manufacturing organizations, despite not being directly involved in revenues or profits. A complete ERP system must therefore support the related business processes. SAP provides extensive support to manage the business processes related to this function in the EAM module.

## Organization levels

As with most other modules, EAM has its own organization levels and the process also interacts with other ERP modules. The organization levels are:

- **Maintenance Plant**: The term refers to any plant in which physical assets are installed. Although the term might seem to refer to a plant that performs maintenance work, it does not. You might recall from prior chapters that SAP uses the term Plant rather flexibly to refer to any unit that produces products or services customers. Thus, the regional office of a consulting company would be defined as a plant, even though it might not have any production equipment. A typical manufacturing plant would also be a plant in SAP. To differentiate between these kinds of plants, SAP uses the term Maintenance Plant to refer to plants that house equipment that may require maintenance.
- **Maintenance Planning Plant**: This term refers to the plant responsible for planning for the Enterprise Asset Management process.

SAP allows for various ways of organizing the planning for maintenance tasks:

- **Decentralized**: Each maintenance plant plans its own activities.
- **Centralized**: We have a single maintenance planning plant that plans for every other maintenance plant.
- **Hybrid**: Many maintenance planning plants with each one responsible for planning for a set of maintenance plants. Thus, SAP also allows us to organize the execution of maintenance activities similarly.

## Master Data

In addition to the organizational levels, we again need to address the master data relevant to Enterprise Asset Management. One example of master data needed for Enterprise Asset Management is the Work Center. Just like production, work centers provide the capacity to perform work. In Enterprise Asset Management, work centers are used to perform maintenance activities. The other master data for Enterprise Asset Management are, broadly termed, Technical Objects. We discuss three types of technical objects:

- **Functional Location:** This term refers to a physical place within the plant. It could be as simple as an office or as complex as a physical location where many pieces of equipment are installed.
- **Equipment**: A piece of equipment is something that might require maintenance and is also something that needs to be tracked autonomously. It is a unique item that can be installed in a functional location or exist in inventory. As an example, we may have a lathe machine (equipment) that is installed in a specific place (functional location) within the plant. From time to time, the lathe may require maintenance. The lathe would be managed as a unique

item. To put things in perspective, keep in mind that plants can be huge and could include thousands of pieces of installed equipment. Proper tracking of where the equipment is installed requires that we create functional locations to identify their precise location. This leads to efficiencies in the maintenance process. Functional locations, by themselves, could also require maintenance, such as the painting of walls or replacement of broken lights.

- **Assembly**: To simplify the planning of materials needed to repair equipment or perform maintenance on functional locations, planners utilize Assemblies. Assemblies are the same as bill of materials, except that the purpose of assemblies in this case is not to facilitate manufacturing, but rather to plan parts needed for maintenance. Assemblies are available for functional locations and equipment. In some cases, to simplify master data creation, material BOMs (bill of materials) can be used as assemblies for equipment.

## Serial Numbers

Serial numbers play an important role in EAM. Serial numbers apply to both materials and equipment.

To understand the idea of serial numbers, consider the difference between the following two scenarios:

- **Individual units need not be tracked**: Many of the products that our company makes use a particular kind of specialty bulb and our company keeps this material in stock and uses it for production as needed -- of course, by issuing these materials against production orders. The company has no need to differentiate between individual bulbs for any business purpose; for all purposes, each one is no different from the rest.
- **Individual units need to be tracked**: Our company uses a certain kind of fan in many parts of the manufacturing plant. The company keeps these in stock and issues them as needed. However, these fans are complex pieces of equipment and need regular maintenance (preventive maintenance) as well as repairs when they break down (breakdown maintenance). These fans need preventive maintenance once every 60 days. This means that each individual fan would have its own preventive maintenance schedule and hence the company would need to track the preventive maintenance schedule for each individual fan. Similarly, the company would also need to maintain the repair history for each individual fan. For these reasons, each individual fan has to be specifically identifiable. Unlike the specialty bulbs mentioned above, these fans cannot be treated as if they were indistinguishable. To facilitate this, we associate a serial number with each individual fan.

Looking at things purely from the viewpoint of materials management, SAP allows us to enter a serial number into the material master record for a material. Associating a serial number with a material allows for inventory management of that individual piece of material. That material can then be treated as an autonomous unit not only for inventory management, but also for maintenance purposes, if applicable. This allows for the company to perform maintenance on that material, essentially treating each individual material as a piece of equipment.

In SAP, Equipment can also be assigned a serial number. Since equipment is already a technical object, EAM processes are allowed on equipment whether or not we have assigned a serial number to each equipment. Assigning a serial number to equipment has the benefit of being able to manage equipment on an individual basis. Managing inventory of equipment and materials with a serial number has an additional benefit. In such cases where a serial number is used, the enterprise can track those materials or equipment which have undergone maintenance, those due for maintenance (planned maintenance), those which have never undergone maintenance, and those that are damaged or no longer in use.

## Process

As we have already seen, a common thread runs through many business processes in SAP. Many processes make use of a document that initiates the process and identifies the need for an action (Sales Inquiry in the sales process, Purchase Requisition in the purchasing process, Planned Order in the manufacturing process and Transfer Request in warehouse management). When the action is to be formally started, we have an Order of some kind (Sales Order in the sales process, Purchase Order in the purchasing process, Production Order in the manufacturing process and Transfer Order in warehouse management).

In EAM, a Maintenance Notification initiates the process. It indicates that something needs to be maintained. A notification could identify a specific equipment at a specific functional location, a functional location itself, or be generic – because it might not always be possible to zero in on the location of a problem, or for that matter, to trace it to a specific piece of equipment. A Maintenance Notification also contains a brief textual description of the problem. The notification could then be converted into a Maintenance Order that would be used as a basis for planning its execution and for estimating costs and as a general document for authorizing further steps in the process.

For example, the maintenance operation could require the use of some stock materials – these can be issued against the maintenance order. The task could also involve the procurement of some material or materials (as consumable(s)). Maintenance Order processing also follows the basic steps in Order-

Related Cost Object Controlling (see Figure 61).

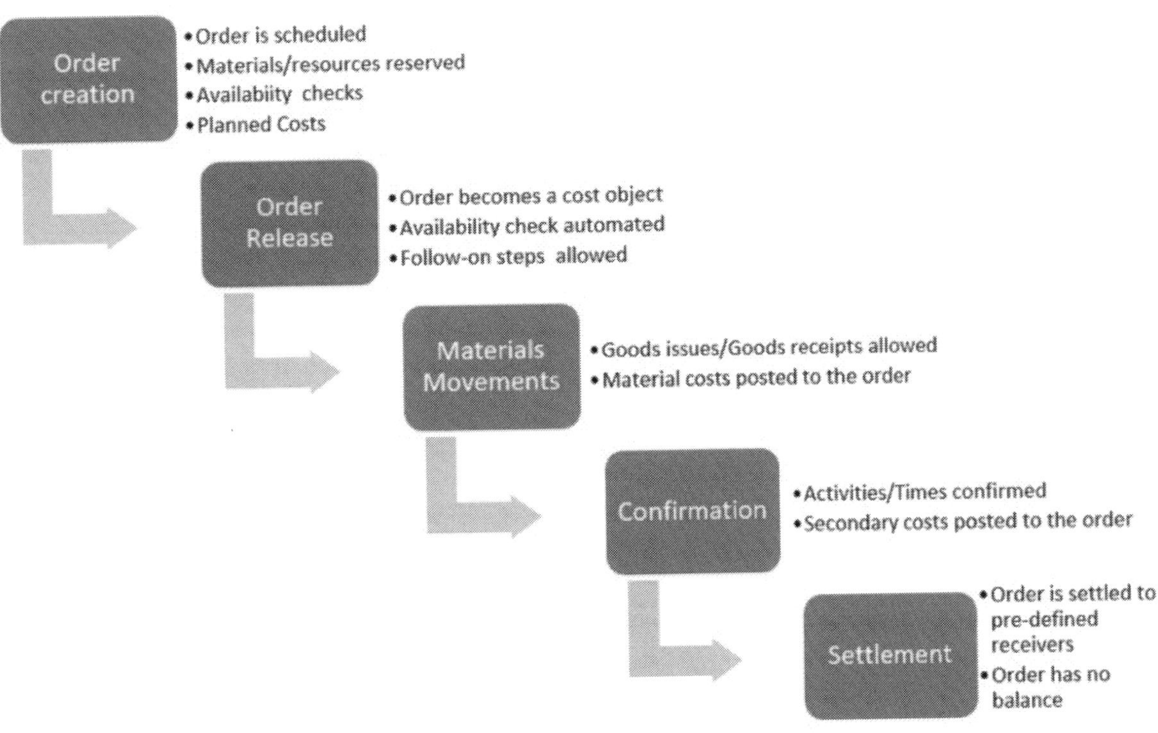


*Figure 61: Order-related cost object controlling*

When the order is created, the order is scheduled, costs are planned, stock materials are reserved in the warehouse, and capacities are reserved in the work centers. In addition to these, should a consumable material be planned on a maintenance order (as described in the previous paragraph), the system will automatically generate a purchase requisition.

Recall from our discussion in management accounting and also observe in Figure 61 that after the order is created, the maintenance order must undergo an order release. At the time of release, the ERP system will perform an automatic availability check and the order will become a cost object. The order is now ready, and goods movements of materials can now take place (goods issues of stock items from inventory and/or goods receipt of materials from purchase orders). Additionally, work centers can begin working on the order and confirming work completed.

In the maintenance order process, a unique step follows the order confirmations. The order status must be changed to Technically Complete (TECO) – see Figure 62. This status means all work planned on the order has been completed and no additional materials or work are needed.

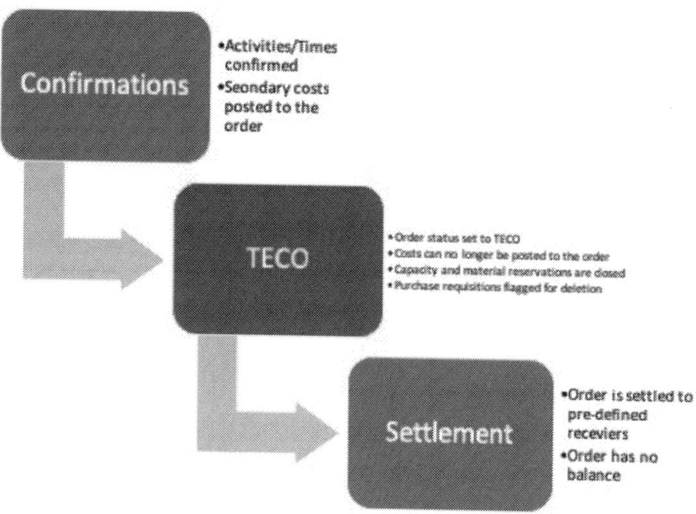


*Figure 62: A maintenance order follows the standard steps in order-related cost object controlling, but also has an additional step of Technical Completion (TECO)*

The status of TECO is not necessary to perform settlement of the order, which is a period-end activity. However, a status of TECO is necessary for business completion of this process. As we know from Order-Related Cost Object Controlling, settlement is the last step in the process.

The SAP TS410 course materials will describe the maintenance process in more detail. Our goal in this chapter was to help you gain an understanding of the organizational levels, master data, and process steps. As you can see, there are many similarities to other processes already covered in this book.

## Review questions: Enterprise Asset Management

(You can find answers on page 238. To answer questions marked with an asterisk (*) at the end, you will need to have studied the official SAP course materials.)

1. When creating a maintenance order, which of the following represent two examples of master data that might require maintenance? (two)

   A. Structure

   B. Functional location

   C. Planner group

   D. Equipment

2. Prior to creating a maintenance order, which of the following documents might be created to support the maintenance process? (one)

   A. Purchase requisition

   B. Transfer order

   C. Maintenance notification

   D. Maintenance requisition

3. Which of the following is considered master data in Enterprise Asset Management? (two)
    A. Maintenance plant
    B. Work center
    C. Technical object
    D. Maintenance planning plant
4. Which of the following are examples of technical objects? (three)
    A. Work centers
    B. BOMs
    C. Functional locations
    D. Equipment
5. What is the role of a functional location?
6. What is the role of equipment?
7. What is the role of assemblies?
8. What is the role of a planner group?
9. What is the role of a maintenance planning plant?
10. What is the role of a notification?
11. What is the role of a maintenance order?
12. What is the significance of releasing a maintenance order?
13. What is the difference between Enterprise Asset Management and Asset Accounting?
14. Which of the following are examples of equipment? (three)
    A. Cafeteria
    B. Oven
    C. Steamer
    D. Cooler
15. When the maintenance order is created, the maintenance notification is deleted. (T/F)
16. Which of the following are different types of maintenance described in this chapter? (two)
    A. Preventive maintenance
    B. Overall maintenance
    C. Breakdown maintenance
    D. Material maintenance
17. Explain the main differences between centralized and decentralized maintenance planning.
18. A maintenance plant is an example of master data. (T/F)

19. Which of the following is considered master data that is responsible for performing maintenance activities? (one)

    A. Maintenance plant

    B. Work center

    C. Technical object

    D. Maintenance planning plant

20. Which of the following is considered master data that is used by planner groups to plan materials for a maintenance order? (one)

    A. Functional location

    B. Work center

    C. Equipment

    D. Assembly

21. A maintenance order is managed using order-related cost object controlling. (T/F) *

# Human Capital Management

*THIS CHAPTER INTRODUCES* Human Capital Management (HCM) concepts as relevant for the SAP TS410 certification examination. HCM is broader than the commonly used business term, Human Resources Management. HCM, among other things, involves having the right number of employees, with the right skill sets, in the right places, at the right time, and at the right price. When it is put in those terms, it can seem a bit simplistic, but do not be fooled. It can involve rather detailed steps and processes to make all of that happen effectively, especially when we incorporate HCM into our ERP environment. As with the other chapters, you might benefit from reading this before proceeding with the SAP TS410 certification course.

Additionally, with the introduction of SAP S/4HANA, SAP has included content regarding Success Factors (cloud solution for HCM) in the new SAP TS410 certification course. We will delve into some Success Factors concepts a little later in this chapter. However, it's important to gain a foundational understanding of HCM before we can discuss the benefits of using Success Factors.

## Human Capital Management Cycle

Several individual components make up what we refer to as the HCM cycle in SAP. Unlike most other business processes, the HCM cycle does not have a well-defined beginning or end (see Figure 63).

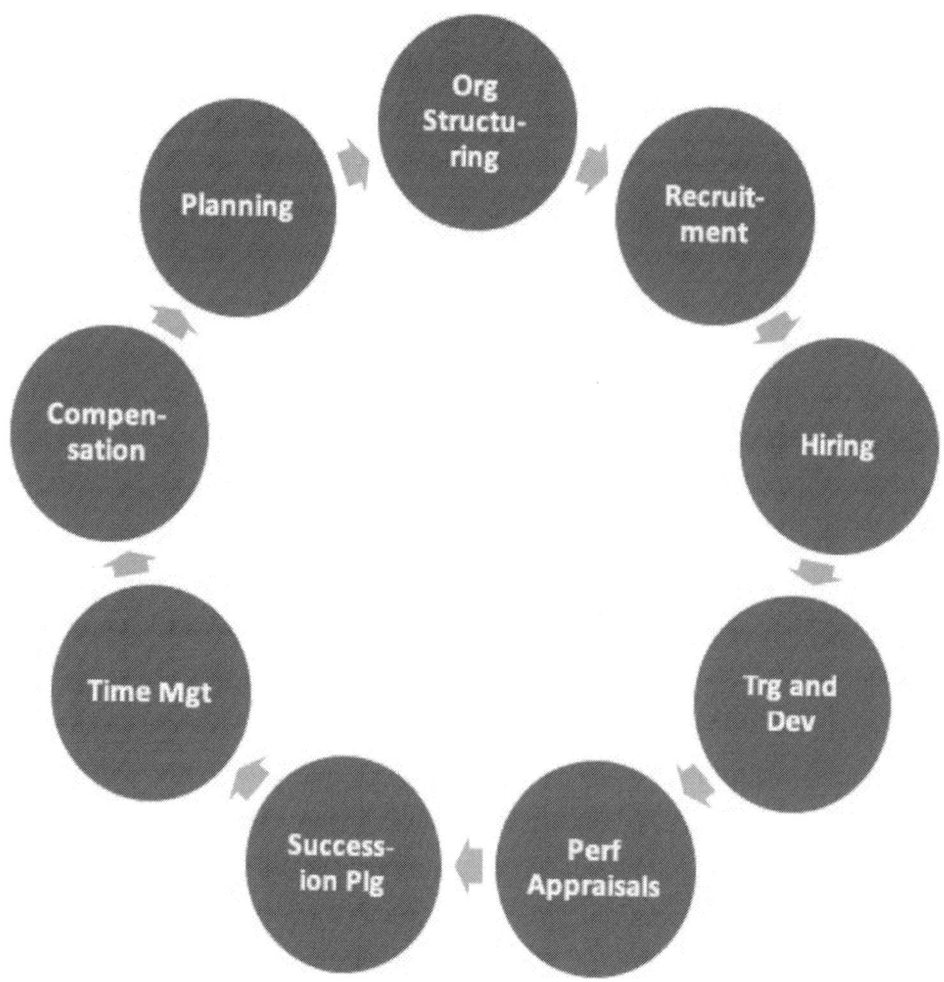


*Figure 63: Human Capital Management (HCM) process*

As we can see, there is a lot involved in the HCM cycle. One might think the cycle begins with recruiting, but it could easily be argued that an enterprise could not recruit employees without having open positions in organizational units (part of the organizational structure). Furthermore, whether an organizational unit exists, needs to be eliminated, or needs to be created depends heavily on planning processes. We could go on and on arguing where the HCM cycle begins and ends, but that is not the purpose of this chapter. The purpose of HCM is to effectively manage these processes in a way that allows an enterprise to have the right number of employees, with the right skill sets, in the right places, at the right time, and at the right price.

## Organizational Structure in HCM

For years, there have been different philosophies on how enterprises should be structured organizationally. In SAP S/4HANA, an organization's structure is organized in an organizational chart depicting the various departments in the company hierarchically. The hierarchy defines the reporting structure amongst these departments (organizational units). Also included in this structure are the various positions that exist in each organizational unit. An example appears in Figure 64.

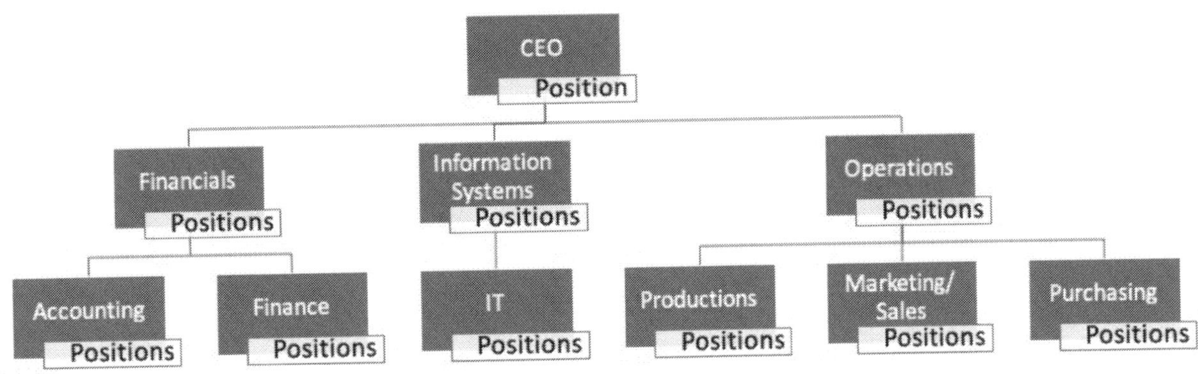


*Figure 64: Organization structure and positions*

Having an organizational chart like the one in Figure 64 is a good start at understanding the organizational structure. However, in a system like SAP S/4HANA, it can get complicated rather quickly. Because such systems are integrated, there is much more that goes into this. SAP refers to the creation and maintenance of the organizational structure as Organizational Management. For purposes of demonstrating this, let us use the production department from the example organizational chart in Figure 64 above. In SAP S/4HANA, the production department is considered an Organizational Unit. As you can see from the example, it must be created in the system and then inserted into the hierarchy; in this case it must be included as part of the Operations organizational unit.

There are several questions which then need to be answered. Those questions may include: How will we track costs for this department? How many different types of jobs will be performed in this department? Are any special skills required for these job types? For the different types of jobs, how many positions will be needed? Will these positions be full-time or part-time positions? How will we pay our employees? What type of an employee will we need? A great deal of planning is required to do this effectively. Perhaps by now, it has become apparent to you as to why planning is a step which precedes the Organizational Structuring in the HCM cycle.

For purposes of understanding how this works, let us simplify things a bit by addressing some of the questions listed above.

- **How will we track costs for this department?** To track costs in SAP, we could use a cost center for the Production department. We discussed cost centers in the Management Accounting chapter of this text. A Cost center is a part of an organization which incurs costs, and to which costs can be allocated.
- **How many different types of jobs will be performed in this department?** In SAP, Jobs are generic descriptions of what people do. A Job should be created and described to be as general

as possible, and as specific as necessary. A department could require many different Jobs. As an example, the Production department could require managers, planners, shop stewards, and shop workers. Each of these would need to have a Job created in the SAP system to describe it.

- **For all the different types of jobs, how many positions will be needed?** Once we know the descriptions of work that will be performed – Jobs – we can then begin planning how many Positions we will need for each of these Jobs. In SAP Positions are described by Jobs. One Job can be used to describe several Positions within one or more departments. For example, as we discussed above, the Production department could require a Job called Manager. The Production department may need three managers. Thus, it will create three Positions described by the Job, Manager. Some or all these positions could be full-time positions. Others may be part-time positions.
- **How will we pay our employees?** Not all employees will be paid in the same manner. As an example, some employees may be paid a salary and receive their paycheck only once a month. Others may be paid a wage and receive their paychecks on a weekly basis.
- **What type of employee will we need?** Just as we may pay employees differently, employees also are categorized differently. For instance, we are likely to have full-time employees and part-time employees. We may also have employees who are contracted on a temporary basis. Another example could be interns. Some interns may receive compensation, while other do not.

These are just some of the questions regarding organizational structuring. There are many other considerations. But for now, the following statement holds true: "An enterprise will hire a Person, into a Position, which is described by a Job, and belongs to an Organizational Unit (Department)."

## Recruitment in HCM

Recruitment in HCM can involve different activities. First, there is the matter of advertising openings for a position. Generally speaking, the advertisements should include a description of the position as well as some requirements associated with these positions. So where do these descriptions and requirements come from? Recall from above that Positions are described by Jobs and that many Positions can be described with a single Job in SAP. To simplify the creation of descriptions for every position in the enterprise, one could use the Job descriptions and then modify those descriptions to satisfy advertisement needs. For example, suppose an Accounting department in the College of Business at a university has an opening for a "Management Accounting Lecturer". In theory, this open Position would be described using a Job labeled, “Lecturer”. That job may be used to describe all lecturer positions at the university. The advertised description for this position could then be modified as needed to customize it to meet the needs of the Accounting Department. Jobs also list specific requirements that are associated with an advertised position. These requirements define the characteristics which candidates must meet to be eligible for consideration for employment. These requirements would also be included in the advertisement. Using the example of the “Management Accounting Lecturer” position, a candidate could be required to hold a Masters' Degree or higher in the field of Accounting.

Part of the recruitment process also involves evaluating candidates. It's only natural that there will be applicants whose qualifications don't meet the requirements of the position. To assist managers, applicants can easily be screened using a tool. In SAP this tool is called the Profile Matchup. Other software vendors have similar tools with different names, but the concept is basically the same. Recall, the enterprise advertises open positions and includes the description as well as the requirements of that position. It's expected that all candidates who apply meet these requirements, but as we noted, that is not true in all cases. A simplified example of a profile matchup can be seen in Figure 65.

| Position requirements | Applicant's Qualifications |
|---|---|
| Master's degree or higher in accounting | ☑ |
| Minimum of three years' teaching experience | ☑ |
| Fluent in English and French languages | ☐ |
| Hold a certification in accounting (CPA or similar) | ☑ |

*Figure 65: Matching a position's requirements to an applicant's qualifications*

Here we have once again used the example of the lecturer position in the Accounting department. Suppose we receive an application from a candidate. Figure 65 shows the position requirements on the left and the applicant's qualifications on the right. You can see that this applicant fails to meet all the requirements of the advertised position. This simple example makes it easy to see how management can use the Profile Matchup for the purpose of evaluating applicants. Those who fail to meet the requirements should no longer be given any consideration for hire into that position.

In today's business environment, it would be difficult for a company to compete for qualified candidates without providing some form of electronic access to advertise these position openings. Once upon a time, a company would do this advertising in newspapers and in rare cases, on radio or in other print media like magazines. Today we go to the Internet to find open positions. There are many online companies like CareerBuilder and Monster to assist enterprises by providing a space where they can post their positions and make them available to the public. Other companies like Gulfstream create their own space (http://www.gulfstream.com/careers/) on the Internet where potential candidates can create a profile and search available openings. However, posting available positions is not exclusively intended for the public. Enterprises realize the value in promoting employees from within. It is a very common practice these days to have a presence on an internal site (intranet) where current employees can also look for opportunities where they work.

Having an online presence can simplify the transition from the recruitment process to the hiring process. Data collected from applicants can be used for automatic transfer during the hiring process to minimize the data entry at hiring. In addition, applicants often have the capability of monitoring and updating their applicant status and information.

All this discussion about advertising positions does not imply that this is all there is to recruitment in HCM. Recruitment could also involve recruiters from the HR department attending career fairs or universities to recruit students. At such events, recruiters could accept resumes from applicants and even screen them using the Profile Matchup and/or interview them for current or future position openings. This is a proactive approach often used by enterprises to help reduce the time and expense required to fill vacancies when they occur.

## Hiring in HCM

The hiring process is the next logical step in the HCM Cycle. After applicants are evaluated, the enterprise must decide which applicant to hire into the position. The hiring process is part of Personnel Management and addresses the needs to fill positions in Organizational Structuring. Personnel Management follows the Recruitment phase in the HCM Cycle. In this phase, the applicant is hired into a position, described by a job, belonging to a department.

Earlier in this chapter, we again referenced Cost Centers, which is a part of SAP Management Accounting (CO), describing where costs occur in an organization. A simple approach for an enterprise is to associate the department where this employee works with a cost center (as described in the Organizational Structuring in this chapter). The position held by the employee also exists in that department and inherits the same cost center. In doing so, when payroll is run for this employee, any labor costs associated with the person being hired will immediately be linked to that cost center. Management accounting isn't the only business function impacted by payroll. We also need to ensure the financial accounting integration with ERP is properly recorded. In this way, the Balance Sheet and Income Statement accurately reflect the impacts of payroll.

Enterprises are also going to want to maintain a Personnel File for employees they hire. A Personnel File is a record of their personal information as well as other information relating that employee to the enterprise. The personnel file contains information that the Humans Resource department needs to maintain for an employee. Some examples include but are not necessarily limited to: address information; employee banking information; pay rate information; and organizational structuring information (see Figure 66). Keep in mind, some of the information applicants entered in the recruitment phase can be copied over into the hiring phase. What does all this mean? It means an enterprise must ensure that this new employee is properly hired into the organizational structure and that necessary information about the employee is maintained.

To manage some of these complexities, SAP uses a form of master data called an InfoType. InfoTypes exist to help maintain all the information the enterprise needs to record for an employee. An InfoType is a collection of related data. The categories (Personal Information, Banking Information, Pay Rate Information, and Organizational Structuring). Figure 66 illustrates this.

Each of the categories is an example of what could be considered a unique InfoType in SAP. The collection of all InfoTypes for an employee makes up the employee's Personnel File. Maintaining InfoTypes in SAP can be performed with something called an Action. Hiring is an example of an Action and would result in the maintenance of the relevant InfoTypes. Often during hiring, the enterprise would need to maintain many InfoTypes at one time. If you can imagine, maintenance of InfoTypes could become a challenge. An enterprise needs to maintain InfoTypes for many reasons other than hiring. Another type of an Action would be termination, which would require further maintenance of InfoTypes. In short, an Action is a process that needs to be performed on an employee (hiring, termination, transfers, and others). When performing an Action, SAP suggests all the relevant InfoTypes to be maintained for that action to ensure all the master data required to complete the action has been entered.

Other reasons could also exist that would require updating an InfoType. Suppose an employee receives a wage increase. Only that one InfoType for that one employee would need to be maintained. On the other hand, we could have several employees who have received a wage increase. It would make sense then to be able to maintain that single InfoType for several employees at one time. To satisfy each of these scenarios, SAP provides three options for InfoType maintenance (see Figure 67). As noted above, to perform an Action, the company would need to maintain several InfoTypes for one employee at one time. SAP refers to this as a Personnel Action.

| Personnel information | Name, address, gender, birth date, etc. |
|---|---|
| Banking information | Bank account details for direct deposit. |
| Pay rate information | Salary/wage, pay rate, hours/week, overtime rate |
| Organizational structuring | **Financial Accounting (CoCd)**<br>• Sub area of Financial accounting (Personnel area)<br>• Additional sub areas (Personnel sub area)<br><br>**Type of employee (Employee group)**<br>• Payment options<br><br>**Organizational assignment**<br>• Department<br>• Position<br>• Job |

*Figure 66: InfoTypes in Personnel File*

For maintaining only one InfoType at a time for one employee, SAP offers Single Screen maintenance. Finally, to maintain a single InfoType for many employees at one time, SAP offers Fast Entry maintenance.

Some InfoTypes can be maintained by employees themselves. For example, if an employee's address changes, it would be inefficient to have management make this change. SAP offers Employee Self-Service (ESS) to enable these types of authorized changes. ESS could also be used for employees to view paychecks and download tax documentation when needed. To summarize the Hiring phase, it is fair to say hiring is supported by the Recruitment phase and integrates directly with the Organizational Structuring phase in the HCM Cycle.

| Infotype maintenance need | Option |
| --- | --- |
| One employee – many InfoTypes | Personnel actions |
| One employee, one InfoType | Single screen |
| Many employees, one InfoType | Fast entry |

*Figure 67: Options for maintaining InfoTypes*

## Training and Development, Performance Appraisals, and Succession Planning in HCM

Training and Development, Performance Appraisals and Succession Planning (Figure 68) are so closely related in the HCM Cycle that it makes sense for us to talk about all three of them at the same time. To begin our discussion, we should note that training and development are not necessarily the same thing. Training could be used for current employees or new hires to improve their skills. To be hired into a position, the employee held the necessary qualifications to meet the position requirements. This does not however mean that new employee is job ready.

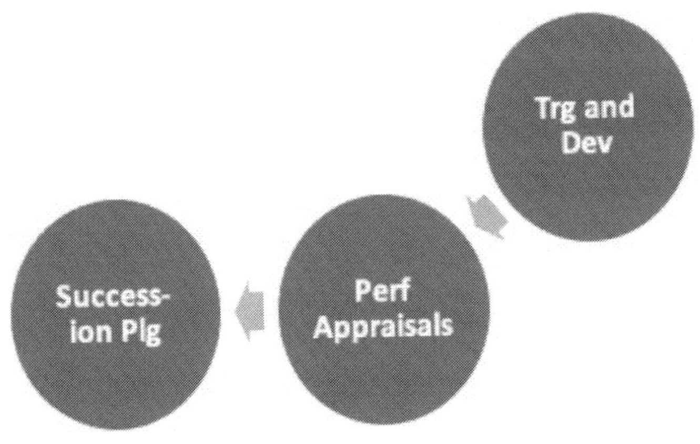


*Figure 68: Training and development, performance appraisals and succession planning in HCM*

The new employee might need some training to improve on their qualifications to suit the needs of the enterprise. Development is different. Development is often used to prepare current employees for future opportunities within the enterprise and to increase their potential value to themselves and to the enterprise.

Training and Development assumes there is a need for either or both. This assumption is what creates the close relationship between them, as well as with Performance Appraisals and Succession Planning. Let's begin by discussing training. Training for the sake of training is generally fruitless. To provide effective training, the enterprise should perform a type of needs assessment. For new hires, this needs assessment generally takes place during the recruitment process. Management, while evaluating and selecting the new employee for the position, makes a determination of this person's capabilities. If they responsibly made this hiring decision, they would have a very good understanding of the new employee's training needs. Current employees also have training needs. The needs assessment for current employees can stem from the use of Performance Appraisals. These appraisals serve many purposes, but one of them is to assist with defining training needs for current employees. Appraisals are primarily based on the requirements of the position held by the employee. The appraisal helps keep the employee informed as to how well he/she is performing in their position. Appraisals also serve other needs, such as compensation decisions; documenting employee successes; documenting employee shortcomings; and building development plans for employees. We will discuss development next.

As noted, development is designed to prepare current employees for future opportunities within the enterprise and to increase their potential value to themselves and to the enterprise. Part of the employee appraisal could include developing a current employee for promotion. The appraisal would help identify the desire for development but doesn't do a very good job of identifying the development needs. Since appraisals are designed to evaluate an employee's performance in their current position, it is not optimized for development. An effective way to build development plans for employees is to once again take advantage of the Profile Matchup. During the appraisal process, the appraiser (supervisor) or the employee might express an interest in the promotion potential for that employee. During the appraisal discussions, a position for promotion could be identified. The Profile Matchup is then used to determine which qualifications an employee currently lacks to be eligible for that position. Let's use the earlier example of the Profile Matchup (see Figure 69). This time we will put it into a different context.

In Figure 69 the qualifications column is now labeled, "Employee's Qualifications" as opposed to "Applicant's qualifications" in Figure 65. This is so because we are not evaluating an external applicant, but rather an existing employee. Suppose the Accounting department in the College of Business has an existing part-time employee who teaches accounting classes as an adjunct lecturer. This adjunct would like to be considered for promotion to a current or future opening of a full-time lecturer's position in the Accounting department. A development plan should be built which addresses qualifications that are missing. In this case, the adjunct lecturer would need to develop his/her language skills to become fluent in both English and French language. If the adjunct currently speaks English, he/she should consider attending available French classes as part of their development plan to meet the development needs.

| Position requirements | Employee's Qualifications |
|---|---|
| Master's degree or higher in accounting | ☑ |
| Minimum of three years' teaching experience | ☑ |
| Fluent in English and French languages | ☐ |
| Hold a certification in accounting (CPA or similar) | ☑ |

*Figure 69: Profile matchup in HCM*

In Figure 69 the qualifications column is now labeled, "Employee's Qualifications" as opposed to "Applicant's qualifications" in Figure 65. This is so because we are not evaluating an external applicant, but rather an existing employee. Suppose the Accounting department in the College of Business has an existing part-time employee who teaches accounting classes as an adjunct lecturer. This adjunct would like to be considered for promotion to a current or future opening of a full-time lecturer's position in the Accounting department. A development plan should be built which addresses qualifications that are missing. In this case, the adjunct lecturer would need to develop his/her language skills to become fluent in both English and French language. If the adjunct currently speaks English, he/she should consider attending available French classes as part of their development plan to meet the development needs.

It becomes apparent that the primary objective of the above example certainly addresses the needs of the employee. However, there are also situations in which the primary objective is not to develop employees for their personal benefit, but to develop employees because it benefits the enterprise. Using the same Profile Matchup in Figure 69, let's again change the context. This time suppose a current full-time lecturer in the Accounting department has announced that he/she will retire at the end of the academic year. The enterprise now has a need to fill a vacancy that will happen in the future. Planning to fill this vacancy is an example of Succession Planning. In this scenario, the head of the Accounting

Department might approach the adjunct lecturer and ask that person to consider applying for the future vacancy. However, the adjunct lecturer does not currently have the necessary qualifications. Addressing this need early in the process helps to get the right person in the right place at the right time. The adjunct lecturer would once again have a development plan which includes attending French classes to satisfy that part of the position requirement. In this example, the primary objective is for the enterprise to have someone readily available and prepared to fill that position as soon as it becomes vacant. This makes a lot of sense but can be difficult to manage. If you think deeply enough, you might soon realize that if a current employee is being prepared to fill a future vacancy, that means their position is also about to become vacant. And so, there will be a spiraling effect associated with Succession Planning that will have to be effectively managed by the enterprise.

## Time Management and Compensation in HCM

Time Management and Compensation are also closely related, so again, it makes sense to include both in a single discussion Figure 70. In the HCM Cycle, times play an important role on several levels. One of those involves using working times to help process payroll. Compensation involves more than simply using recorded times to pay employees for hours they work. Compensation has many additional functions in the HCM Cycle as well.

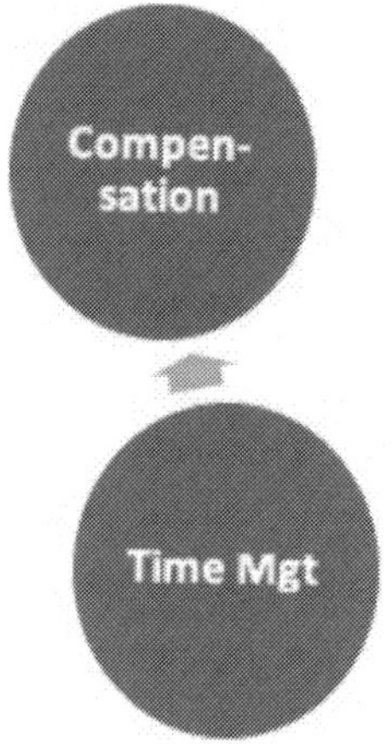


*Figure 70: Compensation and time management in HCM*

If you were asked a question about how times are used in the HCM Cycle, it would only be natural for you to state that times are used for payroll. You would be correct, but that statement is too broad. In the HCM Cycle, we need to look more deeply into what these times are that an enterprise uses for payroll. Naturally we need to record times that people work. These work times are extremely important for calculating pay for an employee. However, each employee is different. If you recall in the hiring phase, we discussed that the organization maintains InfoTypes when hiring employees. Among these includes information the enterprise maintains regarding the type of employee the person is, how they get paid (wage, salary, etc.,), and their pay rate. The collection of working times may be used differently depending on the information maintained in their InfoType records. As an example, a wage worker may receive a rate of pay for all recorded hours up to forty hours. After that, the wage worker may receive a different rate of pay (overtime rate). On the other hand, a salaried employee would receive the same pay regardless of how many hours they work. But that doesn't necessarily mean the enterprise doesn't need to record working times for the salaried employee. Salaried employees could be required to record working times for other reasons. Perhaps the enterprise would like to know how many hours salaried employees work to make sure they are properly being compensated for the amount of work they perform. Or it could be that the salaried employees working times are recorded so they can be used to bill their times to customers. As you can see, working times can be used for more than just payroll.

There are additional forms of time other than working times that an enterprise would also collect in the HCM Cycle. These times include, but are not necessarily limited to: sick time, vacation time, overtime, leave time, maternity time, paternity time, time on sabbatical and travel time. If times are that important in the HCM Cycle, then it's equally important to have an effective tool for recording times. In SAP, there is a tool called, CATS, Cross-application Time Sheet. CATS allows employees, employers, and others to record various times for various business applications, hence its name – Cross-application Time Sheet.

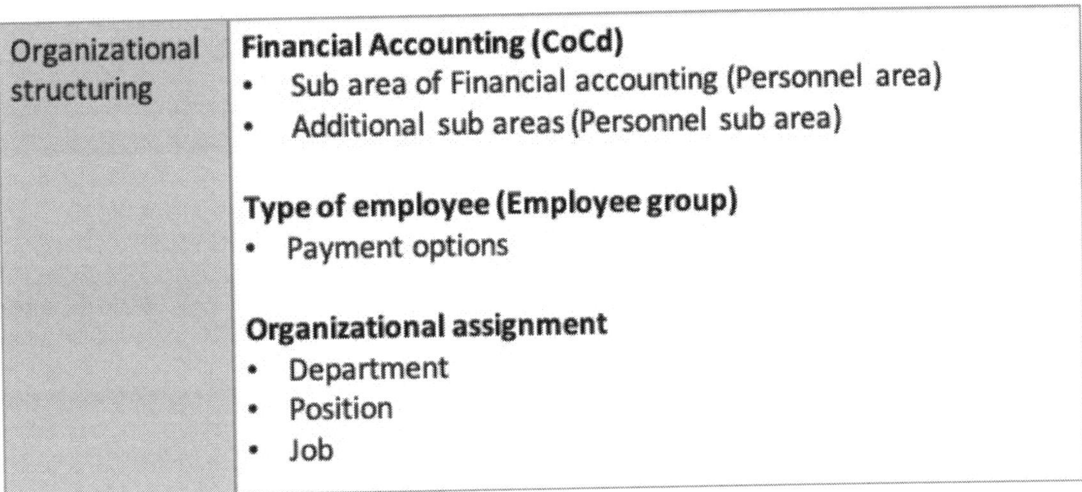

| Organizational structuring | **Financial Accounting (CoCd)**<br>• Sub area of Financial accounting (Personnel area)<br>• Additional sub areas (Personnel sub area)<br><br>**Type of employee (Employee group)**<br>• Payment options<br><br>**Organizational assignment**<br>• Department<br>• Position<br>• Job |
|---|---|

*Figure 71: InfoType for organization structuring*

By now, it should be quite evident that Time Management is closely integrated with Compensation. Up until this point, we've discussed compensation being a result of recording working times. So how does an enterprise determine how much to pay its employees? How is pay rate determined for wage workers and how are salaries determined for salaried employees? A common approach to this is Job Pricing. To learn how job pricing works, we need to reflect on some of the things we've learned so far.

The term Job in SAP is used to describe various positions that can be linked to it. Thus, Jobs describe the work that people in those positions will perform. In addition to this, we looked at InfoTypes for an employee and we learned that an employee is assigned in the organizational structuring. Part of this assignment is for Financial Accounting purposes. You can see in Figure 71, there are sub areas within the Financial Accounting part of Organizational Structuring (Personnel Area and Personnel Sub-area).

Let's use an example to understand how Job Pricing works. In Table 19, you see two employees, Employee A and Employee B. Both employees work for the same enterprise and have some things in common. They both perform the same job and both work in the United States. However, you can see they do not receive the same pay rate.

| Employee | Job | Country | City | Pay rate |
|---|---|---|---|---|
| **Employee A** | Painter | USA | New York City, NY | $35/hr |
| **Employee B** | Painter | USA | Des Moines, Iowa | $25/hr |

*Table 19: Job pricing*

Though both perform the same job, they work in different cities, demonstrating that where you work can impact your rate of pay because cost of living is different in these two cities. From a Financial Accounting perspective, both employees work in the United States, so their payroll expense will report to the same company code. However, in this case, the city may represent the Personnel Sub Area within the United States (CoCd). Based on this scenario, it only makes sense to have a different pay rate based on the city where the employee works, even though they perform the same job. Job Pricing allows the enterprise to analyze a job and to find a pay rate for that job that is competitive within the local market. Recall that HCM involves having the right number of employees, with the right skill sets, in the right places, at the right time, and at the right price.

Pay isn't the only form of compensation. Benefits provide additional forms of compensation. There are many types of benefits for employees. Benefits include health insurance, life insurance, retirement, vacation schedules, leave benefits and others. In some respects, benefits can be used to attract candidates. Should an applicant have more than one job offer, the applicant looks at more than just the rate of pay. The applicant will also consider various forms of benefits that are included in the job offer. The benefits could make the difference between whether or not the applicant accepts the job offer or takes a different offer elsewhere. Benefits also influence retention rates in an enterprise. As an example, an enterprise might provide a fully vested schedule for a retirement benefit after an employee completes ten years of service. If that employee has worked six years and has another job offer from another company, the retirement benefit mentioned may be enough to influence the employee to remain with their current employer, so they could meet the requirements to become fully vested. Benefits can then be considered incentive packages that are a form of compensation. They can be used as a recruiting and a retention tool in the HCM Cycle.

One final form of compensation that bears some discussion is reimbursement. As part of an employee's position requirements, they may need to travel from time to time. The enterprise must consider this and have a mechanism in place by which an employee would be reimbursed for any business expenses they personally paid for during their business travel. Reimbursement is handled as part of compensation and can be included in the employee's paycheck when payroll is run. An employee would complete a travel expense form within the HCM system, and those expenses would need to be evaluated and approved before reimbursement occurs. It's important to note that the reimbursement of these expenses has both a Financial and Management Accounting impact in the system.

Regarding time management and compensation, you should now be aware that these two phases mean more than simply paying employees for the time they work. There is a lot of strategy, integration, and planning that go into these concepts. As for planning, that is next.

## Planning in HCM

Though this is the last phase of the HCM Cycle that we will be discussing, it does not mean that it is the last step in this cycle. Recall from our opening conversation that the HCM Cycle has no clear beginning or end.

There are a couple of aspects of planning that need to be addressed here. To begin, let's focus on organizational structure planning. Of course, planning any changes to the Organizational Structuring phase of the HCM Cycle involves a great deal of integration with the other ERP modules. Changing structures means creating new structures, modifying others, and in extreme cases, the elimination of some. The decisions around these changes are generally driven by profitability. Increased costs could result in restructuring as could increases in revenue. Most cost and revenue planning occur in Management Accounting, so there will be a close relationship between HCM and Management Accounting when it comes to planning.

Planning in HCM also involves planning personnel costs. Personnel costs are dependent on Organizational Structuring. If an enterprise eliminates a department, that will obviously impact personnel costs. Some employees in that department might be absorbed into other departments, but it is very possible that many of their positions will be terminated. Likewise, the creation of a new department may result in an increase in positions. Another input into personnel cost planning is the performance appraisal. Performance appraisals could result in offering pay raises for employees. It would therefore make sense to consider performance appraisal in personnel cost planning as well.

Sometimes external events will also impact planning. Suppose a competing company just opened an office in the same city or in a nearby location. There is likely a threat that some employees may take jobs with the competing company. To offset that threat, the enterprise may re-evaluate their job pricing strategy to become more competitive in hopes of retaining their employees. Furthermore, they might also consider changes to benefits for the same reason. These changes are going to impact future costs and should also be given careful consideration in personnel cost planning.

Planning in the HCM Cycle requires intense management decision making. Therefore, managers must have tools to be able to access the information they need. In SAP S/4HANA, managers can take advantage of a tool in a web-based environment that provides managers with the insight and reporting tools to enable these decisions. Management also needs tools to be able to support other aspects of HCM, and in general these tools are referred to as Manager Self-Service (MSS) tools.

## HR Renewal/HR Professional

SAP offers a modern browser-based interface for Employee Self-Service (ESS) and Manager Self-Service (MSS). This interface is available through the Enterprise Portal or the SAP NetWeaver Business Client. The screens in HR Renewal are more intuitive and provide a consistent user experience. HR Professional is part of HR Renewal and provides HR professionals with access to a more robust set of Organizational Management and Personnel Administration tools. An example of such functionality is the maintenance of InfoTypes. HR Professional includes flexible options for managing several InfoTypes for employees. These are considered Actions in HR Professional. However, it's important to note that this functionality is not the same thing as the Personnel Actions described earlier in this chapter.

## SAP SuccessFactors

SuccessFactors is an SAP cloud-based solution for Human Capital Management. Much of the existing HCM functionality in S/4HANA can be managed in the cloud. Figure 72 depicts SuccessFactors Employee Central and lists some of the functionality available in SuccessFactors.

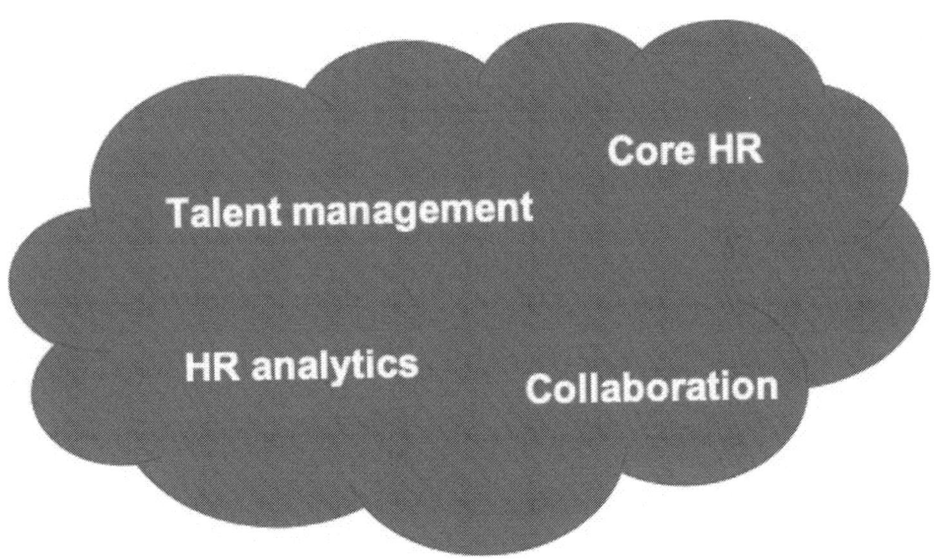


*Figure 72: Success Factors -- Employee Central*

Employee Central Includes a variety of traditional and modern HR capabilities offered in the Cloud. The capabilities are as follows:

- Talent Management and HR Core:
- Recruiting
- Succession Planning
- Compensation (Payroll, Benefits, etc.)
- Learning Solutions (Training)
- Workforce Planning
- Goal Setting
- Performance
- Collaboration
- SAP Jam
- HR Analytics
- Workforce Analytics

The SAP TS410 materials cover these areas in more detail. What is important for you here, is to understand the context surrounding Employee Central. It is a cloud-based solution that allows SAP customers to perform traditional HR functions as well as the most modern functions, such as Analytics and Social Collaboration.

SAP also provides its customers with flexibility regarding the adoption of SuccessFactors. Customers can find easy entry points, such as Analytics in the Cloud while managing all other HCM activities on premise using their existing S/4HANA solution. Table 20 shows scenarios for transitioning to SuccessFactors on the Cloud.

## Review questions: Human Capital Management

(You can find answers on page 240. To answer questions marked with an asterisk (*) at the end, you will need to have studied the official SAP course materials.)

1. Which of the following is not part of the HCM cycle? (one)
   A. Recruitment
   B. Performance appraisals
   C. Time management
   D. Work center planning
2. Define the beginning and end to the HCM cycle.
3. When a person is promoted into a new position, a vacancy occurs. Planning to have that vacancy filled efficiently and effectively is part of... (one)
   A. Recruitment
   B. Hiring
   C. Succession planning
   D. Performance appraisals
4. Keeping track of how much vacation an employee currently has is part of which process in the HCM cycle? (one)
   A. Time management
   B. Compensation
   C. Organizational structuring
   D. Planning
5. The Profile Matchup compares which two things? (two)
   A. Candidate's requirements
   B. Candidate's qualifications
   C. Position requirements
   D. Position qualifications
6. Which processes in the HCM cycle use the Profile Matchup? (two)
   A. Personnel development
   B. Compensation
   C. Recruitment
   D. Planning

| Configuration name | Functionality on the cloud | Functionality in on premise HCM |
|---|---|---|
| **Talent hybrid** | Talent analytics | Time management<br>Payroll<br>Personnel administration<br>Organization management<br>Core HCM |
| **Side-by-side** | Talent analytics<br>Personnel administration<br>Organization management | Time management<br>Payroll<br>Personnel administration<br>Core HCM |
| **Core hybrid** | Talent analytics<br>Personnel administration<br>Organization management<br>Talent management<br>Workforce analytics | Time management<br>Payroll<br>ERP |
| **Full cloud** | Talent analytics<br>Personnel administration<br>Organization management<br>Talent management<br>Workforce analytics<br>Time management<br>Payroll | ERP |

*Table 20: Scenario for transitioning to SuccessFactors on the cloud*

7. Explain how SAP supports the keeping track of costs for various organizational units in SAP HCM.
8. Explain the use of Jobs in SAP HCM.
9. Explain the use of Positions in SAP HCM.
10. The Hiring component in the HCM cycle supports the internal postings of positions for internal candidates. (T/F)
11. Explain how the SAP ERP system supports the integration of data between the Recruitment and Hiring components in the HCM cycle.

12. When someone is hired into a position, explain how this new employee is associated with a cost center.
13. Which transaction in HCM will result in the posting of a cost to a cost center? (one)
    A. Hiring
    B. Payroll
    C. Recruitment
    D. Planning
14. Which of the following best describes an Info Type? (two)
    A. A collection of related data about an employee
    B. A collection of related data about a cost center
    C. Organizational data
    D. Master data
15. Explain a personnel file.
16. Which of the following are possible examples of Info Types? (three)
    A. Personal information
    B. Banking information
    C. Work center information
    D. Pay rate information
17. Which of the following are methods for maintaining Info Types? (three)
    A. Multiple screen
    B. Single screen
    C. Fast entry
    D. Personnel actions
18. Explain personnel actions info type maintenance.
19. Explain single screen info type maintenance.
20. Explain fast entry info type maintenance.
21. It is not possible for an employee to maintain any of their own info type master data. (T/F)
22. Training and development in HCM also takes advantage of the Profile Matchup. (T/F)
23. A company is preparing an employee to fill a future vacancy. As a result, they also need to prepare for the vacancy left behind by this employee. This is an example of __________. (one)
    A. Succession planning
    B. Development
    C. Training
    D. Appraisals

24. A current employee is interested in being promoted to a higher position. The employee works closely with his/her manager to create a plan for achieving this. This is an example of __________. (one)

    A. Succession planning
    B. Development
    C. Training
    D. Appraisals

25. A manager meets with an employee on an annual basis to discuss their performance. This is an example of ______________. (one)

    A. Succession planning
    B. Development
    C. Training
    D. Appraisals

26. Wages, salaries, benefits, and insurance are all examples of _________. (one)

    A. Pay scale
    B. Job pricing
    C. Compensation
    D. Promotion

27. Explain CATS.

28. List various types of times that are used in HCM.

29. Explain the concept of Job Pricing in HCM.

30. Planning is the last phase of the HCM cycle and therefore ends the HCM process. (T/F)

31. Which of the following is available to assist managers in making planning decisions in HCM? (one)

    A. Employee desktop
    B. Manager's desktop
    C. Planning table
    D. Sales and operations plan

32. Which of the following represents SAP's cloud solution to Human Capital Management? (one)

    A. Ariba
    B. SuccessFactors
    C. fieldglass
    D. Concur

33. SAP SuccessFactors Employee Central includes all of the following EXCEPT __________. (one)

    A. Time Management

    B. Payroll

    C. Projects

    D. Organizational Management

# Project Management (PS)

*THIS CHAPTER INTRODUCES* Project Management (PS) concepts as relevant for the SAP TS410 certification examination. While reading through the information in this chapter, it is important to note that the objective of this chapter is to inform you of tools available for project management and how SAP uses those tools for managing projects. Learning how to manage projects and how to become a project manager is NOT an objective here. As with the other chapters, you might benefit from reading this before proceeding with the SAP TS410 certification course.

## Project Characteristics

Projects can serve many purposes and there are many things that can influence a project. From an SAP perspective, it is important to note that the Project Systems (PS) module does not have any organizational levels directly associated with it. Projects get their organizational levels from the other SAP modules with which Project Systems integrates. From an enterprise perspective, projects have some defining characteristics. Projects are generally capital intensive and time intensive. They are usually complex in nature and involve many different functional areas. In addition to these characteristics, projects have a definitive beginning and a definitive end. Identifying the beginning and end of a project can be a lot more challenging than you think.

For purposes of demonstration, let us discuss planning and managing a wedding as a project. Figure 73 lists some important considerations. If you have gotten married, planned a wedding, or know someone who has, you will understand the complexities involved in planning a wedding. If you ask ten different individuals to define when a wedding begins and ends, you are likely to get ten different answers. Whereas this chapter will not help you figure out how to define the beginning and end of a project, it provides you with information on which tools are available that can help manage the project. The beginning, middle, and end of a project can be measured with time but are better represented using other forms of measurement. These other forms of measurement are Work Breakdown Structure (WBS) Elements and Activities.

**Wedding**
- Wedding Ceremony?
- Wedding Reception?
- Wedding License?
- Who will be in the Wedding Party?

*Figure 73: High level considerations in planning a wedding*

## Work Breakdown Structure (WBS) Elements and Activities

Projects have various components which help project managers and teams measure and manage various aspects such as dates, costs, budgets, activities, payments, among other things. If we continue with our example of managing a wedding as a project, we can identify some basic elements which make up the wedding. Figure 74 shows these.

The wedding itself is defined as the top-level element, which defines the project. The items below it represent other elements that must be considered successfully manage the wedding. (Note: this is just a rudimentary example for demonstration purposes only and doesn't necessarily reflect all aspects of a wedding). These elements are called Work Breakdown Structure (WBS) Elements. From a project perspective, we can structure these elements in a hierarchical form to give us a visual representation as a rough-cut WBS.

Figure 74 represents a Work Breakdown Structure (WBS). Thus, a WBS is a hierarchical representation of the project. Realistically, this WBS is a high-level WBS, meaning there are likely to be several additional levels. For example, the Wedding ceremony WBS Element could involve other aspects such as the location, wedding official, flowers, music, etc. Likewise, the Wedding reception WBS element may also have additional aspects associated with it, while the Wedding license and Wedding party WBS Elements may not. Figure 75 shows the WBS hierarchy in greater detail.

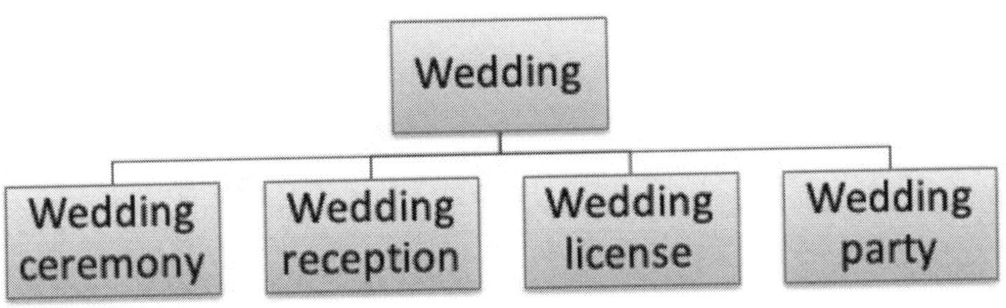


*Figure 74: A rough-cut Work Breakdown Structure*

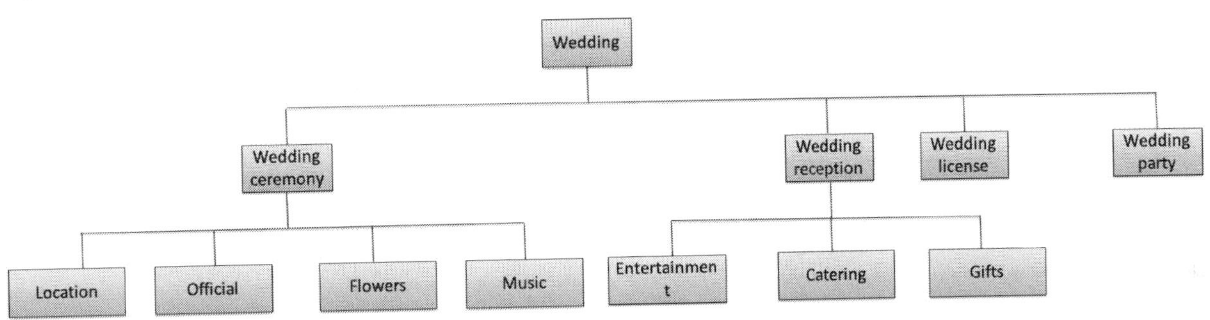


*Figure 75: A more detailed WBS*

The differences between the three previous figures stem from the project phases they represent. At first, the bride and groom to-be might begin working on their wedding by planning it at a very high level. This is considered the concept phase. During the concept phase, there is just some discussion about the wedding, with no detail. That granularity of information can simply be represented with the top-level Wedding as seen in Figure 73. When the planning of the wedding reaches the next phase, it is considered a rough-cut phase. The rough-cut phase would be represented as shown in Figure 74. Ultimately, the wedding progresses to the detailed planning phase. It is the detailed phase that we see in Figure 75.

Interestingly, we have used the term planning to describe these three phases. What does that mean? It means that the WBS can be used to plan the project. The more detailed the WBS, the more detailed the plan. Planning generally includes more than Identifying the WBS Elements. It also involves planning costs, defining a budget, among others. We will discuss other phases of the project a little later in this chapter. For now, these three phases help provide a framework for how WBS Elements and their structure shape a project.

Activities represent the work or steps that need to be accomplished to complete the project. The activities of a project can be linked to one another in a precedence diagram. The precedence diagram describes the relationships (dependencies) between the activities, and the order in which they must be completed. The precedence diagram below is called a Network (Figure 76).

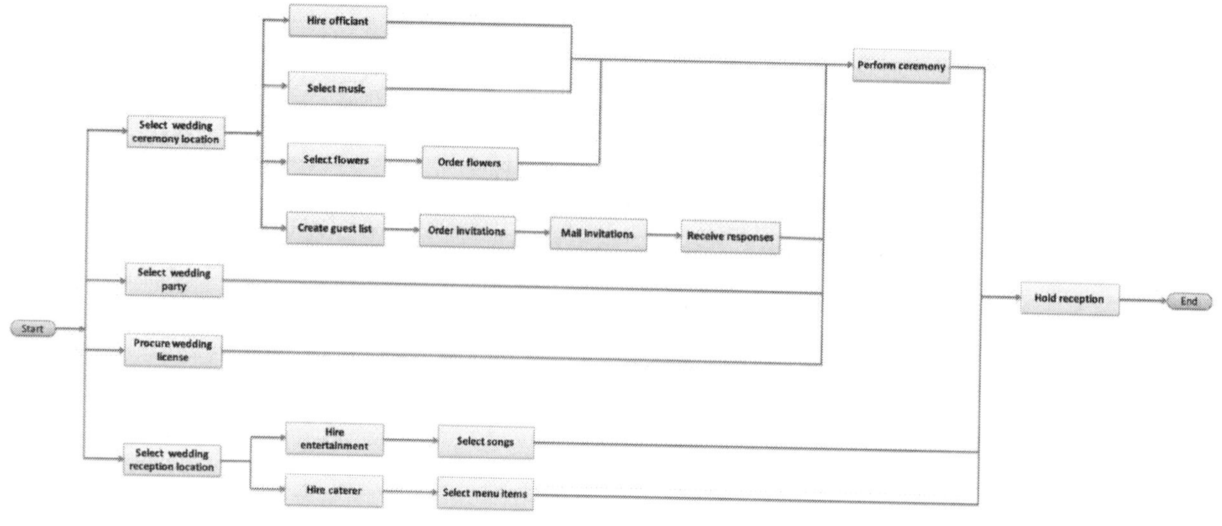


*Figure 76: A Network (or Activity Network)*

As you can see from the network in Figure 76, our wedding project includes many activities. (Note: like the WBS, the network seen here is solely for the purpose of providing an example and does not necessarily reflect all practical activities required for managing a wedding). Let us take a look at some of these activities in more detail to get a better understanding of activities and their relationships. First, an activity (as explained above) is a step in completing the project and involves a type of work that needs to be performed. As you can see, there are four activities which are independent of all others and can be started as soon as the project begins (Select a Location for the ceremony, Select wedding party, Procure a wedding license, and Select a Location for the reception). There are no activities that need to be completed prior to these four and they do not depend on each other. Thus, when the project starts, these activities can be performed independently, and can run concurrently.

If we look at the activity, Perform Ceremony, we clearly see several other activities that must be completed directly prior to performing the ceremony. These activities include: Hire an Officiant, Select music, Order flowers, Receive responses, Select wedding party and Procure a wedding license. The arrows connecting these activities to the Perform Ceremony activity define the relationship between them. From a project perspective, this means the ceremony cannot be performed until these other activities have been completed. You also notice that some of these same activities also have preceding activities upon which they depend. This dependency (called relationships) helps form the network structure. Furthermore, based on this example, the wedding project would only be complete once the reception ends.

This might lead you to wonder why we need WBS Elements if we have Activities, or why we need a Network of Activities if we have WBS Elements in a WBS? Keep in mind, the WBS is a hierarchical representation of the project to help manage costs, budgets, and in some cases revenues, while the Network describes work to be done (Activities), the relationships (dependencies) between them, and the order in which they must be completed.

However, this does not mean WBS Elements and Activities are independent of one another. In fact, when managing projects, activities are assigned to WBS Elements. Doing so facilitates planning, managing, and closing out projects. Figure 77 shows the assignment of activities to WBS Elements for our wedding example. It is important to note that an activity may only be assigned to a single WBS Element, while a WBS element may have none, one, or many activities assigned to it.

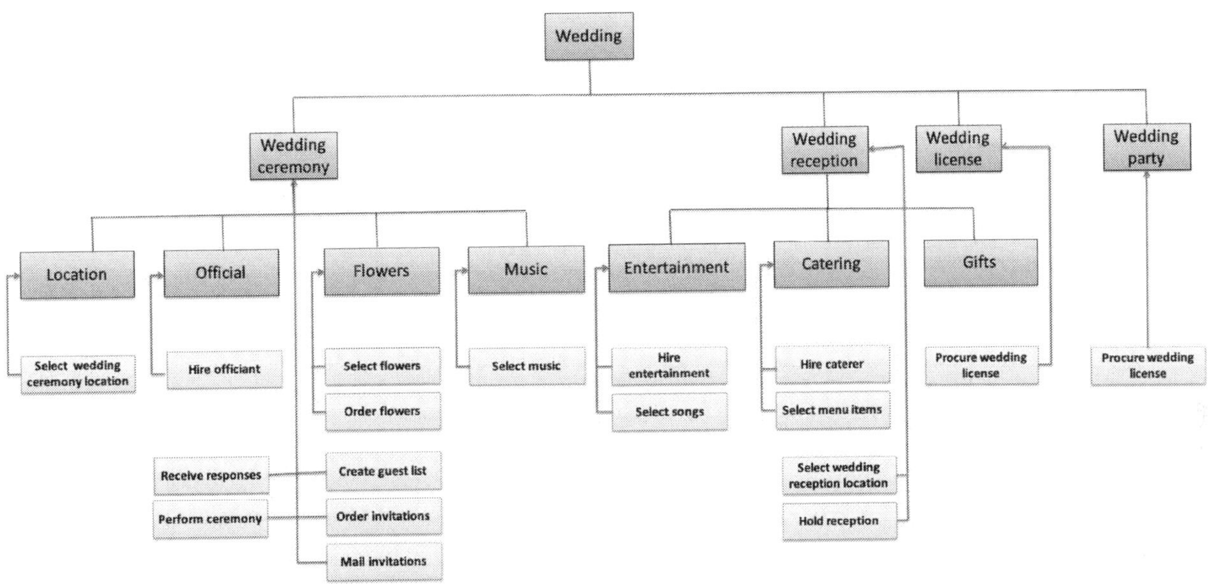


*Figure 77: WBS and activity network shown together with the connections between WBS elements and activities explicitly shown*

## Work Breakdown Structure (WBS) Elements and Operative Indicators

To fully gauge how WBS and Network tools help with project management, we will look at WBS Elements and Activities more closely. SAP provides project teams with some basic functionality surrounding WBS Elements and Activities. Understanding the functionality of each will improve our understanding of the project as a whole. To begin, SAP designates one or more Operative Indicators for each WBS Element in a project. The operative indicators tell project team members whether the WBS Element is used to plan costs (Planning element), collect costs (Account assignment element), and/or collect revenue Billing element). Figure 78 shows the list of Operative Indicators as well as the icons we will use to demonstrate how they are associated with each WBS Element.

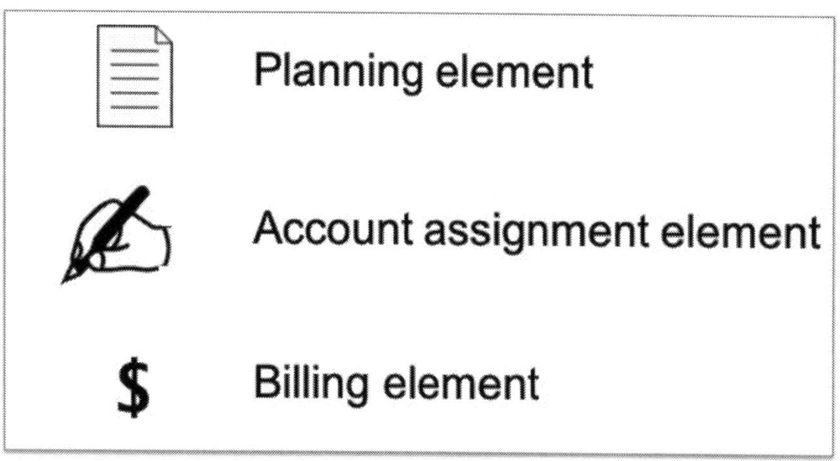


*Figure 78: Operative indicators*

Figure 79 shows operative indicators superimposed on top of WBS elements. This gives us insight into how SAP can help project team members plan, manage, and close a project.

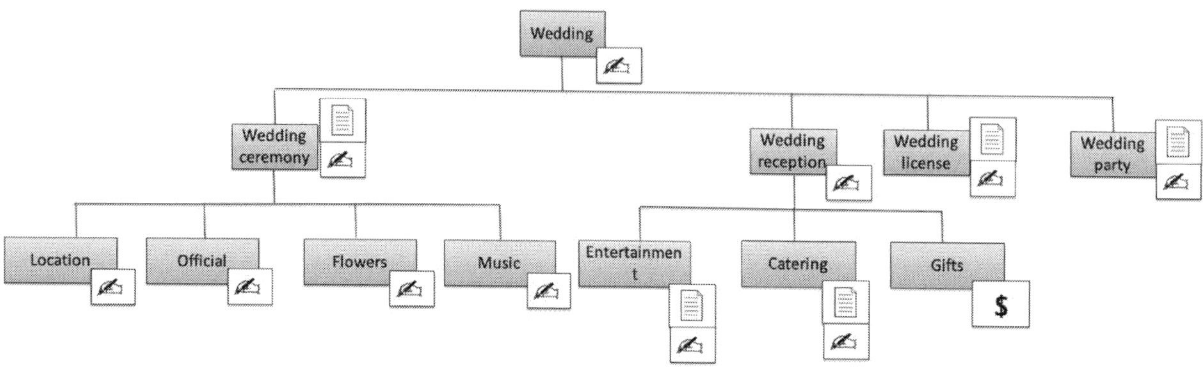


*Figure 79: WBS elements with Operative Indicators superimposed*

Let us begin with planning. If we look closely at Figure 79, we can see that costs are planned at various WBS levels. What should be obvious to you is that the Wedding License and Wedding Party WBS Elements are planned at their own levels. However, the Wedding Ceremony and Wedding Reception WBS Elements are planned at different levels. The Wedding Ceremony WBS Element is planned at a high level, meaning costs associated with the Location, Official, Flowers, and Music are not planned individually, but rather collectively at the Wedding Ceremony level. On the other hand, the Wedding Reception costs are planned on a more detailed level. To support this, the costs of Entertainment and Catering are planned individually at the level below the Wedding Reception level. This exemplifies the flexibility that SAP Project Systems provides for planning project costs.

Each WBS element with the "Account assignment" operative indicator acts as a cost collector (as discussed in Management accounting), and the costs associated with that WBS Element are posted directly to it.

The only Billing Element in our example is Gifts, which we can use to record any monetary or other gifts. These two operative indicators are used to help manage projects as they are progressing. Typically, at period-end closing, those costs and revenues that were posted are settled. We will discuss settlement a little later in this chapter.

As we briefly discussed at the beginning of this chapter, in addition to Operative Indicators, WBS Elements serve several other functions:

- Planning dates and Recording actual dates
- Creating and Managing Budgets
- Posting of cost commitments
- Planning and posting costs and revenues
- Managing payment information (incoming and outgoing)
- Period end closing (settlement)

WBS Elements are used to help plan and manage dates in the project. For rough-cut planning, the project leaders may want to enter some basic dates for each WBS Element to provide an overview of when and how long it will take for starting and completing all aspects of each WBS Element. Other dates will also include dates that get scheduled in the project as well as the actual dates recorded for the WBS Elements. We now know that WBS Elements can be used for planning costs, which is generally a method for requesting a budget for the project. As costs are planned at the Planning Element levels, these costs can be rolled up to the Project Definition to support the request for a budget.

Funds can be made available to WBS Elements according to the budget using Availability Control in SAP, which we discuss later in this chapter. While discussing budgeting as one of the functions of WBS Elements, it makes sense to also address the concept of Commitments as a function of WBS Elements. A commitment can occur when we have a planned expense against budgeted funds, usually in the form of a purchase requisition (PR) or purchase order (PO). For a commitment to take place, the purchasing document (PR or PO), must include the WBS Element as the account assignment object in the line item. When that happens, the user can see committed costs against assigned budgeted funds for a WBS Element.

While WBS Elements with the Planning operative indicator allow for the planning of costs, we know that WBS Elements with the Account Assignment indicator are used for posting actual costs. Additionally, WBS Elements with the Billing operative indicator are used for posting revenue. Thus, the planning and posting of costs, and the posting of revenue are also functions of WBS Elements.

Payment information can also be seen in a WBS Element. From a business perspective, payments are outgoing for costs and incoming for revenue. Any incoming or outgoing payments, planned or posted, can also be managed in the WBS Element.

Finally, project team members will want to periodically evaluate the progress of a project and ensure that all costs and revenues are accurately posted and settled accordingly. These actions are generally performed at period-end closing. Settlement is among a number of action items performed at period-end closing.

Similar to WBS Elements, there are functions associated with Activities:

- Activities can be Internally processed
- Activities can be Externally processed
- Activities can be Service activities
- Activities can be Cost activities
- Materials can be planned on activities
- Milestones can be managed on activities
- Period-end closing (settlement)

Activities can be either internally processed or externally processed. To help make sense of the difference, we will look at two different activities in our wedding example. We have identified the mailing of invitations as an activity. This is an activity that would be considered internally processed, because we will use internal resources to perform it. Each invitation needs to be addressed, stamped, and placed in the mail to the invitees. Assuming that these steps are not outsourced as a service, members of the wedding party, family, and/or friends will perform these tasks. Their ability to successfully complete these steps depends on their availability to do so. We refer to this availability as capacity. Recall from the Manufacturing Execution chapter that work performed internally requires a work center and available capacity. That same concept applies to internally processed activities. In a business sense, internally processed activities could include production orders, maintenance orders or even internal orders. These are all typically performed internally by the enterprise.

An externally processed activity is procured externally. This generally requires a purchase order for services performed. Using our wedding example, we can identify catering as externally processed. We might hire a caterer to perform this activity. In other words, that service is a purchased activity for the project. In the purchase order, it would make sense then to include the Catering WBS Element as the account assignment object in order that costs can be posted to it when the activity is completed. There are other forms of activities (Service and Costs) which will be addressed in your certification course materials.

Materials are another function of activities and can only be planned for activities, not WBS Elements. For example, the physical invitations must be purchased before they are to be mailed to invitees. The invitations would be considered materials used in the project. Those materials are required for the activity

Mail Invitations. When purchased, the materials are listed in a purchase order, again with an account assignment object. Before they are received for the project, a commitment can be seen for the costs associated with these materials. Once received, the committed costs will become actual costs. Thus, the posting of actual costs is also a function of Activities.

The completion of an activity can also be used as a milestone for billing in projects. Our wedding example is not a very good representation of this, but if we were to associate billing with our wedding example, the activity, Mail invitations could serve as a milestone. Once invitations are placed in the mail, it generally triggers invitees to send gifts to the wedding couple. Although the gifts may or may not arrive until the wedding reception, the mailing of the invitations can be identified as a milestone from which revenue will soon be posted.

Finally, as with WBS Elements, project team members will want to periodically evaluate the progress of a project from an activity perspective. All costs need to be accounted for and settled. Again, these actions are generally performed at period end closing.

## Phases of a Project

Now that we have a pretty good understanding of WBS Elements and Activities, we can once again look into the various phases associated with a project. Projects can differ, but generally speaking, the different phases for each project are relatively unchanged and Figure 80 shows them.

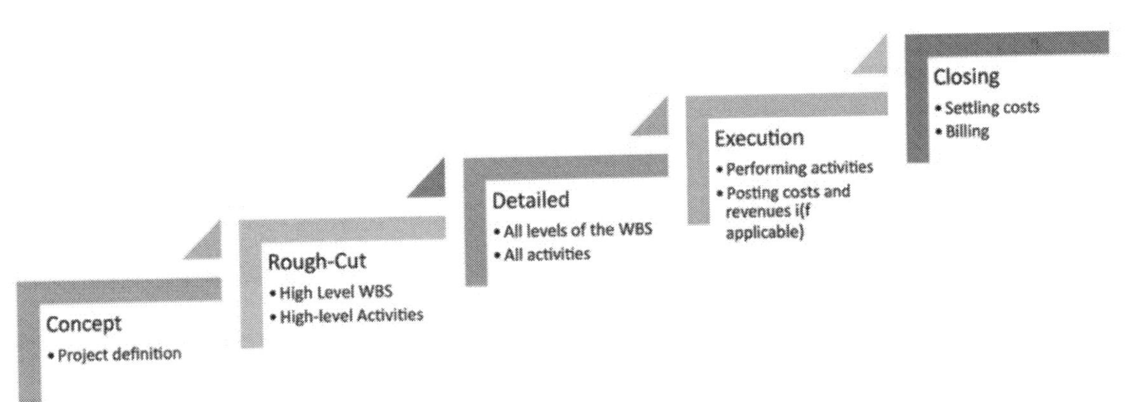


*Figure 80: Phases of a project*

Let us apply Figure 80 to what we know about WBS and Activities. Using the wedding example, the Concept phase occurs when the wedding couple begins discussing the wedding. That phase is represented in Figure 81 (which we saw earlier as Figure 73).

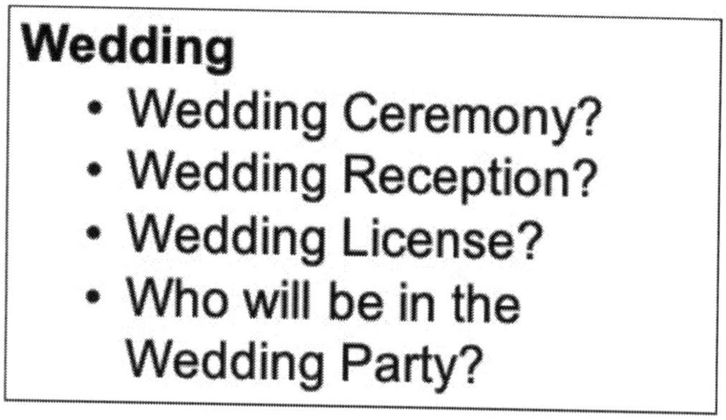

Wedding
• Wedding Ceremony?
• Wedding Reception?
• Wedding License?
• Who will be in the Wedding Party?

*Figure 81: The high-level considerations that we looked at earlier in Figure 73 represents the concept phase for this wedding*

The concept phase can be used to initiate the planning of the project at a very high level. No detail at all is included. The Project Definition is clearly identified and then a basic idea of other things to be considered is also included. The project then moves to the Rough-Cut phase. Here, WBS Elements are added to the Project Definition and are organized in a hierarchy as Figure 82 shows. (We saw this earlier as Figure 74).

Wedding
Wedding ceremony
Wedding reception
Wedding license
Wedding party

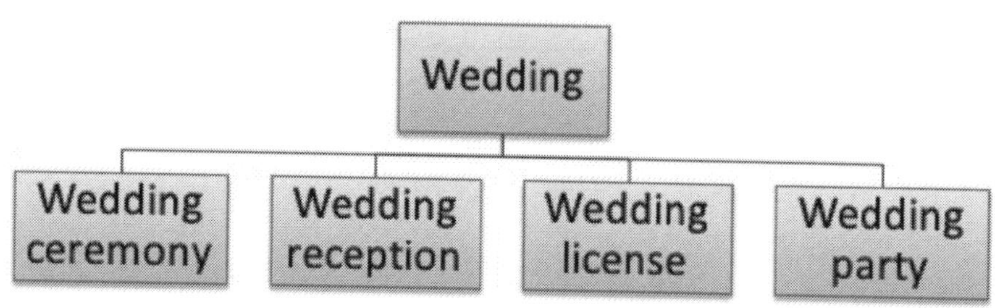

*Figure 82: Rough-cut phase of the wedding project (shown earlier as Figure 74)*

Notice the absence of activities in the rough-cut phase of our example. As a matter of fact, the project is still shown at a high level, with no detail included. In our example, we haven't included activities. It is possible to include activities during the rough-cut phase. However, any activities included here would also be at a high level, with no detail.

It is at the next phase of the project where all the Activities and WBS Elements are included. This is the Detail phase shown in Figure 83.

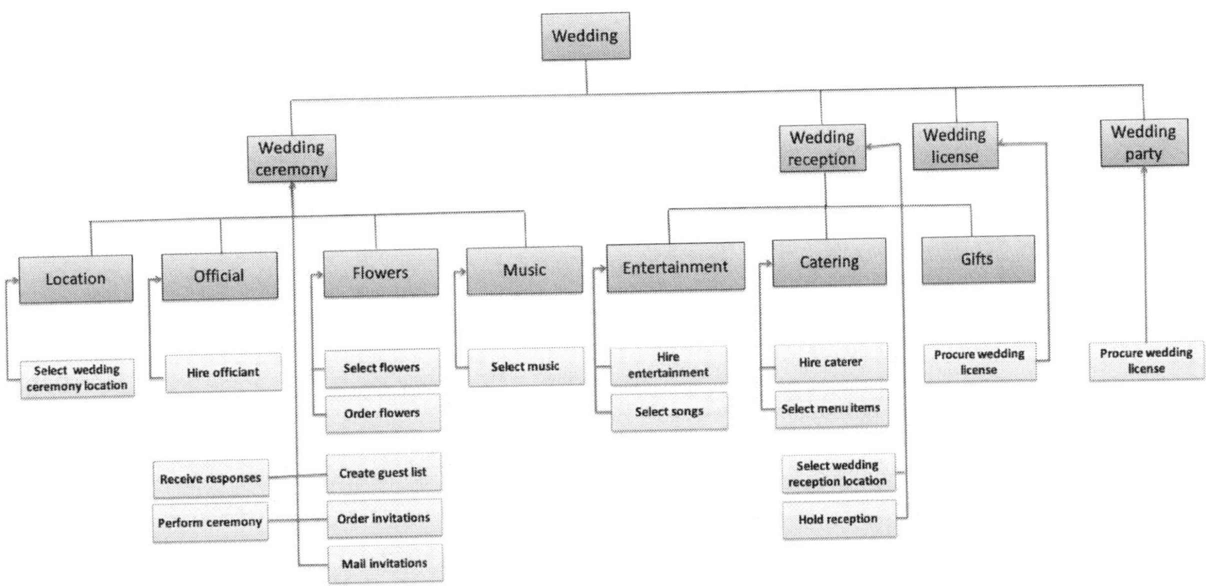


*Figure 83: Detail phase of the wedding project (previously shown as Figure 77)*

The discussion about the WBS Elements and Activities helps put the project phases into perspective. Though we discussed them to a small degree earlier in this chapter, only now can we start piecing all of this together. The remaining phases in the project are the Execution and Closing phases.

## SAP Tools in Project Systems

SAP provides project team members with an assortment of tools to work with projects. There are many similarities between them, which allow users to work with the tools with which they are most familiar and comfortable. One of the primary objectives of this text is to provide you with business context to increase your knowledge and to facilitate your learning of the SAP TS410 materials. However, it is necessary at times to deviate somewhat and provide you with more in-depth insight into SAP. This is one of those times.

There are two primary tools that SAP provides for working with projects. They are the Project Builder and the Project Planning Board. Both provide users with the capability of achieving the same results. Users can create, save, release, and edit projects using either or both tools. For simplicity, we will focus on the similarities and differences between these two tools. Figure 84 illustrates these.

As you can see, the major differences between the Project Builder and the Project Planning Board are mostly navigational. Having both tools available allows users to work comfortably in an environment they are used to. The Project Builder offers an indented tree navigational feature with expandable and collapsible menu objects and manages data editing in a main work window. A user can call up a template of a project, or portion of a project and create a new project by copying it. In addition to this, users can also call up a worklist of recently accessed projects to simplify navigation. The Project Planning Board offers a more graphical experience for the user. The key interface is an interactive Gantt chart where users can call up and work with both WBS Elements and Activities. In addition, the Project Planning Board offers users access to graphical overviews of materials, capacities, and cost/revenue information in the project. Like the Project Builder, the Project Planning Board also allows users to call up a template of a project, or portion of a project and create a new project by copying it.

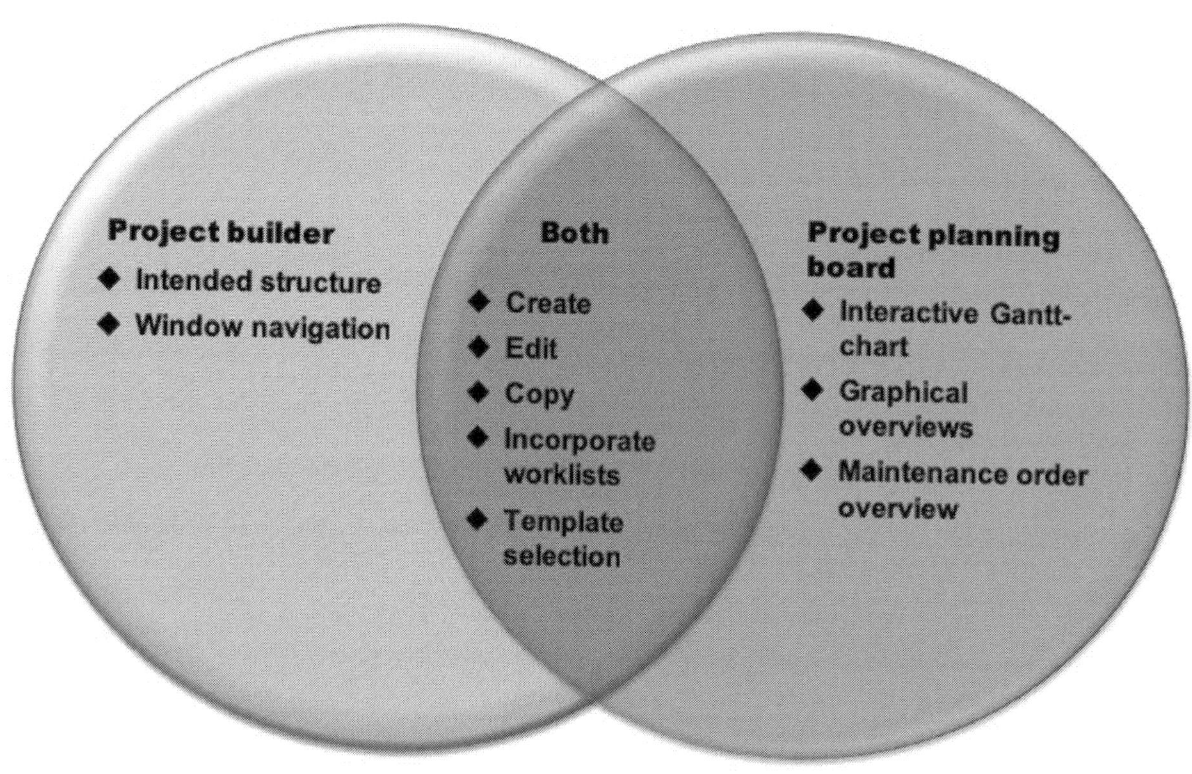


*Figure 84: Features supported by Project Builder and Project Planning Board*

Finally, the Project Builder and the Project Planning Board have links to viewing and working with the project using additional graphical tools. Users can view the WBS in a Hierarchy Graphic, and the Activities in a Network Graphic. The user can also edit both WBS Elements and Activities from these two additional views.

## Cost Planning and Budgets in Project Systems

Perhaps one of the most important aspects of projects is the planning of costs. There are many different methods for planning costs, but we will focus on just a few of them. To assist us in understanding cost planning, let us again refer to our wedding example. Recall that not all of the WBS Elements received the Planning operative indicator. Only those WBS Elements with the Planning Operative indicator will be used for planning of costs. We saw the WBS with operative indicators in Figure 79. We repeat that in Figure 85.

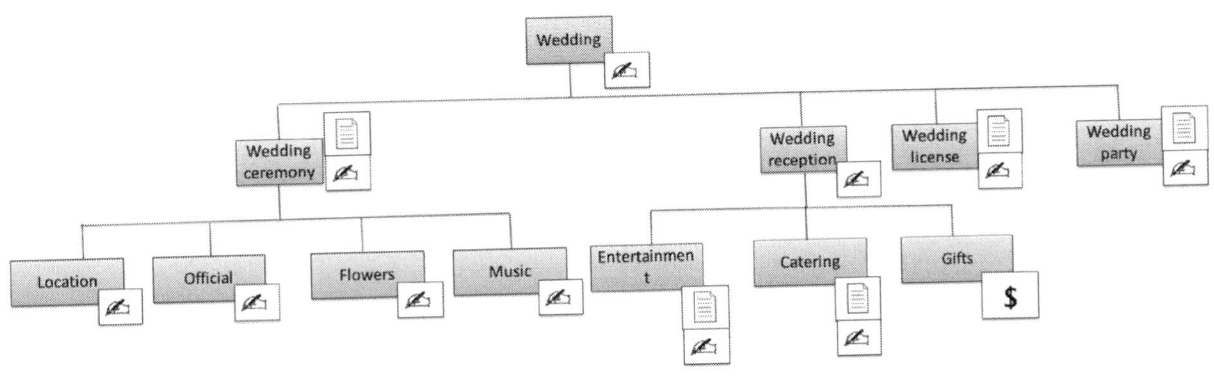


*Figure 85: WBS with operative indicators*

As noted earlier, the costs associated with the Wedding Ceremony WBS Element are planned at its own level. While costs associated with the Wedding Reception WBS Element are planned at the WBS level beneath it. Let us first consider the planning of costs for Wedding Reception. Since these costs are planned at the lower-level WBS Elements, we need to take those into consideration. We would then have to plan costs for Entertainment and Catering individually. To plan these costs, we could use the activities associated with each of them as shown in Figure 86.

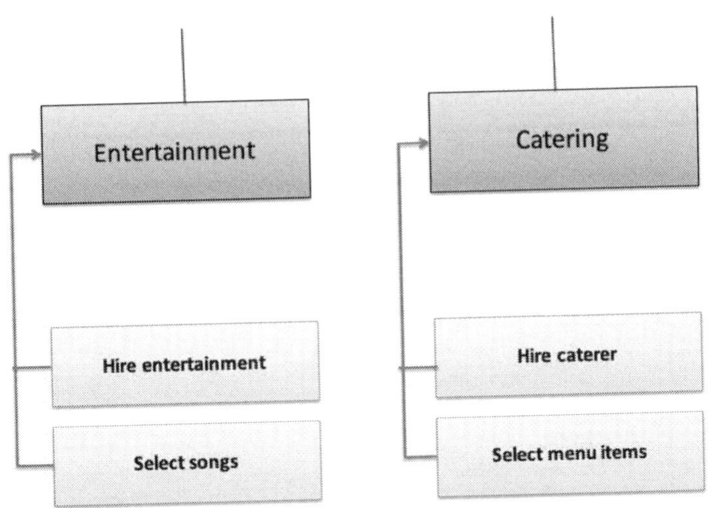


*Figure 86: We can plan costs for Entertainment and Catering WBS elements through the costs of their associated activities*

Since there are costs associated with the activities assigned to these WBS Elements, one could plan the costs on these activities and use those costs to plan the cost at the WBS level. While planning these costs for the wedding, suppose a band provided a cost quotation to the wedding couple. Should the wedding couple decide to hire that band, they could plan the costs for this externally processed activity of hiring entertainment, which is then used to plan the cost at its respective WBS Element: Entertainment. Likewise, as we discussed earlier, the hiring of a caterer is also an externally processed activity. Similarly, costs for catering could be planned in the external activity, and those costs used to plan the costs at the Catering WBS Element. Once we have the planned costs for these two WBS Elements, they can be used to determine the planned costs for Wedding Reception.

In the case of the Wedding Ceremony WBS Element, those planned costs are not derived from lower-level WBS Elements or Activities. The planning of these costs will have to be done differently. One potential method for planning these costs is a method called, Overall Planning. In this case, the wedding couple could simply research and get some insight into what a wedding ceremony normally costs and use that overall value as the planned cost for the Wedding Ceremony WBS Element.

There is not a single method for cost planning that can be labeled as being the best. The method which is best is the method that is most appropriate for the situation. Cost planning is not only one of the most important aspects of working with projects; it can also be one of the most challenging. SAP offers an alternative tool called SAP Easy Cost Planning. SAP Easy Cost Planning offers the use of planning templates and simple data entry fields to help with complex cost calculations.

One of the reasons cost planning is so important is that it provides the basis for budget requests. To see how this works, consider our wedding example again. Looking at Figure 87 we can see that costs are planned for WBS Elements labeled with the Planning operative indicator. Those planned costs can then be rolled up to higher WBS Elements, and ultimately to the Project Definition (upward arrows). This method forms the basis of the budget request. Once a budget request is made, an approved budget is created and released top-down in the WBS.

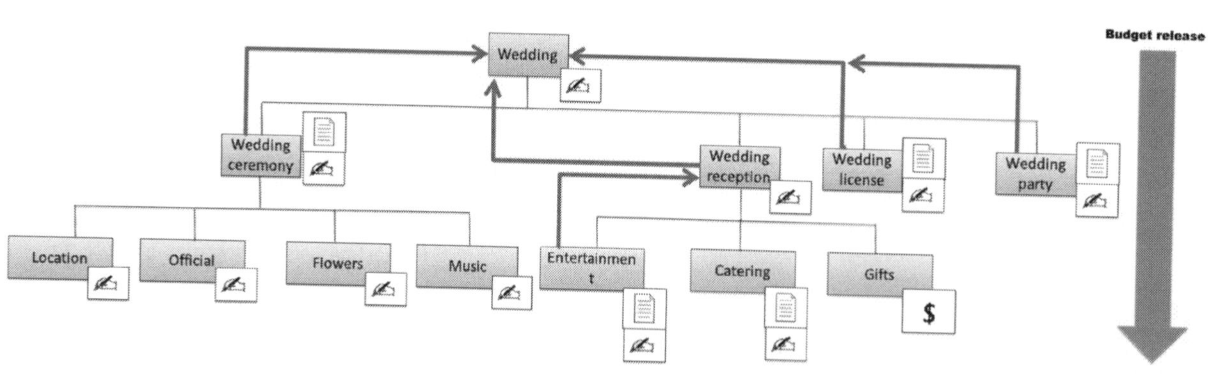


*Figure 87: Costs roll up based on the WBS hierarchy whereas budget is released top-down*

In SAP, the budget release is managed with Availability Control. Availability Control provides flexibility in managing the project budget. Availability Control manages changes to the budget which may include changes in budgeted values as well as reallocation of budgeted funds. It also offers flexibility regarding how much and when to release budgeted funds. Funds can be released and allocated to all levels of the WBS at one time or the budget can be released in increments at different WBS levels.

Project team members will also want to have visibility into the budgeted funds, planned costs, actual costs, and committed costs for WBS Elements. SAP provides two options to help manage this visibility.

Users can take advantage of Passive Availability Control or Active Availability Control. Passive Availability Control gives project team members the capability of running cost and budget reports on WBS Elements. From these reports, the user can see budgeted funds, planned costs, actual costs, and committed costs. In doing so, the project team members can manage their costs against the budgeted funds and see where they are at risk of exceeding the budget. There are times when project team members may want the system to generate a warning message when planned, actual, or committed costs are close to exceeding the budgeted funds for a WBS Element. For such cases, SAP also offers Active Availability Control.

## Posting Actual Costs and Dates in Project Systems

After having spent significant time discussing the planning and budgeting of projects, we now move on to the execution phase. While we spend time on this phase, you should be reminded of the functions of WBS Elements and Activities, as well as their relationship to one another.

Remember that actual dates, costs, and payments are posted to WBS Elements. Functions of Activities include the association with materials, actual costs, and milestones for billing. Let us take a look at one of the activities and WBS Elements in our wedding example (Figure 88).

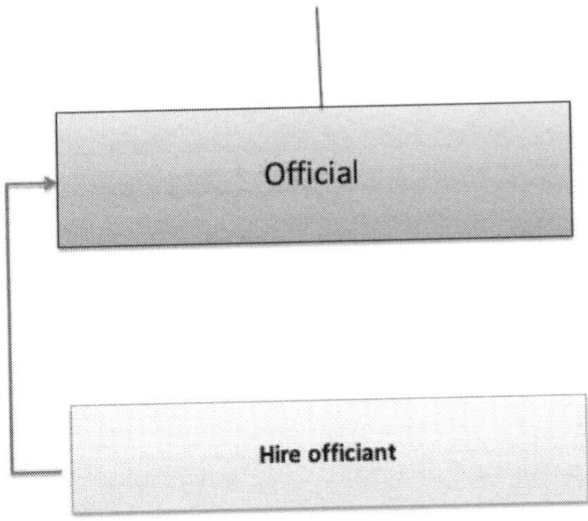


*Figure 88: An externally processed activity*

We can identify the activity, Hire an Officiant as an externally processed activity. This means, it will require the use of the purchase process for consumption in MM Procurement which we discussed in an earlier chapter. If we were using SAP to procure the services of an officiant, we would create a purchase order and include the WBS Element, Official as the account assignment object. We can use that WBS Element as an account assignment object because in our example, we gave it the operative indicator, Account Assignment, which means it is used to collect costs. When the purchase process is completed, dates associated with the purchase as well as actual costs are collected in the WBS Element, Official.

Now let us look at another example, except this time we will demonstrate how this works with an internally processed activity. Since we are familiar with the activity, Mail invitations, let us use that example (Figure 89).

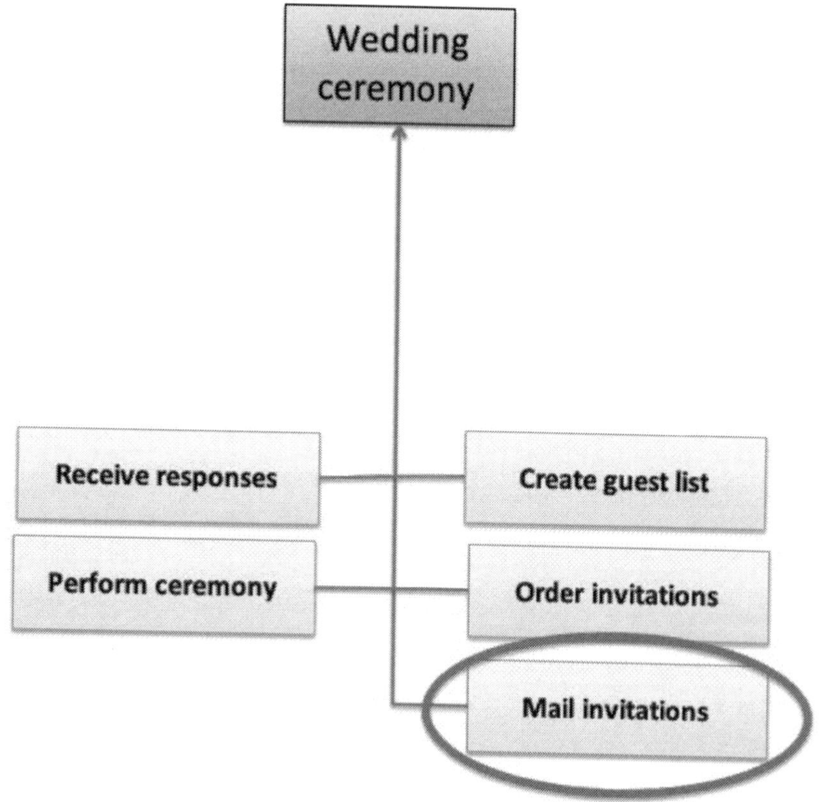


*Figure 89: An internally processed activity*

Again, we will look at this example from the perspective of using SAP. In this example, we have a lot of things to consider. First off, we could create an order in SAP for this activity so that it can be managed as an internally processed activity. An activity that is internally processed would contain operations. These operations are similar to what we discussed in routings for production. The operations are assigned to a resource, like a work center, so that capacity can be checked, and the work can be scheduled. When the work is completed, a confirmation is performed, and costs are posted to that Activity.

In the context of our wedding example, the mailing of the invitations is being performed by one or more family members. The family is essentially a work center in that the scheduling of the family members to do this work is dependent on their availability. When the invitations have been mailed, the operation is complete, and this is considered the confirmation.

At this stage for the internally processed activity, notice that the actual costs have only been posted to the Activity and not the WBS Element, again reinforcing what we already know. That is, functions of Activities include materials and actual costs. That may lead you to ask, when and how does the cost of the Activity, Mail invitations get posted to the WBS Element Wedding Ceremony? That is a very good and insightful question, and the answer to that is: At period-end closing when we perform settlement. That is the next topic of discussion.

## Settlement in Project Systems

At period-end closing, project team leaders will want to evaluate the progress of the project, but equally important, they will want to properly allocate costs and revenues. The further allocation of costs and revenues is referred to as settlement. Settlement is not foreign to us as we have discussed it in earlier chapters, notably during the discussion on Order-Related Cost Object Controlling. Settlement occurs using a Settlement Rule. A Settlement Rule defines who the receiver(s) will be for the allocation of costs or revenues. SAP offers two options for settlement in Project Systems. One of these options is Direct Settlement. During Direct Settlement, the sending cost object (WBS Element or Activity) will settle directly to one or more receivers as defined in the Settlement Rule. To demonstrate how this works we will again refer to our wedding example. Suppose the bride-to-be's family has agreed to pay for the entire wedding. In SAP we would create a cost center for the family. At the end of the period (typically at month end), all costs will be settled to that family (Settlement Rule). Using the examples from the previous section, the WBS Element, Official and the activity, Mail invitations would settle their costs directly to the family cost center. This form of Direct Settlement can be seen in Figure 90.

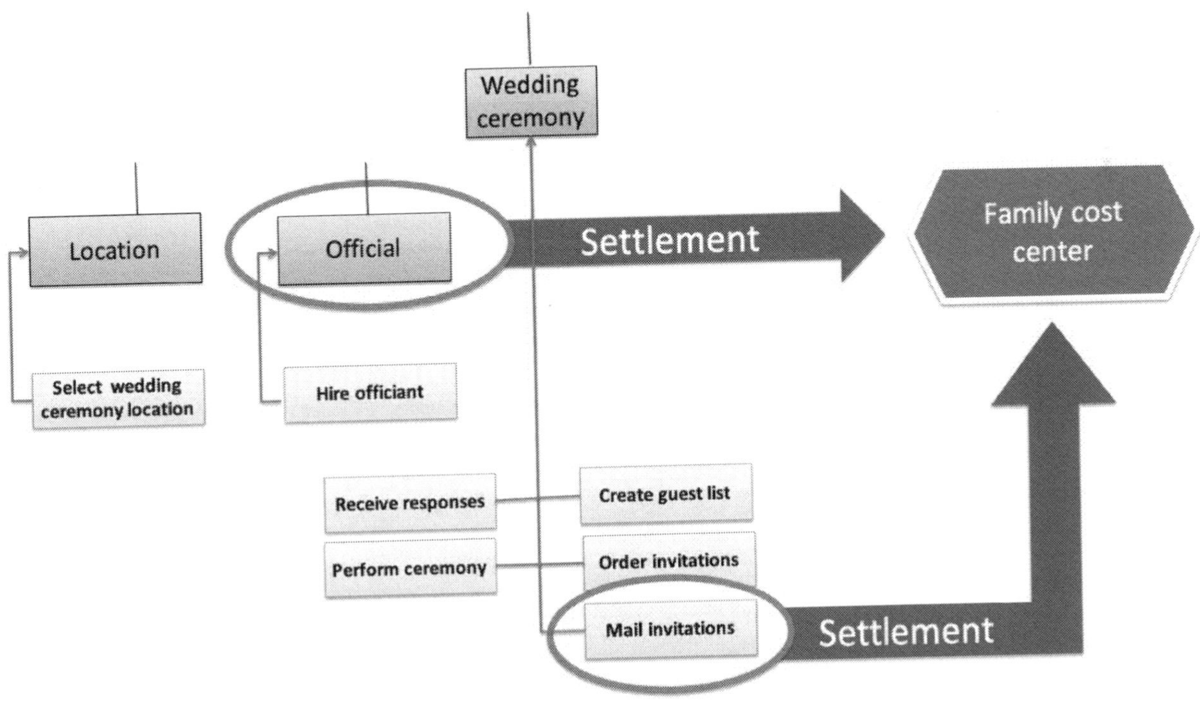


*Figure 90: Direct settlement*

The second option for settlement is called Multi-level Settlement. In Multi-level Settlement, the Activities are settled upwards in the project to their respective WBS Elements, and WBS Elements are settled upwards in the project to the next level WBS Element. This continues until all costs are eventually settled to the Project Definition. The Project Definition then settles to a predefined settlement receiver according the Settlement Rule. Using the same example as above we will perform settlement again, only this time we will demonstrate Multilevel Settlement.

Once again, assume the bride-to-be's family has agreed to pay for the entire wedding, except this time we are not going to settle WBS Elements and Activities directly to the Family cost center. This time we will use Multi-level Settlement and settle the costs of the Internal Activity, Mail invitations to its respective WBS Element, Wedding Reception. We will also settle the Official WBS Element up to the Wedding Ceremony WBS Element since that is the WBS Element at the next level. Since Wedding Ceremony is assigned to the Project Definition Wedding, it must then be settled there as seen in Figure 91

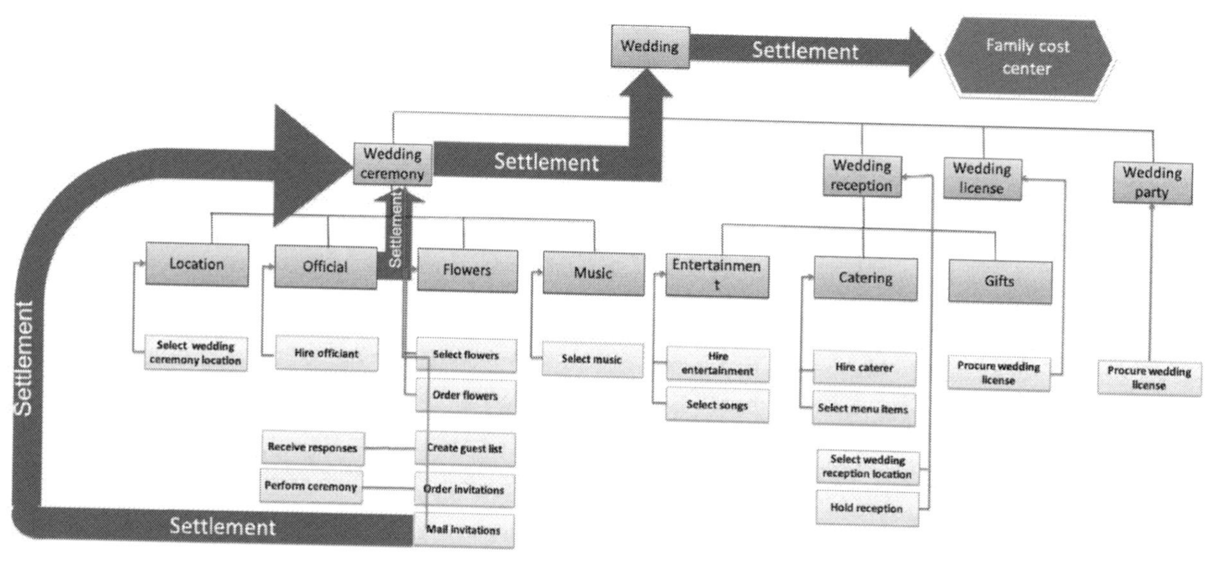


*Figure 91: Multi-level settlement*

## Summary of Project Systems

By now you should have noticed that SAP Project Systems involves a great deal of integration across various SAP modules. Keep in mind that this chapter – like the unit on Project Systems in the TS410 certification course – is not designed to teach one how to manage a project. Its intent is simply to provide you with information on the tools available to project managers and project team members.

## Review questions: Project Management

(You can find answers to these questions on page 245. To answer the questions marked with an asterisk (*), you will need to have read the official SAP course materials.)

1. Which of the following represent the organizational levels specific to project management? (one)
   A. Company code
   B. Plant
   C. Storage location
   D. Project management in SAP has no organizational levels to itself
2. Define the characteristics of projects.
3. Which objects of a project are structured hierarchically? (one)
   A. Project builder
   B. Project planning board
   C. Work breakdown structure
   D. Network
4. Activities in a project are linked together using relationships to form the ________. (one)
   A. Project builder
   B. Project planning board
   C. Work breakdown structure
   D. Network
5. Define a Work Breakdown Structure.
6. Define Activities.
7. Define Networks.
8. Describe the relationship between WBS Elements and Activities.
9. List the operative indicators for WBS Elements.
10. A WBS element that has the operative indicator "Planning Element", is an element for which __________. (one)
    A. costs and revenues are planned
    B. materials are planned
    C. MRP will create planned orders
    D. a G/L account is assigned
11. A WBS element that has the operative indicator, "Account Assignment", is an element for which ______________. (one)
    A. costs are planned
    B. costs are posted
    C. revenues are posted
    D. a G/L account is assigned

12. A WBS element that has the operative indicator, "Billing Element", is an element for which ____________. (one)
    A. costs are planned
    B. costs are posted
    C. revenues are posted
    D. a G/L account is assigned
13. List the functions of WBS Elements.
14. List the functions of Activities.
15. List the five phases of a project.
16. Describe the concept phase of a project.
17. Describe the rough-cut phase of a project.
18. Describe the detailed phase of a project.
19. Describe the execution phase of a project.
20. Describe the closing phase of a project.
21. Which of the following are functions of the Project Builder? (three)
    A. Menu navigation
    B. Create projects
    C. Edit projects
    D. Gantt chart navigation
22. Which of the following are functions of the Project Planning Board? (three)
    A. Menu navigation
    B. Create projects
    C. Edit projects
    D. Gantt chart navigation
23. Which of the following are additional graphical tools that are available in SAP Project Systems? (two)
    A. Activity graphic
    B. Network graphic
    C. WBS graphic
    D. Hierarchy graphic
24. The Hierarchy graphic can be accessed from both the Project Builder and Project Planning Board (T/F)
25. Which of the following are graphical overviews available in the Project Planning Board? (three)
    A. Activity overview

B. Capacity overview

C. Material overview

D. Cost overview

26. In order to plan costs on a WBS Element, that WBS Element must be assigned the Account Assignment operative indicator. (T/F)

27. For planning costs for WBS Elements with one or more activities, costs can be planned at the activity level and rolled up to the WBS Element level. (T/F)

28. List different methods for planning costs on projects in SAP.

29. Cost planning in projects is important because it provides the basis for ______. (one)

A. the budget request

B. the budget release

C. Easy Cost Planning

D. settlement

30. Which of the following controls how the budget on a project is released? (one)

A. Budget balance

B. Availability control

C. Activity control

D. Easy Cost Planning

31. List two different versions of Availability Control for projects in SAP.

32. Describe the difference between Active Availability Control and Passive Availability Control.

33. Explain how costs are posted to the project using the MM Procurement process.

34. Explain how costs are posted to the project using activities.

35. Which of the following are settlement options in projects? (two)

A. Single-level settlement

B. Multi-level settlement

C. Direct settlement

D. Indirect settlement

36. Explain the difference between direct settlement and multilevel settlement.

# Answers to review questions

This chapter contains suggested answers to all review questions.

## In-chapter review questions in Big Picture

***Review 1:*** *Look around you and select an object. Make up a BOM for it.*

**Answer**: Obviously, since you could have picked any object whatsoever, we do not provide the answer You should have identified an object and listed the components that might have been assembled to make the object.

***Review 2:*** *If TRUS has to make 50 tables and already has 100 legs, 12 tops, 60 liters of primer and 80 liters of paint in inventory, how much of each material would it need to buy or procure?*

**Answer**: Not considering the materials already in stock, to make 50 tables TRUS would need 200 legs, 50 tops, 100 liters of primer and 100 liters of paint. Subtracting what is already in stock we get: 100 legs, 38 tops, 40 liters of primer and 20 liters of paint.

***Review 3:*** *Refer to tables 2 and 3. If we have to make 10 pieces of material A and have no stock of materials B, C, D and E, how much of each of these materials would we need to procure?*

**Answer**: From Table2 we can see that making 10 units of A requires 30 units of B and 10 units of C. However, B itself has a BOM. Referring to Table 3 we see that to make 30 units of B we will need 60 units of D and 150 units of E. Putting all this together, to make 10 units of A, we will need 10 units of C, 60 units of D and 150 units of E.

***Review 4:*** *Answer the following:*

1. What information does a BOM contain? **The BOM for a material A tells us what other materials and how much of each we need in order to make one unit of A.**

2. What information does a routing contain? **The steps or operations needed to make a material. The routing also shows the work center where each operation needs to be performed and the time required to perform each operation.**
3. What is purchasing lead time? **The time between the placement of the purchase order and the receipt of goods.**
4. What is lot size? **A number such that the material to which the lot size applies can only be purchased in multiples of that number. For example, if a material has a purchasing lot size of 50, then the organization can only order multiples of 50 units of that material.**
5. How many different lot sizes have been mentioned in this document? What are they? **Four lot sizes have been mentioned – one for each of the raw materials.**
6. What is the name of the document that indicates to a vendor what materials and in what quantities we want to buy them? **Purchase order**
7. Where is information about a particular material stored? **Material Master Record**
8. What is the name given to the entity that keeps information about all materials? **Purchase Order**
9. What contains information about a particular vendor? **Vendor Master Record**
10. What is the name given to the entity that keeps information about all vendors? **Vendor Master**
11. To store information about the vendors mentioned in *Table 5*, how many vendor master records would we need? Explain. **Two – one for each vendor**
12. To store information about the materials mentioned in *Table 1* as well as information about a TRUS table itself, how many material master records would we need? Explain. **Five. Four for the raw materials (legs, top, primer and paint) and one for the finished good (the table).**
13. What type of material is a TRUS table? **Finished good**
14. What type of material is paint in the context of TRUS? **Raw material**
15. List the different types of materials discussed in this chapter. **Raw material, Finished good and Trading good**
16. What is a Trading Good? **A material that the company buys and resells without further processing.**

***Review 5:** Answer the following:*

1. How many tables are to be made on March 31? **140**
2. How many legs are needed? **140*4 = 560**
3. How many tops are needed? **140**
4. How many liters of primer are needed? **140 tables * 2 liters per table = 280 liters**
5. How many liters of paint are needed? **140 tables * 2 liters per table = 280 liters**

6. At the latest, when should the purchase order for legs go out? **Legs have a lead time of 1 month. S0 the order has to go out on or before the last day of February.**
7. How many legs should be ordered? **140*4 = 560. However, legs have a lot size of 100 and so we should order 600.**
8. At the latest, when should the purchase order for tops go out? **Lead time is 2 months. So, we should order by the end of Jan.**
9. How many tops should be ordered? **140 tops are needed. With the lot size at 25, we would order 150.**
10. At the latest, when should the purchase order for primer go out? **Lead time is 2 weeks. Hence order should be placed by March 15.**
11. How many liters of primer should be ordered? **280 liters needed. Lot size is 100. So, order 300 liters.**
12. At the latest, when should the purchase order for paint go out? **Lead time is 3 weeks. So, order by March 7.**
13. How many liters of paint should be ordered? **280 liters needed. Lot size is 25. Hence order 300 liters.**

*Review 6: Answer the following:*

1. What is BOM explosion? **Given a material, say X, with its BOM, BOM explosion is the process of computing the raw materials and the quantities needed to make a certain quantity of X. For example, if we have to make 50 cars, what materials and in what quantities would be needed? We will need 200 tires, 50 steering wheels, 50 accelerator pedals, 50 brake pedals, and so on.**
2. What is MRP? Don't just expand the acronym. Instead, give a concrete example of your own. **Given a plan to sell certain quantities of materials (say finished goods), MRP is the process of determining how much of each of the many materials are needed at what times and also adjusting this to reflect what the company already has on hand and the shipments it expects to receive for Purchase Orders already placed.**
3. In the TRUS case, what information should be considered in determining when a purchase order should be sent out? **The purchasing lead time as well as the date on which the material is needed.**
4. What information determines the quantity of an item to be ordered? **BOM explosion to determine the quantity needed for making the items, quantity already on hand and the lot size.**
5. In the TRUS case, all materials needed for producing a table are bought from vendors and therefore MRP only has to produce purchasing documents. Suppose some of the parts to assemble a table are themselves assembled in our own factory, using materials bought from outside, then what additional considerations enter the MRP process? **In this case MRP will also have to account for the time needed to produce these intermediate products.**

*Review 7: Explain in your own words the terms Configuration and Customization.*

**Answer**: in the context of computer software packages, Configuration occurs when organizations use the features provided by a product to select the specific options that they need. For example, what fields should appear on a particular screen. Customization occurs when an organization adds new programming language code to change how a product works.

***Review 8:*** *Find two reasons why Customization might require more time and resources than Configuration.*

**Answer**: Customization requires time and resources for determining the functionality needed and for the whole process of specifying, coding and implementing the new functionality. Developing new functionality through programing requires many people and takes up a lot of time. In addition, there is the risk of the new code not working correctly under new versions of the product. Configuration does not require any new software development and the process of determining the necessary functionality is a lot less complex.

***Review 9:*** *Answer the following:*

1. Name two company codes in ERPI that cannot share costs with company code 7000.
2. Name two company codes in ERPI that can share costs with company code 3000. **Any company code that is not in the same controlling area as Company code 3000. Thus 4000. 5000. 6000, 7000 and 8000 would all be valid answers.**
3. Can company codes 1000 and 4000 have a common purchasing department? Why or why not? **They cannot, since they do not belong to the same controlling area,**
4. Can company codes 6000 and 7000 share a power generating plant? Why or why not? **They can, since they belong to the same controlling area.**

## In-chapter review questions in Financial accounting

***Review 1:*** *For each of the following items, indicate whether it is an Asset, Liability, Owners' Equity or none of those:*

a. New shares worth $450,000 that the company issued. **Owners' equity**
b. Shares worth $100,000 that this company purchases in other companies as a way of investing some of its earnings. **Asset**
c. $26,500 that the company is yet to pay its suppliers for goods already supplied. **Liability**
d. The value of goods supplied in the above item ($26,500, lying in inventory and not yet used) **Asset**
e. Money in a checking account maintained by the company. **Asset**
f. Money that the company has paid as salary to its employees in the current month. **None of these**

g. The value of a power generation plant that the company maintains to supply power to one of its factories. **Asset**
h. Bank loans amounting to a total of $700,000 that the company has taken out to finance its business operations. **Liability**

***Review 2:*** *In your own words, explain the logic behind the accounting equation.*

**Answer:** It represents the common-sense point that any asset that a company has ought to have been acquired only through money obtained from one of the following: liabilities (loans, accounts payable, etc.,), owners' equity (shares and retained earnings).

***Review 3:*** *Draw up a balance sheet from the following information about John, a kid who operates a lemonade stand:*

- John borrowed $15 from his parents and put $7 from his profits back into his business
- John has equipment (glass jugs, drinking glasses, mixing spoons, etc.,) worth $10.
- John has borrowed 10 lemons from mom and will pay them back after the next weekend. These lemons cost $5.
- John has stocks of sugar worth $5
- Some of John's friends bought lemonade worth a total of $7 during the past weekend and have promised to pay him soon.
- John has $5 in his cash box.

**Answer**:

- **Assets: $27**
    - Equipment: $10
    - Sugar stock: 5
    - Accounts receivable (amount that friends owe): $7
    - Cash: $5
- **Liabilities: $20**
    - $15 borrowed from mother
    - $5 borrowed lemons
- **Owners' equity**
    - $7 profits invested back into the business

***Review 4:*** *For each of the following business transactions, explain whether the total of assets (and therefore liabilities and owners' equity) will have a different value at the end of the transaction than it had at the beginning. If there will be a change, explain which components on the two sides of the accounting equation change. If the total does not change, explain whether there will be any redistribution among the components* *within a particular side of the equation. We have given two examples:*

***Example 1:*** *Company uses cash to buy raw materials worth $500.*

***Answer 1:*** *No change to total assets. Redistribution occurs only within the assets side. Cash decreases by $500 and inventory increases (the company now has additional raw material worth $500).*

***Example 2:*** *Company takes out a new long-term loan for $100,000*

***Answer 2:*** *Total assets increase because the company now has $100,000 more in cash (on the left-hand side of the equation). To compensate, there is now also an additional long-term liability (the new bank loan that the company now has to pay back) of $100,000 on the right-hand side. The two balancing entries therefore ensure that the accounting equation balances.*

a. The company receives raw material worth $50,000 and has been invoiced by the vendor in full. The company has not yet paid for this purchase. **Since the company now has an additional $50,000 worth of raw material, assets have increased**

   by $50,000. The company owes the supplier $50,000 and hence its accounts payable – a liability – has increased by $50,000.

**b.** The company uses $200,000 of its cash to buy back (repurchase) some of its own stock. **Assets decreased by $200,000 because the company now has that much less cash. Owners' Equity decreased by $200,000 because the value of outstanding shares with shareholders went down as well.**

c. The company pays back $100,000 of its outstanding loan. **Cash decreased by $100,000. At the same time, loans – a liability – also decreased.**

**d.** The company pays $50,000 to the vendor mentioned above. **Cash decreased by $50,000. Accounts payable – a liability – also decreased on $50,000.**

e. The company places a new purchase order with a vendor to supply goods worth $35,000. **No financial accounting impacts. Impact only starts when the company receives the good ordered as that will change the value of material stock.**

**f.** The company sells some of its land for $1,000,000. **Value of land – an asset – decreases by $1,000,000. Cash – also an asset – increases by $1,000,000. Thus, this transaction only impacts the assets side of the balance sheet.**

***Review 5:*** *For each account mentioned in the Chart of Accounts in Table 9, identify the category to which it belongs (asset, liability, etc.). Do you see any pattern?*

Answer*:*

1000, 1100 and 1200 are all assets.

2000 and 2100 are liabilities

3000 and 3200 are owners' equity

4000 and 4100 are revenue accounts

5000, 5200, 5300 and 5400 are all expense accounts

Pattern is obvious – all accounts of the same type have the same first digit.

***Review 6:*** *NA*

***Review 7:*** *What is the relationship between the Chart of Accounts and the General Ledger?*

**Answer:** The Chart of Accounts specifies the various accounts that a company wants to use, and assigns a number to each. It represents the structure that a company uses or wants to use for its financial accounting. We could say that it represents the design of a company's accounting structure. Specifically, the Chart of Accounts does not have any details of actual transactions. The General ledger on the other hand represents the actual accounts and holds the various transactions posted to each account. The general ledger (GL) is based on a Chart of Accounts. All the accounts with their account numbers specified in the Chart of Accounts exist in the G/L and we can see the various postings as well in the G/L.

Carrying the design analogy further, the G/L represents a product based on the design that a Chart of Account represents.

***Review 8:*** *If two different company codes use the same Chart of Accounts for their General Ledger, does this mean that they will always have identical transactions posted for each account? Explain.*

**Answer**: No. The Chart of Accounts is just the structure. Each company will post its transactions to its own general ledger. For example, suppose the account number for the expense Account rents in the shared Chart of accounts is 5400. Each company posts rent expenses to this account number in its own general ledger. Obviously therefore the actual transaction amounts posted will differ for the two companies.

***Review 9:*** *What is impact on profits if a company charges less depreciation than it should?*

**Answer:** If we look at the computation of profits in the income statement, we see that various costs as well as depreciation are subtracted from the sales revenues to arrive at the profit. If a company charges a lower depreciation than it should, then it will clearly end up with higher profits.

## End of chapter review questions for Financial accounting

1. What are reconciliation accounts?

   **Answer**: Accounts that accumulate the postings made in subledger accounts. Example: Accounts Receivable account at the Balance Sheet level. This account accumulates all the postings made to individual customer accounts.

2. At what level is the G/L managed?

   **Answer:** Company code

3. What is the organization level corresponding to a legal entity in SAP?

   **Answer:** Company code

4. Which is the smallest SAP entity that supports a full set of books?

   **Answer:** Company code

5. Which organization element supports the creation of Balance Sheet and Income Statements that cut across company codes?

   **Answer**: Segment (or Business Area)

6. Which organization element is concerned with tracking of profits within a component of a company code?

   **Answer**: Profit center

7. Which organization element is concerned with tracking the performance of external market segments?

   **Answer**: Operating concern

8. How many company codes can be in a client?

   **Answer**: Many

9. To how many company codes can a business area be linked?

   **Answer**: Many

10. How many business areas can a company code be linked?

    **Answer**: Many

11. Where does the controlling area fit into the organizational elements of SAP?

    **Answer**: It exists within the Client and has one or more Company Codes assigned to it.

12. How many company codes can be allocated to a controlling area?

    **Answer**: Many

13. What restriction applies to a company code when it is assignment to a controlling area?

    **Answer**: All company codes associated with the same Controlling Area must use the same Operative Chart of Accounts

14. At what level are charts of accounts maintained?

    **Answer**: Client

15. How many charts of accounts can a company code use?

    **Answer**: One (This is true for legal reporting. However alternative charts of accounts are frequently used for consolidation -- such as the case when assigning a company code to a controlling area.)

16. How many company codes within a client can use the same Chart of Accounts?

    **Answer**: Many

17. From where do G/L accounts get their definition?

    **Answer**: Chart of accounts

18. What are the two segments that make up a complete G/L master record?

    **Answer**: Chart of Accounts segment and company code segment

19. Which segment of the G/L master contains general information which describe the account?

    **Answer**: Chart of Accounts segment

20. Which segment of the G/L master contains specific information about how a company chooses to use an account?

    **Answer**: Company code segment

21. **Reconciliation accounts** allow for "real-time integration" of G/L accounts with sub-ledger accounts.
22. The account for an individual vendor or customer would be found in the **sub-**ledger.
23. The Accounts Receivable G/L balance sheet account used to consolidate individual customer receivables is an example of a **reconciliation** account.
24. The feature of the G/L that allows for postings within a document to be broken out into different categories, such as profit centers and segments is called **document splitting**.
25. SAP customers can take advantage of light-weight management accounting functionality by using **profit centers** within FI.
26. In SAP FI, there is a single ledger at the client level called the **leading ledger.**
27. It is always possible to drill down into the line item list of an account from the balance display for a G/L account. T/**F**?

    **Answer**: F: Drilling down into the details of an account is possible only if it is enabled for that account.

28. The vendor business partner includes the following three roles: **General**, **FI Vendor**, and **Supplier**.
29. The reconciliation account number for Accounts Payable in the G/L is stored in which role and which organizational level of the vendor business partner?

    **Answer**: FI Vendor at the Company Code

30. Information about purchasing data for a vendor can be found in which role and which organizational level of the vendor business partner?

    **Answer**: Supplier and Purchasing Organization

31. The customer business partner has information in the following three roles: **General, FI Customer**, and **Customer**.

## In-chapter questions for Management accounting (CO)

***Review 1:*** *Explain in your own words why the information gathered for financial accounting might not be readily usable for decision-making.*

**Answer:** Financial accounting gathers information needed for accurate external financial reporting. This might not always have the level of detail needed for decision-making.

***Review 2:*** *Explain why financial accounting might not be well-equipped for the profitability computations mentioned in the previous paragraph.*

**Answer:** Financial accounting does not necessarily have to disaggregate the information to the extent needed. It only has to do what is necessary for external reporting.

***Review 3:*** *Explain how you might go about calculating the profit margin separately for the two products. Just mention the approach – you do not have enough information to come up with a number.*

**Answer:** Get the direct costs for each product. Get the fair share of the indirect costs for each product. This will give the total costs for each product. Divide the cost for each product by the number of units produced to get the unit cost. Subtract this from the price to get the margin.

***Review 4:*** *From the above description, which costs can we directly attribute to the individual products?*

**Answer:** Direct labor, cost of dedicated machinery and raw materials.

***Review 5:*** *Choose any one of the indirect costs mentioned above (costs of the foremen, supervisors, top management, marketing and sales) and explain one way by which you can allocate the cost to the two products. We cannot specify a single correct answer but thinking about it can aid understanding.*

**Answer:** Foreman and supervisors: Time spent on each product or even an estimate of the level of difficulty of managing the production of each product.

*Review 6: Identify at least one indirect cost that the above narrative has not explicitly mentioned. Rent/space cost, electricity and other utilities, other overheads like cost of accounting department. Cost of IT infrastructure*

**Review 7:** Identify at least two decisions that might be influenced by your calculation of the profit margins of the two products. Discounts to offer, Pricing, Distribution channel choices, Salesperson commissions, Distribution channel commissions.

***Review 8:*** *Suppose we allocate a third of the foreman's cost to product A and two thirds to product B. If it actually turns out that the foreman actually spends an equal amount of time on both products. How would this affect our cost estimates for products A and B.*

**Answer:** We will then under-allocate the cost to Product A and over allocate to product B. We will underestimate product A's cost and overestimate product B's cost.

**Review 9**: *Explain how under or over-allocating indirect costs to a particular product might affect the quality of the decisions you identified in an earlier question.*

**Answer:** We could price a product incorrectly based on an inaccurate cost estimate. We could make poor decisions on commissions.

**Review 10**: *Suppose our company uses machine X only for product A. The company produced 10,000 units of product A during the previous year. How can we compute cost per unit of machine X per unit of product A for the previous year?*

**Answer**: Take the depreciation for the machine for the previous year – say it is $20,000. Divide this across 10,000 units to get $2 per unit of product A.

**Review 11:** *Would it make sense to treat the accounting department of a company as a profit center? Why or why not?*

**Answer:** Usually not. Accounting departments do not generate revenues and hence cannot be seen to generate profits. However, it is possible for a company to actually charge user departments for the use of the services of the accounting department and also allow the accounting department to use its skills and resources to provide services to external clients in addition to their own company. In this situation, it is conceivable, although very un- likely, for an accounting department to be treated as a profit center (as well as a cost center).

**Review 12**: *We know that, in SAP, a client represents a conglomerate company and can have several company codes within it. Given this scenario, can management accounting cut across company code boundaries? Support your answer with examples.*

**Answer**: If the various company codes share common resources – like a purchasing department, manufacturing facilities, buildings, power generation, etc., then these shared costs will need to be allocated across company code boundaries.

**Review 13**: *List three utility costs that might be assigned to the "Administration" cost center.*

**Answer:** Electric, water/sewerage, telephone, Internet services.

**Review 14**: *Name three other possible cost centers in a typical organization. Do not take the easy path and go off the same theme as utilities and name other utilities. Try harder!*

**Answer:** Marketing, IT, Production, etc.

**Review 15**: *Having a cost center called "Administration" helps the company keep track of utility costs and manage them. Suppose a company found that it spent $1,200,000 on utilities during a specific quarter. How might this impact the profit margin that the company calculates for a particular product?*

**Answer:** The fair share of this cost has to be allocated to each of the products that the company makes and hence this plays a role in computing the profit margin.

***Review 16:*** *Through an example, bring out the difference between a cost element and an occurrence of a cost element.*

**Answer:** Cost element is a category of cost. It does not have an actual monetary value associated with it. When an instance of the cost element occurs, that instance has the monetary value. For example, from a personal viewpoint, "food expense" could be a cost element. When we go out and spend $25 at a restaurant, that becomes an instance of the cost element "food expense."

*For a company, "Rent" could be a cost element and the rent of $3,000 that it pays this month would be an occurrence of the "rent" cost element.*

## End of chapter review questions for Management accounting

1. Which of the following questions might relate to the Overhead Cost Controlling component of CO? (two)
   A. What is the unit cost of Product A?
   **B. How much did we spend on utilities in July 2018?**
   **C. How should we allocate the costs of our IT department?**
   D. Did Profit Center X meet its target profit?
2. Which of the following questions might relate to the Product Cost Accounting component of CO? (two)
   **A. What is the unit cost of Product A?**
   B. How much did we spend on utilities in July 2018?
   **C. What was the total cost of production order Y?**
   D. Did Profit Center X meet its target profit?
3. Which of the following questions might relate to the Profitability Analysis component of CO? (one)
   A. Did Profit Center X meet its target profit?
   **B. How profitable was company code 1000 in the Northern Region?**
   C. How much did we spend on utilities in July 2018?
   D. How much did production order Y cost as a whole?
   E. How much did project X cost?
4. Name a cost that might flow from the noted SAP module to CO. Also indicate the component within CO where it might be used. (five)
   A. FI (general): **utility expense – overhead cost controlling**
   B. FI-AA (Asset Accounting): **depreciation – product cost accounting**
   C. HCM (Human Capital Management): **payroll – overhead cost controlling**

D. MM (Materials Management): **purchasing of materials for consumption – overhead cost controlling**

E. PP (Production planning and execution): **product cost – profit center accounting**

F. SD (Sales and distribution): **cost of goods sold – profitability analysis**

5. Indicate one way in which CO might have an impact on FI.

   **Answer:** Product costing, which is an aspect of management accounting (CO), impacts valuation of finished goods.

6. In which organizational element will you find Overhead Cost Controlling?

   **Answer:** Controlling area

7. In which organizational element will you find Product Cost Accounting CO-PCA?

   **Answer:** Controlling area

8. One controlling area can have multiple company codes assigned to it. **T**/F?

9. One company code can belong to multiple controlling areas. T/**F**?

   **Answer:** False. A **Company** Code can belong to only one Controlling Area

10. A Client (in the SAP sense) has many Controlling Areas with each containing multiple cost centers. Cost centers can allocate costs between Controlling Areas. T/**F**?

    **Answer: False.** Cost allocations can occur only between cost centers belonging to the same Controlling Area.

11. Scenario: Two company codes (1000 and 2000) belong to the same controlling area. Account 100000 in company code 1000 is an expense account and account 200000 in company code 2000 is an asset account. What other facts can you infer from these two facts?

    **Answer:** Because these two company codes must use the same Operative Chart of Accounts, the same account numbers must reflect the same type of account in each company code.

12. Explain the mechanism used to transfer accounting information from FI to CO.

    **Answer:** Every expense account in FI is now considered a primary cost account. Whenever an expense is posted in FI, the posting to that primary cost account results in a posting to a cost object in CO.

13. What type of cost elements exist as account types in FI?

    **Answer:** In S/4HANA, both, primary cost elements and secondary cost elements are now account types in the General ledger.

14. Which master data in CO is used to track where costs are incurred within the enterprise?

    **Answer:** Cost center

15. How are cost centers structured in SAP?

    **Answer:** Cost centers are assigned to cost center groups, which are structured hierarchically in SAP

16. What do the cost center groups enable?

    **Answer:** They enable the ability to track and allocate costs across multiple related cost centers.

17. The unit price of an activity in Activity Based Costing is determined by the combination of **cost center** and **activity type**.

18. A company has determined that rental costs will be allocated based on square footage used by various departments. The square footage is fixed across time periods. This is an example of a **01 or fixed** Type Statistical Key Figure.

19. You are preparing an assessment in SAP ERP Management Accounting. Which type of cost element is used to perform an assessment? (one)

    A. Primary

    **B. Secondary**

    C. Revenue

    D. Cost object

20. In SAP S/4HANA, expenses in FI are tracked using which account type? (one)

    **A. Primary cost account**

    B. Secondary cost account

    C. Balance Sheet account

    D. Sub-ledger account

21. A company accumulates costs associated with its cafeteria in a cost center and allocates this cost to other cost centers at the end of each month. What is this process broadly called?

    **Answer**: Allocation

22. A company accumulates costs for a training event in an internal order and then allocates this cost to other cost centers at the end of the month. What is this process broadly called?

    **Answer:** Settlement

23. What is the difference between CO postings to primary cost elements and to secondary cost elements in CO?

    **Answer:** Primary cost elements represent the flow of expenses from FI to CO. Secondary cost elements represent allocations across various cost objects within CO.

24. What two entries must be made for a journal posting in FI to properly post in CO?

    **Answer:** It requires a line entry to a primary cost account as well as the account assignment object responsible in CO.

25. What is the purpose of a periodic allocation?

    **Answer:** To accumulate costs in a cost center that will be allocate to other CO objects at the end of the accounting period.

26. Which of the following is not an example of periodic allocation? (one)

    **A. Direct activity allocation**

    B. Assessment

    C. Distribution

D. Periodic reposting

E. Template allocation

27. For which of the following scenarios would you suggest using an Internal Order? (three)

A. The company is going to produce finished goods and wants to have a mechanism to accumulate production costs.

**B. The company is organizing a promotional seminar and needs to track all costs incurred for this purpose.**

**C. The company is buying a new machine and wants an object to which to charge the cost of the machine as well as future costs incurred on the machine.**

**D. The company is constructing a new parking lot and wants to accumulate the costs incurred.**

28. When does settlement occur for internal orders?

**Answer:** End of each settlement accounting period, or at the end of the life of the order.

29. Which of the following cannot be a receiver when the costs of an internal order are settled? (One)

**A. Profit center**

B. Cost center

C. Project

D. Asset

E. Profitability segment

30. What is the difference between a true cost object and a statistical object?

**Answer:** True cost objects can be allocated costs. Statistical costs are only for information purposes and cannot be allocated.

31. What is the purpose of a statistical cost object?

**Answer:** To collect or compute specific cost statistics for information purposes without having a need for reallocation

32. Which of the following are examples of characteristics used in profitability segments? (three)

**A. Sales region**

B. Cost of goods sold

C. Sales revenue

D. Product

E. Customer

33. What is the effect on the material master when the material standard cost estimate is marked?

**Answer:** The material master record now has a "future" standard price.

34. What is the effect on the material master of releasing a material standard cost estimate?

**Answer:** The "future" standard price becomes the "current" standard price and the "current" price becomes the "previous" price.

## End of chapter review questions for Procurement (MM)

1. Which of the following represent organization levels at which stock levels can be viewed? (four)
   - **A. Storage location**
   - **B. Client**
   - C. Business area
   - **D. Company code**
   - **E. Plant**
2. Which of the following represent valid assignments of the purchasing organization? (three)
   - A. Cross client
   - **B. Cross company code**
   - **C. Cross plant**
   - **D. Dedicated to a single plant**
   - E. Cross storage location
3. A storage location may be assigned to how many plants?

   **Answer**: One
4. How many storage locations can be assigned to a single plant?

   **Answer**: Many
5. A plant may be assigned to how many company codes?

   **Answer**: One
6. How many plants can be assigned to a company code?

   **Answer**: Many
7. Can more than one plant be assigned the same number?

   **Answer**: No
8. What combination is required to uniquely identify a storage location?

   **Answer:** Plant number and storage location number
9. Which of the following represent levels at which material master data is defined? (three)
   - **A. Plant**
   - **B. Client**
   - C. Company code

D. Purchasing organization

**E. Storage location**

10. Which of the following represent the roles of the vendor business partner? (three)

A. Reconciliation role

**B. General role**

**C. FI Vendor role**

**D. Supplier role**

11. Which of the following represent organizational levels at which the vendor business partner is defined? (three)

A. Plant

**B. Client**

**C. Company code**

**D. Purchasing organization**

E. Storage location

12. Which master data contains information about the combination of a material and a vendor?

**Answer:** Purchasing Info Record

13. Which of the following is not part of the standard SAP procurement process? (one)

A. Supply source determination

**B. Goods issue**

C. Purchase order monitoring

D. Invoice verification

E. Goods receipt

14. Which of the following is not a valid scenario in SAP procurement? (one)

A. Procuring a stock item with a material master record

B. Procuring an item without a material master record for consumption

C. Procuring an item with a material master record for consumption

**D. Procuring a stock item without a material master record**

15. Which of the following represent ways by which a purchase requisition can be created in SAP? (four)

**A. Via SAP SRM**

B. Via SAP CRM

**C. Via SAP SCM**

**D. Manually**

**E. Automatically via MRP**

F. From a purchase order

16. For what reason would one maintain a material master record for a material that is being managed in inventory on a quantity base, but not a value base?

    **Answer:** A consumable, such as office supplies (pens, markers, post-it notes) is an example. For many of these items, inventory management on a quantity base is helpful for purposes of reordering.

17. When purchasing material for which there is no material master, how does the material description get populated in the purchasing document (PR or PO)?

    **Answer**: A description is entered manually

18. Which of the following purchasing scenarios requires an account assignment object? An account assignment object is mandatory for procuring: (two)

    A. Any material that is subject to value-based inventory management

    **B. Any material that is not subject to value-based inventory management**

    **C. Any material without a material master record**

    D. Any material for stock which will later be consumed for production of finished goods

19. Which of the following are examples of valid account assignment categories? (four)

    **A. Cost center**

    B. Profit center

    C. Vendor

    **D. Project**

    **E. Asset**

    **F. Order**

20. What is the difference between an account assignment category and an account assignment object?

    **Answer:** Account assignment category: Represents the general types of cost objects that can be used as account assignment objects while purchasing for consumption. Object: The actual object that is serving as the cost collector. For example, "Cost center" is an account assignment category. The specific Cost center 1000 is an example of an account assignment object. Similarly, "Asset" is a category. A particular asset number is be an account assignment object.

21. How does the procurement of a stock item differ from that of a consumable?

    **Answer:** For a stock item, the balance sheet inventory account is debited at the goods receipt posting, with no impact to Controlling. For a consumable, an expense is incurred as soon as the goods receipt is posted. This posts to an expense in FI and a primary cost element linked to that expense account will be used to debit the account assignment object in CO.

22. What type of a purchase order is used when materials are purchased from another plant?

    **Answer:** Stock Transport Order

23. While checking the status of a purchase order, SAP supports status checking for the entire orders as well as individual items in the order. T/F?

    **Answer:** True

24. Which of the following is not part of a purchase order? (one)

    A. Header

    B. Item overview

    **C. Schedule lines**

    D. Item detail

25. Which item category is used for vendor owned inventory? This is inventory that is ordered and received but is still owned by the vendor until it is used. (one)

    A. Standard

    B. Subcontracting

    **C. Consignment**

    D. Third party

    E. Stock transfer

26. Which of the following is not an effect of a goods receipt of materials for a PO? (one)

    A. Creation of a material document

    **B. Posting to a vendor account**

    C. Creation of an accounting document

    D. Update of the purchase order

27. A company wants to select a specific stock type for a material in a PO. How is this set?

    **Answer:** This can be set during the goods receipt on the line item or item detail for each material.

28. When material is received into stock type: quality inspection, will the value of stock increase before it clears inspection?

    **Answer:** Yes

29. The Stock overview is said to be a static view. What does this mean?

    **Answer:** This means this overview shows only the current stock situation and does not automatically update or refresh should there be any goods movements.

30. A material was in a storage location, awaiting quality inspection. After it was inspected, it was changed to unrestricted use stock. Is this goods movement an example of a stock transfer or a transfer posting?

    **Answer:** Transfer posting

31. Will a stock transfer of a material from one storage location to another within the same plant have any financial impact?

    **Answer:** No.

32. All goods movements result in the creation of material documents. T/F?

    **Answer:** True

33. If warehouse management is active, how does a goods-receipt impact warehouse management?

    **Answer:** If the storage location/plant combination assigned for the goods received is linked to a warehouse number, then the goods receipt creates a Transfer Request for Warehouse management and the materials are booked into an interim storage area.

34. Does a goods-receipt for a PO impact the material master?

    **Answer:** If the material received is a stock item, at the time of the goods receipt, the material master will show an increase in stock level and stock value.

35. What is the impact of a goods receipt if QM is active?

    **Answer:** An inspection lot is created.

36. What step completes the logistics portion of the procurement process?

    **Answer:** Posting of the vendor's invoice (invoice verification)

37. Under what conditions would an invoice-posting result in the update of the moving average price in the materials master record?

    **Answer:** If the price on the invoice differs from the price on the PO, then the difference is applied, updating the moving average price.

## End of chapter review questions for Material planning

1. At which organizational level is material planning generally performed? (one)

    A. Client

    B. Company code

    **C. Plant**

    D. Storage location

2. Which of the following represent master data required in Materials Planning? (three)

    **A. Materials**

B. Work centers

**C. Routings**

**D. Bill of materials**

3. Which of the following represent required views in the material master record for Material Planning? (one)

   **A. MRP**

   B. Work scheduling

   C. Accounting

   D. Forecasting

   E. Quality management

4. Explain how each of the following fields in the material master is used:

   MRP Type: **Determines how MRP will plan materials**

   Procurement type: **Determines whether the material is internally produced or externally procured**

   Strategy group: **Determines how independent requirements behave – that is, if a sale occurs, is it treated as forecast sales or as new sales. This has an impact on how material requirement is calculated.**

5. When creating a material master record, you assign it a material type. Which of the following are valid material types? (three)

   A. In house production

   **B. Raw material**

   **C. Finished good**

   D. Externally procured

   **E. Operating supplies**

6. What does the material type determine? (two)

   **A. What views are displayed for maintaining the material**

   **B. How the material number is assigned**

   C. The strategy group assigned to the material

   D. The MRP Type for the material

7. All BOM master records in SAP are single-level. T/F?

   **Answer:** True, A component in a BOM may also contain its own BOM master record, allowing the user to see a multi-level BOM report.

8. What is the difference between the header quantity and the component quantities in the BOM?

**Answer:** The header quantity defines how many or how much of the header item will be produced. That is, it specifies the quantity of the header product which that BOM represents. Component quantities indicate how many or how much of each of the component items are needed to make the quantity specified in the header.

9. In SAP it is possible for a material to have multiple BOMs. These are referred to as versions. Explain BOM versions.

   **Answer:** Many BOMs may exist for the same material. This allows flexibility of producing different output batches of the same material. Also, different plants use different sets of materials to produce the same product.

10. What does the BOM usage field in the BOM header determine?

    **Answer:** It determines the business function for which the BOM is used. Thus far we have seen BOMs for manufacturing. Later we will see that BOMs are also used in *Enterprise Asset Management*, The usage field in the BOM tells us what business process the BOM will support.

11. Which of the following represent valid item categories in a BOM? (three)

    A. In house production

    B. External procurement

    **C. Stock item**

    **D. Non-stock item**

    **E. Variable-size item**

12. Can a consumable material be included as a component in a BOM?

    **Answer:** Yes – that component would require the item category, "non-stock item".

13. In SAP ECC, planning is managed using a Sales and Operations Planning (SOP) table. In SAP S/4HANA, the SOP is being replaced with which process? (one)

    A. COPA planning

    B. Production Planning

    **C. Integrated Business Planning (IBP)**

    D. MRP Planning

14. What is a product group?

    **Answer:** A product group is a group of products with similar planning characteristics. It creates efficiencies in the planning process.

15. The lowest level of a product group hierarchy contains ________ ____________.

    **Answer:** Finished products

16. With respect to requirements in MRP, which of the following statements are true? (two)

A. Planned independent requirements represent customer orders

B. Customer independent requirements are based on forecasts and plans

**C. Planned independent requirements can be based on forecasts and plans**

**D. Customer independent requirements are sales orders**

E. Dependent requirements can be based directly on forecasts and plans

17. Demand management results in the creation of independent requirements. What does MRP create to meet these independent requirements? (one)

    **A. Planned orders**

    B. Purchase requisitions

    C. Production orders

    D. Schedule lines

18. To plan procurement proposals, MRP performs a supply v demand calculation known as the Net Requirement Calculation. Which of the following make up the demand side of that calculation? (one)

    A. Purchase orders

    **B. Safety stock**

    C. Firmed planned orders

    D. Confirmed purchase requisitions

19. The MRP type is used to define how materials are planned. Some materials are planned based on independent requirements, other forms of planning are based on ___________.

    **Answer:** Consumption

20. Which of the following are valid procurement proposals generated by MRP? (three)

    A. Sales orders

    **B. Planned orders**

    **C. Purchase requisitions**

    **D. Schedule lines**

    E. Purchase orders

21. MRP Live is part of SAP S/4HANA. Which of the following is not a feature of MRP Live? (one)

    A. Faster run times

    **B. Planning at individual plants**

    C. More frequent MRP runs possible

    D. Real time insight

22. Which of the following control parameters determines the scope of the MRP run in SAP S/4HANA? (one)

    **A. Processing Key**

    B. Purchase Requisitions

    C. Planned Orders

    D. Schedule Lines

23. Which of the following processing keys is no longer needed in SAP S/4HANA? (one)

    A. NEUPL

    B. NETCH

    C. **NETPL**

24. What is the main difference between the stock/requirements list and the MRP list?

**Answer:** The MRP list is valid ONLY for the current MRP run. If MRP is run again, the original MRP list becomes obsolete. The stock requirements list is dynamic and can be refreshed after additional MRP runs.

## End of chapter review questions for Manufacturing

1. At which organizational level are costs managed in a production order? (one)

    A. Client

    **B. Controlling area**

    C. Company Code

    D. Plant

2. During the manufacturing execution process, which steps include a material availability check?

    **Answer:** An availability check can be performed manually or automatically at the time of the creation of the production order. It is always automatically performed when the order is released.

3. When a production order is created, costs are planned, and the order is scheduled. Which master data is responsible for the scheduling of the order? (two)

    A. Material

    **B.** BOM

    **C. Routing**

    **D. Work center**

4. When a production order is created, materials are reserved. Which master data is responsible for these reservations? (one)

A. Material

**B. BOM**

C. Routing

D. Work center

5. A production order can be confirmed before the release of the order. (T/F)

   **Answer:** False: The order must be released before any goods movements or confirmation can occur.

6. What procurement type would you suggest in the material master for finished goods?

   **Answer:** In-house production

7. What are task lists and what are the different types of task lists in SAP?

   **Answer:** Task lists indicate the steps used in making an item. *Routing* is one type of task list used for discrete manufacturing. For process manufacturing, the set of steps needed to make a product is called a *master recipe*. For repetitive manufacturing (assembly line) it is called a *rate routing*.

8. What are PRTs and what type of data are they?

   **Answer:** Production resources and tools are master data.

9. What field in a work center master record links the work center with a CO object?

   **Answer:** The Costing tab in the work center master record has a field linking the work center to a cost center in CO.

10. Which of the following represent categories of data stored in the work center master record? (three)

    A. Actual cost determination

    **B. Scheduling**

    **C. Costing**

    **D. Capacity planning**

11. What combination in the work center master record is used to define activity prices?

    **Answer:** The costing tab of the work center master record contains a link to a cost center as well as activity types available at that work center. The combination of cost center/activity type is used to derive the activity price.

12. Operations in the routing include time elements. What is an example of a fixed time assigned to an operation?

**Answer:** Setup time. This is the time required to set up the work center to perform the operation. This is a fixed time and does not depend on any quantities produced.

13. Operations in the routing include time elements. What is an example of a variable time assigned to an operation?

    **Answer:** Time per unit – that is, how much time does it take to complete the operation for a single unit of a product. Thus, if the order has "n" pieces, we can calculate the total time for the operation for that order.

14. BOM components not assigned to an operation in a routing default to which operation?

    **Answer:** Components default to the first operation

15. In addition to BOM components, name other master data that can be assigned to an operation.

    **Answer:** PRT

16. Master data in manufacturing support various logistics steps. Which master data in manufacturing also integrates directly with SAP HCM?

    **Answer:** Work Center master data

17. Which of the following steps in the manufacturing process can be automated? (two)

A. Order creation

**B. Order release**

C. Material staging

**D. Material withdrawal posting**

E. Order archiving

18. Which of the following can be directly assigned to operations on a production order? (three)

**A. Materials**

B. Cost center

**C. PRT**

**D. Trigger points**

E. Profit center

19. Which step in the manufacturing execution process will results in the initial financial impact?

    **Answer:** Material withdrawal (Goods Issue)

20. At which step in the manufacturing execution process will labor costs post to the production order?

    **Answer:** Confirmation

21. In what status must the production be before a goods issue can be posted for the order?

    **Answer:** Released

22. In which steps of the manufacturing execution process do availability checks occur?

    **Answer:** Availability checks occur at order creation and release

23. What are the inventory impacts of posting a goods issue to a production order?

    **Answer:** Reservations are reduced. When the order is created, reservations for stock items are generated for the order. Once materials have been issued to the order, the reserved quantity is then reduced by the quantity issued. To be concrete, suppose an order has reserved 200 units of a material. When 50 units are issued, the reservations are reduced to 150.

24. Which of the following accounts are impacted when a goods issue occurs against a production order? (two)

    **A. Stock/inventory**

    B. Product

    C. Overhead

    **D. Consumption expense**

25. The production order is updated when goods are issued against a released production order. T/F?

    **Answer:** True

26. When goods are issued to a production order, does the SAP system create a Controlling document?

    **Answer:** Yes. When goods are issued against a production order an expense is posted in FI for the consumption of the materials issued. A primary cost element will then post this expense as a material cost to the production order. A controlling document is generated to track this cost posting.

27. What two options exist for confirming production?

    **Answer:** Order-based and operation-based confirmations

28. Can goods movements be automated during the manufacturing process?

    **Answer:** When an order is confirmed we can automate the posting of the goods receipt. It is also possible for the goods issue to be automated via the backflush process.

29. Explain the process of backflush and the automated goods issue posting during backflush.

    **Answer:** *Backflush* postings occur when specific steps in manufacturing occur automatically, and in reverse order. Consider this example: Suppose we are producing cars. It is possible to manually post a good issue of 4 tires for each car. The alternative approach is to simply keep the tires on the shop floor, and when a confirmation is posted for the completion of 20 cars, the system can automate the goods issue posting of 80 tires. This process of backflush improves efficiency and reduces errors.

30. Materials from a production order are received into a storage location/plant combination assigned to a warehouse number. What automation occurs in warehouse management because of this goods receipt?

    **Answer:** In warehouse management, a Transfer Requirement is automatically generated for the putaway of those materials.

31. Which accounts are updated when goods are received against a production order?

    **Answer:** Stock account and plant activity account (Primary Cost/Revenue Account)

32. When a production order is settled, what mechanism determines the receiver(s) of the settlement?

    **Answer:** Settlement Rule

33. In the manufacturing process, which step follows the goods receipt? (one)

A. Release

B. Confirmation

**C. Variance Calculation**

D. Settlement

## End of chapter review questions for Chapter 9: Sales order processing

1. Which of the following define a sales area? (three)

    **A. Division**

    **B. Sales organization**

    C. Sales Group

    **D. Distribution channel**

    E. Plant

2. Which of the following organization levels are unique to Sales and Distribution? (two)

    **A. Shipping point**

B. Sales Order

**C. Sales organization**

D. Sales location

E. Product Group

3. How many sales organizations can be assigned to a single company code?

   **Answer:** Many

4. To how many company codes can a sales organization be assigned?

   **Answer:** One

5. Which of the following are examples of distribution channels? (two)

   **A. Internet sales**

   **B. Wholesale sales**

   C. Distribution center

   D. Shipping point

   E. Loading dock

6. What does the Division represent in Sales and Distribution?

   **Answer:** It represents a product line. For example, the Dell computer company may have several Divisions such as: Desktops; laptops; tablets; and servers. These represent different product lines and hence different divisions in Sales and Distribution.

7. Which of the following statements about sales areas are true? (two)

   A. One division can be part of only one sales area

   **B. A single sales organization could exist in several different sales areas**

   **C. A division can be used in defining several different sales areas**

   D. The same combination of sales organization, distribution channel and division can occur in multiple sales areas

8. How many sales areas can a plant be associated with?

   **Answer:** Many – because a plant can be linked with one or more sales organizations.

9. Are sales areas automatically defined based on combinations of existing sales organizations, distribution channels and divisions?

   **Answer:** No. Sales areas must be manually defined for each combination through which sales will occur.

10. What is the role of the plant in SD?

**Answer:** It is the organizational level from which materials are issued for sales and distribution.

11. How would you describe the relationship between plants and shipping points?

    **Answer:** This relationship is many to many. One plant can have many shipping points, and one shipping point can serve many plants.

12. Which component in SAP S/4 HANA determines a customer's creditworthiness when a sales order is created? (one)

    A. Quality Management

    B. Management Accounting

    C. Financial Accounting

    **D. Financial Supply Chain Management**

13. Which steps in the sales order process directly impacts a customer's available credit? (two)

    A. Order creation

    B. Goods Issue

    **C. Billing**

    **D. Payment**

14. Which step in the standard sales order process represents the first financial accounting impact? (one)

    A. Creation of the sales order

    B. Creation of the outbound delivery

    **C. Goods Issue**

    D. Billing

15. Which of the following represent master data relevant to a sales order? (three)

    A. Plant master

    **B. Customer master**

    **C. Output master**

    **D. Condition master**

    E. Price master

16. Which of the following represent mandatory partner functions in the customer master record? (two)

    **A. Sold to party**

    B. Contact persons

    **C. Ship to party**

    D. Billing party

E. Forwarding agent

**Explanation:** Although some of these items are valid partner functions, they are not valid choices here because they are not **mandatory**. Contact person and forwarding agent are not mandatory. Billing party is not a valid choice, however *bill-to party* would have been.

17. Which role of the customer master record contains the partner functions?

    **Answer:** Customer Role (Sales Area)

18. Which role of the customer master record contains the G/L reconciliation account for receivables?

    **Answer:** FI Customer Role (Company Code)

19. What master data determines how documents are communicated or sent to various parties?

    **Answer:** Output master

20. Which of the following are examples of condition master data? (four)

    A. **Material Price**

    B. **Customer/Material Price**

    C. **Discount**

    D. Payment terms

    E. **Surcharges**

21. Which of the following represents the sequence of steps in the standard sales order process? (one)

    A. Sales order> Inquiry> Billing> Payment

    B. **Inquiry> Sales order>Delivery> Billing> Payment**

    C. Inquiry> Sales order> Billing> Delivery>Payment

    D. Sales order> Delivery> Payment> Inquiry

22. A sales order can be created by referencing which documents? (two)

    A. **Sales Inquiry**

    B. Purchase order

    C. **Quotation**

    D. RFQ

23. The structure of a sales order document includes which of the following? (three)

    A. **Header**

    B. Billing

   C. **Line items**

   D. **Schedule lines**

24. Which of the following is required to create a sales order? (three)

   A. Sales group

   B. **Sales area**

   C. **Customer**

   D. **Required delivery date**

   E. Customer material number

25. Which of the following represent flexibility in terms of how sales orders are created? (two)

   A. A purchase order can be the reference document for a sales order

   B. **Can be created independently of any other sales document**

   C. **Multiple pre-sales documents can be combined into one sales order**

   D. Can be based on prior scheduling agreements

26. Which partner functions appear in the header of a sales order? (two)

   A. **Sold-to party**

   B. Payer

   C. **Ship-to party**

   D. Bill-to party

27. Which of the following scenarios would require separate schedule lines for a single line item on a sales order? (one)

   A. **Customer orders 500 units of a material and wants them to be delivered in two separate shipments**

   B. Customer orders two different materials in the order and specifies a different delivery date for each material

   C. Customer places two separate sales orders with separate delivery dates, and one item on each order.

   D. The customer wants all the pieces of the materials on each order to be delivered on the date specified in the respective orders.

28. While placing a sales order, the system determined that the requested date for a material could not be met. What kind of scheduling is used to make this determination?

   **Answer:** Backward scheduling

29. In the above scenario, what kind of scheduling might the system use to propose a new delivery date?

   **Answer:** Forward scheduling

30. The ______________ ____ can be used to find out required fields are missing when creating a sales order.

    **Answer:** Incompletion log

31. Sales orders are considered __________ __________ requirements in MRP.

    **Answer:** Customer independent

32. Under what conditions can multiple sales orders be combined into a single delivery document? (three)

    **A. The delivery dates are the same**

    B. Sold-to party is the same

    **C. Ship-to party is the same**

    D. Plant is the same

    E. **Shipping point is the same**

33. Which of the following documents contain schedule lines? (one)

    A. Billing documents

    B. Invoices

    **C. Sales orders**

    D. Outbound deliveries

    E. Inbound deliveries

34. Picking lists are used to support which logistics process? (one)

    **A. Warehouse management**

    B. Shipping

    C. Billing

    D. Order processing

35. Under what conditions would a transfer requirement be created for an outbound delivery?

    **Answer:** If the plant/storage location combination in the delivery has a warehouse number assigned.

36. You are in the process shipping an item against a sales order. You have created an outbound delivery and look at the stock/requirements list. In a different session, you proceed to a post goods issue for the outbound delivery. When you go back and refresh the stock/requirements list, what changes will occur?

    **Answer:** The stock quantity will be reduced and the requirement for the material associated with the order has been satisfied and no longer appears.

37. Which G/L accounts are affected when a goods issue is posted against for an outbound delivery?

    **Answer:** Stock (inventory) is credited and a stock change account (COGS) is debited

38. Which accounts are affected when a billing document is generated for a delivery?

    **Answer:** The Revenue account is credited, and the customer sub-ledger account is debited. When the posting to the customer sub-ledger occurs, the accounts receivable reconciliation account in the G/L is also debited.

39. Which feature displays all the related documents generated during the sales order process and allows the user to navigate to anyone of these documents?

    **Answer:** Document flow

40. Which of the following modules has direct integration with Sales and Distribution? (three)

    **A. Materials management**

    **B. Warehouse management**

    C. Manufacturing execution

    **D. Material planning**

## End of chapter review questions for Inventory and warehouse management

1. In which of the following scenarios would a goods receipt be required? (two)

    **A. Arrival of materials from a purchase order**

    B. Materials from inventory are needed for a production order

    **C. Finished product for a production order need to be put away in the warehouse**

    D. Materials for a sales order need to be shipped to a customer

2. In which of the following scenarios would a goods issue be required? (two)

    A. Arrival of materials from a purchase order

    **B. Materials from inventory are needed for a production order**

    C. Finished product for a production order need to be put away in the warehouse

    **D. Materials for a sales order need to be shipped to a customer**

3. In which of the following scenarios would a transfer posting be required? (two)

    A. The warehouse confirms a transfer order for an inbound delivery

    **B. Materials on consignment are now needed**

    C. Stock is moved from one plant to another within the same company code

    **D. A material in stock type, "Quality Inspection" is now cleared for use**

4. Which of the following are true about one and two step stock transfers? (two)

A. One step stock transfer results in the creation of two material documents

**B. One step transfer results in the creation of one material document with two line items**

C. Two step stock transfer results in the creation of two material documents with two line items on each

**D. Two step stock transfer results in the creation of two material documents each with one line item**

5. What is an advantage of a two-step stock transfer procedure over a one-step procedure?

   **Answer:** A two-step procedure can be managed with authorization. This means the issuing a receiving party only have authorization in their ow plants. (This obviously does not apply to a Storage location to storage location stock transfer). Additionally, after the first step of the two-step procedure the materials are marked as ***"in transfer"*** at the receiving location.

6. After the first step of a two-step procedure, at which location can the material be found?

   **Answer:** The material appears *in-transfer* in the receiving location because it has not yet been physically received.

7. If valuation occurs during a two-step procedure, at which step does the valuation take place?

   **Answer:** Valuation always occurs at the time of goods issue.

8. Will an accounting document be generated for a stock transfer?

   **Answer:** An accounting document will be created any time there is a change in valuation. This is true for all plant-to-plant and company code-to-company code stock transfers. Valuation does not generally occur for a storage location-to-storage location stock transfer.

9. If valuation takes place during a stock transfer, when is the accounting document generated?

   **Answer:** Valuation always occurs at the time of the goods issue. For a two-step procedure, this occurs during the first step. For a one-step procedure it occurs during the only step.

10. Under what conditions will an accounting document be created for storage location-to-storage location stock transfer?

    **Answer:** An accounting document will be created in this case only when the material is split-valuated. This means the value for the same material is different in each storage location.

11. During a one-step storage location-to-storage location stock transfer, the material can be issued from any stock type and received into any stock type. (T/F)

    **Answer:** True. A one-step stock transfer between two storage locations within the same plant can be issued and received from any stock type into any stock type.

12. Which of the following scenarios is correct for a storage location-to-storage location stock transfer? (one)

A. A material in unrestricted stock from the origin can be moved to stock in QI at the destination

B. A material in unrestricted stock from the origin can be moved to blocked stock at the destination

**C. A material in unrestricted stock from the origin can be moved to unrestricted stock at the destination**

D. A material in QI stock at the origin can be moved into QI stock at the destination

13. Describe the financial accounting impacts of a company code-to-company code stock transfer.

**Answer:** Since the stock transfers involves two company codes, two accounting documents are created (one for each company code) at the time of goods issue.

14. Suppose you are planning to move stock from one plant to another and would like to include additional costs such as freight charges associated with this move. What form of stock transfer would be best? What other benefits does this approach provide over the alternative approaches?

**Answer:** In this case, it would be best to use a stock transport order (STO). An STO acts as an internal purchase order. In this special form of a purchase order, conditions can be entered in the STO just as any other PO. Other advantages of an STO include: it is MRP relevant; the material can be received into any stock type; inspection can be planned; receipts can be planned; the material can be entered as a consumable.

15. When an STO is used for the purposes of a stock transfer, what is the restriction on the issuing plant and where do the materials appear after the posting of the goods issue?

**Answer:** Though the material can be received into any stock type at the receiving plant, the issuing plant must issue the materials out of unrestricted use stock. Upon posting the goods issue, the materials appear ***in transit*** in the receiving plant's inventory. AN accounting document is also generated at the time of the goods issue.

16. How is inventory management integrated with warehouse management?

**Answer:** A warehouse number is assigned to a plant/storage location combination. Goods movements which are subject to a warehouse number, would then require additional logistic execution steps within warehouse management.

17. Is a goods issue posting part of inventory management or warehouse management?

**Answer:** It is part of inventory management.

18. Is the execution of a transfer order part of inventory management or warehouse management?

**Answer:** It is part of warehouse management

19. Which field in a goods movement transaction defines the purpose of the goods movement?

**Answer:** The movement type. This field defines the purpose of the goods movement and provides default values as well as additional required fields in the transaction.

20. With respect to warehouse management which of the following statements is correct? (one)

    E. **Multiple plant/storage location combinations can be assigned to a single warehouse number**

    F. All the storage locations assigned to a warehouse number must have the same storage location number

    G. Different storage locations of a given plant cannot be allocated to different warehouse numbers

    H. If one storage location of a plant is allocated to a warehouse number, then all storage locations in that plant must be allocated to warehouse numbers, but not necessarily the same one

21. Which document is required to perform logistics execution steps in warehouse management?

    **Answer:** In warehouse management, all logistics execution steps are completed with a transfer order

22. Which document is required to perform warehouse tasks in extended warehouse management?

    **Answer:** In extended warehouse management, all warehouse tasks are completed with a delivery order

23. What is the structure of the warehouse number in warehouse management?

    **Answer:** A warehouse number is composed of a storage type; storage section; and bin.

24. Which of the following is not an additional feature of extended warehouse management? (one)

    A. **Bin management**

    B. Yard management

    C. Cross-docking

    D. Wave management

    E. Slotting

25. Describe the difference between centralized warehouse management and decentralized warehouse management.

    **Answer:** In centralized warehouse management, the WM system and the ERP system run on the same machine. In decentralized warehouse management, the WM and ERP system are being run on separate machines.

# End of chapter review questions fo Enterprise asset management

1. When creating a maintenance order, which of the following represent two examples of master data that might require maintenance? (two)

   A. Structure

   **B. Functional location**

   C. Planner group

   D. Equipment

2. Prior to creating a maintenance order, which of the following documents might be created to support the maintenance process? (one)

   A. Purchase requisition

   B. Transfer order

   **C. Maintenance notification**

   D. Maintenance requisition

3. Which of the following is considered master data in Enterprise *Asset Management*? (two)

   A. Maintenance plant

   **B. Work center**

   **C. Technical object**

   D. Maintenance planning plant

4. Which of the following are examples of technical objects? (three)

   A. Work centers

   **B. BOMs**

   **C. Functional locations**

   D. **Equipment**

5. What is the role of a functional location? **A functional location refers to a physical place where we may have equipment installed. It helps us keep track of various locations in our plant that may require maintenance or has equipment installed that may require maintenance.**

6. What is the role of equipment? **Equipment are items that need to be managed individually from a maintenance perspective. A material that has been assigned a serial number is also managed as a piece of equipment. Examples of equipment are vehicles, machines, etc. Equipment can be kept in inventory or installed in functional locations.**

7. What is the role of assemblies? **Assembly is another term for bill of materials. For Enterprise Asset Management, assemblies are used by planners to plan materials needed for maintenance purposes. Assemblies exist for functional locations, equipment, and materials. If a material BOM is being used to manage a piece of equipment, it is assigned in the master record for that piece of equipment.**

8. What is the role of a planner group? **Planner groups are individuals or groups of individuals and they are assigned to a maintenance planning plant. The planner group is responsible for creating notifications of maintenance items and planning the maintenance in the maintenance order.**

9. What is the role of a maintenance planning plant? **A maintenance planning plant is the plant designated for planning maintenance requirements. When a maintenance item is identified, the maintenance plant is where the planning will take place. Planner groups assigned to the maintenance planning plant perform the planning tasks.**

10. What is the role of a notification? **A notification is generally the first step in the maintenance process. When a maintenance need occurs, the planner groups are contacted. The planner groups gather as much information as possible in order to be able to plan the maintenance. The notification may contain one or more technical objects (it may also contain no objects), items to be maintained, description of the issues, tasks, and activities. The maintenance notification is managed in parallel with the maintenance order.**

11. What is the role of a maintenance order? **The main planning and execution aspects of maintenance are contained in the maintenance order. The order also collects all costs associated with the maintenance process. Planner groups create the order and can plan work to be performed as well as materials required. Maintenance orders follow the order-related cost object controlling process.**

12. What is the significance of releasing a maintenance order? **Because a maintenance order follows order-related cost object controlling, maintenance orders must be released for work to be performed and costs posted. The maintenance order cannot collect any costs associated with the maintenance until it is released. Thus, the release sets the order as a cost object.**

13. What is the difference between *Enterprise Asset Management* and *Asset Accounting*? **Enterprise asset management deals with the physical maintenance of assets. Asset accounting deals with managing these assets from an accounting point of view.**

14. Which of the following are examples of equipment? (three)

    A. Cafeteria

    **B. Oven**

    **C. Steamer**

    **D. Cooler**

    **Cafeteria could be a functional location.**

15. When the maintenance order is created, the maintenance notification is deleted. (T/F) **False, the maintenance notification is managed in parallel with the maintenance order.**

16. Which of the following are different types of maintenance described in this chapter? (two)

    **A. Preventive maintenance**

    B. Overall maintenance

    **C. Breakdown maintenance**

    D. Material maintenance

17. Explain the main differences between centralized and decentralized maintenance planning. **Centralized maintenance planning occurs when a single maintenance planning plant is used to plan the maintenance at other maintenance plants. Decentralized maintenance planning occurs when each maintenance plant is responsible for planning its own maintenance. Thus, it is also a maintenance planning plant.**

18. A maintenance plant is an example of master data. (T/F) **False, maintenance plants are considered organizational levels.**

19. Which of the following is considered master data that is responsible for performing maintenance activities? (one)

    A. Maintenance plant

    **B. Work center**

    C. Technical object

    D. Maintenance planning plant

20. Which of the following is considered master data that is used by planner groups to plan materials for a maintenance order? (one)

    A. Functional location

    B. Work center

    C. Equipment

    **D. Assembly**

**21.** A maintenance order is managed using order-related cost object controlling. (T/F) **True. The maintenance order must be released to become a cost object. It will collect costs from goods movements and confirmations. At period end, the order is settled to one or more receivers. It is managed using order-related cost object controlling.**

---

## End of chapter review questions for Human capital management

1. Which of the following is not part of the HCM cycle? (one)

    A. Recruitment

    B. Performance appraisals

    C. Time management

    **D. Work center planning**

2. Define the beginning and end to the HCM cycle.

    **Answer:** There is no definitive beginning and end to the HCM cycle. Each of the process steps in the cycle is dependent on one another.

3. When a person is promoted into a new position, a vacancy occurs. Planning to have that vacancy filled efficiently and effectively is part of... (one)

A. Recruitment

B. Hiring

**C. Succession planning**

D. Performance appraisals

4. Keeping track of how much vacation an employee currently has is part of which process in the HCM cycle? (one)

**A. Time management**

B. Compensation

C. Organizational structuring

D. Planning

5. The Profile Matchup compares which two things? (two)

A. Candidate's requirements

**B. Candidate's qualifications**

**C. Position requirements**

D. Position qualifications

6. Which processes in the HCM cycle use the Profile Matchup? (two)

**A. Personnel development**

B. Compensation

**C. Recruitment**

D. Planning

7. Explain how SAP supports the keeping track of costs for various organizational units in SAP HCM.

**Answer:** An organizational unit in HCM is like a department where people work. In order to keep track of costs for these departments, a cost center is often used.

8. Explain the use of Jobs in SAP HCM.

**Answer:** Jobs are generic descriptions of work that people will do. They are used to describe one or more positions as well as evaluating pay rates for people who hold those positions. Jobs should be created to be as general as possible, but as specific as necessary.

9. Explain the use of Positions in SAP HCM.

**Answer:** Positions are described by Jobs. Several positions could be described by the same Job. People are hired into positions in SAP HCM. A person can hold only one position, but a position can be occupied by more than one person. Positions can be entirely vacant, filled, or partially filled.

10. The Hiring component in the HCM cycle supports the internal postings of positions for internal candidates. (T/F)

    **Answer:** False – the Recruitment component supports this.

11. Explain how the SAP ERP system supports the integration of data between the Recruitment and Hiring components in the HCM cycle.

    **Answer:** Data can be transferred from the Recruitment component to the Hiring component in SAP HCM. When an applicant is hired, their application information can be transferred to an Info Type to facilitate the hiring process.

12. When someone is hired into a position, explain how this new employee is associated with a cost center.

    **Answer:** When someone is hired into a position, this position is assigned to an organizational unit (department). Typically, this department is assigned a cost center and the employee will inherit that cost center from their position.

13. Which transaction in HCM will result in the posting of a cost to a cost center? (one)

    A. Hiring

    **B. Payroll**

    C. Recruitment

    D. Planning

14. Which of the following best describes an Info Type? (two)

    **A. A collection of related data about an employee**

    B. A collection of related data about a cost center

    C. Organizational data

    **D. Master data**

15. Explain a personnel file.

    **Answer:** A personnel file is a record of an employee's personal information as well as other information relating that employee to the enterprise. The personnel file contains information that assist the Humans Resource department in managing various aspects associated with an employee. Some examples include but are not necessarily limited: to address information; employee banking information; pay rate information; and organizational structuring information. Thus, a personnel file is a collection of various info types that have been maintained for an employee.

16. Which of the following are possible examples of Info Types? (three)

**A. Personal information**

**B. Banking information**

C. Work center information

**D. Pay rate information**

17. Which of the following are methods for maintaining Info Types? (three)

A. Multiple screen

**B. Single screen**

**C. Fast entry**

**D. Personnel actions**

18. Explain personnel actions info type maintenance.

**Answer:** In personnel actions, many info types will be maintained at one time for one personnel number. The info types appear and are maintained in sequential order according to the type of Action that is being performed. (An Action is a process that is completed for an employee. Examples of Actions include: Hiring; termination; transfer; promotion.)

19. Explain single screen info type maintenance.

**Answer:** In single screen info type maintenance, only one info type can be maintained at one time for one personnel number.

20. Explain fast entry info type maintenance.

**Answer:** In fast entry info type maintenance, only one info type can be maintained at one time but can be maintained for more than one personnel number. Upon saving the info type, the next personnel number will appear sequentially.

21. It is not possible for an employee to maintain any of their own info type master data. (T/F)

**Answer:** False – through Employee Self-Services (ESS), an employee may have access to change information in an info type as long as they have authorization to do so. For example, using ESS an employee could update their address information which in turn will update their info type master data.

22. Training and development in HCM also takes advantage of the Profile Matchup. (T/F)

**Answer:** True – in training and development, an existing employee may be interested in a promotion. Because of this, they will need to know what the requirements are for being eligible for this promotion. The Profile Matchup will compare their current qualification to the desired position to find shortfalls that can be used for a development plan.

23. A company is preparing an employee to fill a future vacancy. As a result, they also need to prepare for the vacancy left behind by this employee. This is an example of __________. (one)

    **A. Succession planning**

    B. Development

    C. Training

    D. Appraisals

24. A current employee is interested in being promoted to a higher position. The employee works closely with his/her manager to create a plan for achieving this. This is an example of __________. (one)

    A. Succession planning

    **B. Development**

    C. Training

    D. Appraisals

25. A manager meets with an employee on an annual basis to discuss their performance. This is an example of ______________. (one)

    A. Succession planning

    B. Development

    C. Training

    **D. Appraisals**

26. Wages, salaries, benefits, and insurance are all examples of _________.(one)

    A. Pay scale

    B. Job pricing

    **C. Compensation**

    D. Promotion

27. Explain CATS.

    **Answer:** CATS is Cross-Application Time Sheet. It is used by employees and third-party business partners for time entry. Those times can be transferred to various business applications, one being HCM. As an example, an employee can enter their working times using CATS and have those times transfer to HCM for payroll processing.

28. List various types of times that are used in HCM.

    **Answer:** Sick time; vacation time; overtime; leave time; maternity time; paternity time; time on sabbatical; and travel time.

29. Explain the concept of Job Pricing in HCM.

**Answer:** Job pricing is used to determine if the pay compensation offered to employees is competitive in the market place. The location where an employee works can greatly influence their rate of pay.

30. Planning is the last phase of the HCM cycle and therefore ends the HCM process. (T/F)

    **Answer:** False – There is no definitive beginning and end to the HCM cycle. Each of the process steps in the cycle is dependent on one another.

31. Which of the following is available to assist managers in making planning decisions in HCM? (one)

    A. Employee desktop

    **B. Manager's desktop**

    C. Planning table

    D. Sales and operations plan

32. Which of the following represents SAP's cloud solution to Human Capital Management? (one)

    A. Ariba

    **B. SuccessFactors**

    C. fieldglass

    D. Concur

33. SAP SuccessFactors Employee Central includes all of the following EXCEPT __________. (one)

    A. Time Management

    **B.** Payroll

    C. **Projects**

    D. Organizational Management

## End of chapter review questions for Project management

1. Which of the following represent the organizational levels specific to project management? (one)

    A. Company code

    B. Plant

    C. Storage location

    **D. Project management in SAP has no** organizational **levels to itself**

2. Define the characteristics of projects.

    **Answer:** Projects are unique in purpose, generally capital intensive and time intensive. They are usually complex in nature and involve many different functional areas.

3. Which objects of a project are structured hierarchically? (one)
   - A. Project builder
   - B. Project planning board
   - **C. Work breakdown structure**
   - D. Network
4. Activities in a project are linked together using relationships to form the ________. (one)
   - A. Project builder
   - B. Project planning board
   - C. Work breakdown structure
   - **D. Network**
5. Define a Work Breakdown Structure.

   **Answer:** A WBS contains WBS Elements arranged hierarchically to manage costs, budgets and dates for the project.
6. Define Activities.

   **Answer:** Activities represent the work or steps that need to be accomplished to complete the project.
7. Define Networks.

   **Answer:** The activities of a project can be linked to one another in a precedence diagram. The precedence diagram describes the relationships (dependencies) between the activities, and the order in which they must be completed. The precedence diagram is called a Network.
8. Describe the relationship between WBS Elements and Activities.

   **Answer:** Activities are assigned to WBS Elements. A WBS Element may have many activities assigned to it, but an activity may only be assigned to a single WBS Element.
9. List the operative indicators for WBS Elements.

   **Answer:** The operative indicators include: Planning element; Account assignment element; Billing element.
10. A WBS element that has the operative indicator "Planning Element", is an element for which ___________. (one)
    - **A. costs and revenues are planned**
    - B. materials are planned
    - C. MRP will create planned orders

D. a G/L account is assigned

11. A WBS element that has the operative indicator, "Account Assignment", is an element for which ______________.(one)

    A. costs are planned

    **B. costs are posted**

    C. revenues are posted

    D. a G/L account is assigned

12. A WBS element that has the operative indicator, "Billing Element", is an element for which ____________. (one)

    A. costs are planned

    B. costs are posted

    **C. revenues are posted**

    D. a G/L account is assigned

13. List the functions of WBS Elements.

    **Answer:** WBS Elements are associated with the following functions:

    - Dates
    - Budgets
    - Commitments
    - Costs and revenues
    - Payment information
    - Period end closing

14. List the functions of Activities.

    **Answer:** Activities are associated with the following functions:

    - Internally processed
    - Externally processed
    - Materials
    - Costs
    - Milestones
    - Period-end closing

15. List the five phases of a project.

    **Answer:** The five phases of a project include:

    Concept

    Rough-cut Planning

    Detailed Planning

    Execution

    Closing

16. Describe the concept phase of a project.

    **Answer:** During the concept phase of a project, the project definition is created, and discussion of the project is at a very high level. No detail is present in this phase.

17. Describe the rough-cut phase of a project.

    **Answer:** During the rough-cut phase of a project, WBS Elements are defined at a high level. It does not include all WBS Elements that will be required for the project. Activities are not essential at the rough-cut phase but may also be present at a high level.

18. Describe the detailed phase of a project.

    **Answer:** During the detailed phase of a project, all WBS Elements are created and included in the Work Breakdown Structure. In addition, all Activities are created, assigned to WBS Elements, and included in a Network.

19. Describe the execution phase of a project.

    **Answer:** During the execution phase of a project, the project must be placed in released status. At that time, work on the project can be performed and the functions of WBS Elements and Activities are activated. Actual dates, costs, and revenues can be posted to the project.

20. Describe the closing phase of a project.

    **Answer:** During the closing phase of a project, period-end activities occur. Billing can take place and aspects of the project are settled. Project evaluation and analysis also occurs.

21. Which of the following are functions of the Project Builder? (three)

    A. **Menu navigation**

    B. **Create projects**

    C. **Edit projects**

    D. Gantt chart navigation

22. Which of the following are functions of the Project Planning Board? (three)

A. Menu navigation

**B. Create projects**

**C. Edit projects**

**D. Gantt chart navigation**

23. Which of the following are additional graphical tools that are available in SAP Project Systems? (two)

A. Activity graphic

**B. Network graphic**

C. WBS graphic

**D. Hierarchy graphic**

24. The Hierarchy graphic can be accessed from both the Project Builder and Project Planning Board (T/F)

**Answer:** True

25. Which of the following are graphical overviews available in the Project Planning Board? (three)

A. Activity overview

**B. Capacity overview**

**C. Material overview**

**D. Cost overview**

26. In order to plan costs on a WBS Element, that WBS Element must be assigned the Account Assignment operative indicator. (T/F)

**Answer:** False, in order to plan costs on a WBS Element, that WBS Element must be assigned the Planning operative indicator.

27. For planning costs for WBS Elements with one or more activities, costs can be planned at the activity level and rolled up to the WBS Element level. (T/F)

**Answer:** True

28. List different methods for planning costs on projects in SAP.

**Answer:** Overall Planning, SAP Easy Cost Planning, Activity and Network Planning, Planning with Orders, Cost Element Planning

29. Cost planning in projects is important because it provides the basis for ______. (one)

**A. the budget request**

B. the budget release

C. Easy Cost Planning

D. Settlement

30. Which of the following controls how the budget on a project is released? (one)

A. Budget balance

**B. Availability control**

C. Activity control

D. Easy Cost Planning

31. List two different versions of Availability Control for projects in SAP.

**Answer:** Active Availability Control; Passive Availability Control

32. Describe the difference between Active Availability Control and Passive Availability Control.

**Answer:** When Active Availability Control is in use, the system will generate a message when the budget has or will be exceeded. Passive Availability Control allows users to evaluate costs on the project to see if the budget has been exceeded, but it does not generate any messages.

33. Explain how costs are posted to the project using the MM Procurement process.

**Answer:** In MM procurement, consumable items needed for the project require an account assignment category. The user could select account assignment category "Project" or "Network". As a result, an account assignment object will be required pending the account assignment category selected. At the time of the goods receipt posting, the cost will post to the appropriate account assignment object in the project.

34. Explain how costs are posted to the project using activities.

**Answer:** Activities could be internally processed or externally processed. Externally processed activities will post costs to the project using the MM Procurement process. Internally processed activities are performed by work centers. When an activity is confirmed, those costs post to the project activity and update the costs to the WBS Element.

35. Which of the following are settlement options in projects? (two)

A. Single-level settlement

**B. Multi-level settlement**

**C. Direct settlement**

D. Indirect settlement

36. Explain the difference between direct settlement and multilevel settlement.

**Answer:** If direct settlement is used in the project, all WBS Elements and Activities that need to be settled are settled directly to the receiver of the project. If multi-level settlement is used, all activities are settled to their respective WBS Elements, and the WBS Elements are settled upward in the hierarchy until everything is settled to the top level WBS Element. Once settlement reaches the top level WBS Element, it is then settled to the receiver for the project.

Made in the USA
Columbia, SC
07 August 2021